CANADA UNDER SIEGE

This is the US version of Canada Under Siege. This is not for sale in Canada and can not be returned to credit in Canada.

CANADA UNDER SIEGE

HOW PEI BECAME A FORWARD OPERATING BASE FOR THE CHINESE COMMUNIST PARTY

MICHEL JUNEAU KATSUYA and GARRY CLEMENT
with DEAN BAXENDALE

OPTIMUM PUBLISHING INTERNATIONAL
LONDON | MONTRÉAL | TORONTO

Canada Under Siege, How PEI became a Forward Operating Base for the CCP
© Ottawa, 2025 Garry Clement, Michel Juneau-Katsuya and Dean Baxendale

First Edition published in Canada and United States.
Published by Optimum Publishing International.

All rights reserved. No part of this publication may be reproduced in any form or by any means whatsoever or stored in a data base without permission in writing from the publisher, except by a reviewer who may quote passages of customary brevity in review.

LIBRARY AND ARCHIVES CANADA CATALOGUING IN PUBLICATION

Title: Canada Under Siege, How PEI Became a Forward Operating Base for the CCP
Garry Clement, Michel Juneau-Katsuya, Dean Baxendale
Subjects: Elite Capture, Transnational Repression, Religion Freedoms, Tibet Buddhism, CCP, Belt And Road Initiative, Geo-politics, Uyghur Genocide, United Front Works Department | Description: Optimum Publishing International US edition

ISBN 978-0-88890-376-1(US Trade Paperback)
ISBN 978-0-88890-369-3 (ePub)

Jacket and Interior design by Jessica Albert

This book can not be sold in Canada.

For information on rights or any submissions, please e-mail:
deanb@opibooks.com

Optimum Publishing International
Dean Baxendale, President & CEO
Toronto, Canada

www.optimumpublishinginternational.com
www.opibooks.com
Twitter @opibooks | Instagram @opibooks

OTHER GREAT BOOKS FROM OPTIMUM

Hidden Hand

Wilful Blindness (3rd Edition)

China Nexus

Under Cover

China Freedom Trap

Unbroken

CONTENTS

CHAPTER 1.
Anne of Green Gables: How Greed Ruins Legacy — 1

CHAPTER 2.
Getting to the Island — 11

CHAPTER 3.
Paradise Patterned: From Honiara to Charlottetown — 19

CHAPTER 4.
The United Front: From Beijing to Charlottetown — 26

CHAPTER 5.
Prince Edward Island's Engagement with the People's Republic of China — 38

CHAPTER 6.
Elite Capture and the Whistleblower: Susan Holmes and the PEI Provincial Nominee Program Scandal — 46

CHAPTER 7.
The Island Awakens — 53

CHAPTER 8.
Voices of Devotion: The Journey of the Great Wisdom Buddhist Institute — 59

CHAPTER 9.
Tibetan Buddhism Under Siege: The Panchen Lama and Taiwan's Role, A Faith Under Occupation — 70

CHAPTER 10.
Custodians of the Flame — 79

CHAPTER 11.
Shadows on the Island: An Immigration Consultant's Story — 85

CHAPTER 12.
The Poor Guru Who Wears Prada: The Intelligence Analysis — 92

CHAPTER 13.
The Fall of Zhong Gong and the Rise of Mary Jin — 99

CHAPTER 14.
The King Government: Part of the Solution or the Problem? — 108

CHAPTER 15.
Land Grab and No Accountability: The Legacy of Several Premiers — 115

CHAPTER 16.
A Conversation with Wayne Easter — 135

CHAPTER 17.
Evidence of Money Laundering — 129

CHAPTER 18.
72 Hours in Taipei — 163

CHAPTER 19.
The Reckoning: Final Testimonies from the Front Lines — 190

CHAPTER 20.
The Forward Operating Base You Didn't See Coming — 202

EXHIBITS — 206
PHOTOS — 220
AKNOWLEDGEMENTS — 231
GLOSSARY — 233
APPENDICES — 242
ENDNOTES — 247
ABOUT THE AUTHORS — 255
INDEX — 257

CHAPTER 1
ANNE OF GREEN GABLES
HOW GREED RUINS LEGACY

"Parva sub ingenti."[1]
(LATIN: *"The small under the protection of the great."*)

From out over the breakers to where the first morning schooners bob lazily amid the summer cruise ships and the squawking gulls, the bells atop St. Dunstan's Cathedral ring in the morning. Charlottetown slides gently down to Victoria Park, the nose of the city swelling into the four-pronged crossroads of the harbour, where the great Atlantic Ocean streams into the heart of the Island and spreads its arms east and west through rivers with the slightest kiss of ocean salt water that feed their way all through the province. The city glows in the early sunlight, morning settling on the boardwalk before bursting to life in the tourist-packed downtown between Great George and Queen streets, under the tall iron gate of Victoria Row's cobblestone arteries and up to the iconic ice cream stands across from looming old hotels and clean new museums and theatres. The city of just 36,000 balloons each summer with more than a million tourists, busloads of visitors in the iconic straw hats and mock red pigtails of Lucy Maud Montgomery's classic novel walking along the bright red beaches and touring the rolling countryside, the endless lighthouse points and coves, the winding north coast down to Malpeque Bay, and the recreation of Green Gables itself. An endless supply of potato trucks streams from the earth out of the big Cavendish farms and the hundreds of little family plots. A child might grow up believing dirt could be no other colour than the deep brick-red hue that accumulates under grass and fingernails alike. Prince Edward Island is more than the salt of the earth: it's a land where the earth and sea themselves seem to glimmer and shine in a way found nowhere else. Leaving the capital, it's almost pointless to ask for directions; the province winds and turns, dips and rises through green and blue on and on forever, and nowhere is ever too far to go. Cresting out against the horizon, the Confederation Bridge is the only proof that an outside world exists. In fact, it's hard to imagine anything but peace and serenity amid the rolling red earth and the sea, as if all the world's darkness and corruption stops with the last ferry and washes away with the Maritime rain.

Yet dark clouds still manage to roll over the Island and into the public eye. The province so storied in tradition, seeming almost frozen in time in its identity as the home of Anne of Green Gables, is still not immune to the ever-rocky landscape of Canadian politics, and the Richmond Street Legislative Assembly stands out as a constant reminder of reality against the romantic backdrop of Province House. In 2014, enjoying near-universal popularity and a healthy lead in all major polls, Prince Edward Island premier and Liberal leader Robert Ghiz resigned under a cloud of suspicion. After eleven years as the head of the Island's ruling party and considered by many to be the ideal candidate for federal leadership, the 41-year-old Ghiz seemingly chose to go out on his own terms. The bombshell resignation was a true bolt from the blue, with the premier's closest caucus ministers only finding out fifteen minutes before Ghiz made an official statement to the media, an appearance that left the Islanders with more questions than answers. Why did a young, beloved premier with re-election seeming certain suddenly disappear? In his eight years as premier, Robert Ghiz's political résumé had only one black mark, an allegation of bribery against bureaucrats within his party, a scandal from which Ghiz himself had emerged seemingly untouched. Though memories floated around during the confusion of the premier's sudden resignation, the chaos that ensued—a derailed legislative agenda and total reset of the political landscape—saw any notions of fraud left firmly in the rearview, and there they stayed, until a 2019 whistleblower lawsuit brought it all roaring back.

Ten thousand years ago, back before PEI had split from the mainland and floated off into the sea, the Mi'kmaq, the first inhabitants of the Island, arrived here via the Northumberland Strait. The Mi'kmaq Nation's culture and traditions remain ingrained in the land today, part of a rich civilization built over centuries in Epekwitk, with communities still active today in Lennox Island and Abegweit. The first European to document the territory was Jacques Cartier, considered by many a Canadian Columbus, during his inaugural 1534 voyage to the New World.

When the British seized Île Saint-Jean in 1758, it marked more than just a wartime victory in the Seven Years' War—it was the beginning of an island's transformation by imperial ambition. The French settlers, mostly Acadians who had built lives and communities here for generations, were rounded up and forced from their homes in a brutal act of state-sanctioned ethnic cleansing. It was the tail end of *Le Grand Dérangement*, the Great Deportation (1755) that scattered thousands of Acadian families across the Americas. That same year, British troops burned their farms, loaded them onto overcrowded ships, and deported them under threat of bayonet. Many never made it. Their crime? Being on the wrong side of the empire.

With the French removed and the land cleared, the Crown wasted no time in imposing a new colonial order. Samuel Holland's 1764 survey sliced the island into perfectly measured lots, not for settlers, but for absentee landlords—British elites who had never touched the soil but now owned vast swaths of it. Promises of land and freedom drew Scottish and Irish families across the Atlantic, only for them to discover they were tenants, not owners. They were expected to pay rent, improve the land, and keep quiet. The political class in London had turned the island into a feudal experiment—one that left farmers poor and landlords rich.

But Islanders are not easily broken. By the 1860s, the people rose in protest—rent strikes, rallies, and a full-fledged revolt. The government feared it would spiral into open rebellion. It took Confederation and a political bargain in 1873 to finally resolve the crisis, as Ottawa agreed to buy out the landlords and hand over the land to those who had earned it through generations of labour. That federal intervention paved the way to the island becoming the seventh province. The legacy still matters. Because on Prince Edward Island, the land is never just land. It is a battleground for justice, identity, and the quiet resolve of those who refuse to be tenants of their own destiny.

Home to the assembly that penned the founding documents of Canada, the land nicknamed the "Birthplace of Confederation" ironically became a province by resolving issues surrounding land ownership, an issue that is at the heart of the controversy in 2025. Once home to a healthy agricultural and industrial scene and humming trade, dwindling mainland connections and empty absentee land saw the colony's economy stagnate enough to push it to join the dominion in return for the Canadian government agreeing to take over the loan payments on its newly constructed railway. While Canadian status brought modernity along the railways and security from debt, PEI remained a poor rural province for much of its history, scrounging at the eastern tip of the continent far from the booming industrial heartlands of Ontario and Quebec. The Second World War brought new life to the Island's ports and airfields as homes to a burgeoning national air force and navy, while the province boasted the highest per capita enlistment rate in the country. The harrowing aftermath of so many lives lost in the war made the need for newcomers on the impoverished Island ever more important, and many of the great masses of immigrants, part of the postwar global diaspora, who arrived at Pier 21 in Halifax made the short final journey to settle on PEI. Slowly but surely, the province grew into the gem it has become known as, a traditional place with one eye always fixed on the past. Its history, and its heartbeat of immigration, are the inheritance of Robert Ghiz.

The Ghiz family has a long history with both PEI and the Island's legacy of immigration, with its power to make a "better island, and country." Robert's grandfather, Atallah Joseph Ghiz, emigrated from Lebanon to Charlottetown and earned a living as a corner store owner in the 1940s and '50s. His son, Harvard-educated lawyer Joe Ghiz, became the 27th premier of Prince Edward Island, from 1986 to 1993, the first Canadian provincial leader not of European descent. Ghiz helped oversee the federal government's constitutional reform after the Quebec Referendum, became a provincial Supreme Court judge, and was a key player in Brian Mulroney's push for global free trade, becoming a national figure for his support of the Meech Lake Accords. Known primarily as PEI's great road-builder, he began construction on many of the Island's major highways, presiding over the ever-controversial debate surrounding the need for a "fixed link" between PEI and the mainland. Just weeks before his death in 1996, he took a private tour of the half-built Confederation Bridge, the final answer to that divisive question. Widely beloved, Joe, like his son Robert, resigned before he could be voted out, when his campaign for proposed constitutional amendments to the Charlottetown Accords was defeated. When Robert Ghiz won the 2003 Liberal leadership, there was but one Liberal in the Legislature. The election in the Fall would return the Pat Bins Conservatives to power, but Ghiz and three others won their seats: Carolyn Bertram, Richard Brown, and Ron MacKinley. However, the Bins government began to fall out of favour, and on May 28, 2007, built on their commitment to strengthening rural communities, the Robert Ghiz Liberals went on to a resounding political victory—23-4—reversing an eleven-year reign. Ghiz became the Island's 31st premier, and not only did it reaffirm the clan's great immigrant success story, it cemented the Ghiz name among PEI's first families. His election platform focused on economic development, transparency, and ethics. Ironically, Ghiz's government became entangled in the controversial Provincial Nominee Program (PNP), especially as allegations surfaced that the program disproportionately benefited insiders during his tenure. This contrast became a focal point of criticism during and after his time in office.

In a twist of fate that borders on the ironic, the issue of immigration has become the defining legacy of the son of PEI's "Canadian Dream" premier. In 2011, three former provincial employees alleged that the Liberal Party was involved in a conspiracy to funnel money to political allies. They claimed that senior government officials had directed hush money through the PNP[2] to secure approvals for immigration applications that should have been rejected.

The PNP was designed to attract potential immigrants by allowing them to invest in local businesses, thereby gaining approval for immigration. However, the program quickly became a national controversy. It was labelled a "$400 Million Scandal"[3] by locals and media alike, highlighting a financial scheme where funds were disbursed long before any returns materialized. The early program (shut down in 2008) targeted wealthy individuals, particularly Chinese investors, and required new immigrants to stay for a minimum of one year and invest in a local business. Yet, initial challenges, including mandatory language levels and good-faith deposits, proved to be significant barriers.

Amid the program's early turmoil, three government workers, including a contractor for the Educational Secretariat, raised concerns about rampant corruption. Cora Plourd (later Plourd Nicholson) and Svetlana Tenetko[4] alleged that the program was rife with bribery and fraud, allowing numerous immigrants to bypass the necessary paperwork and security clearances. Susan Holmes, the third whistleblower, had her contract terminated when she refused to change the score for a multimillion dollar contract that that would qualify the premier's number one go-to-guy for immigration, as well as his wife, who owned Study Abroad and the English as a Second Language[5] program that would help immigrants learn the English required to get their deposits back and integrate with the Island community.

Court File No:

SUPREME COURT OF PRINCE EDWARD ISLAND
(GENERAL SECTION)

BETWEEN:

SUSAN HOLMES, CORA PLOURD NICHOLSON, and SVETLANA TENETKO

Plaintiffs

- and -

THE GOVERNMENT OF PRINCE EDWARD ISLAND,
ROBERT GHIZ, ALLAN CAMPBELL, and MICHAEL MAYNE

Defendants

STATEMENT OF CLAIM

TO THE DEFENDANTS:

A LEGAL PROCEEDING HAS BEEN COMMENCED AGAINST YOU by the plaintiff. The claim made against you is set out in the following pages.

IF YOU WISH TO DEFEND THIS PROCEEDING, you or a lawyer acting for you must prepare a statement of defence in Form 18A and a designation of address for service (Form 16A.1), prescribed by the Rules of Civil Procedure, serve it on the plaintiff's lawyer or, where the plaintiff does not have a lawyer, serve it on the plaintiff, and file it, with proof of service, in this court office, WITHIN TWENTY DAYS after this notice of action is served on you, if you are in Prince Edward Island.

If you are served in another province or territory of Canada or in the United States of America, the period for serving and filing your statement of defence is forty days. If you are served

As it turned out, many applicants were reportedly willing to forfeit their deposits, showing little intention of fulfilling their commitments to learn English or French or to remain on the Island for a year. In fact, many never intended to stay in PEI at all. After six years of intermittent investigation, during which Premier Robert Ghiz dismissed the allegations as "wild accusations" by disgruntled employees, both the RCMP and a provincial commission found clear signs of mismanagement bordering on fraud in the PNP. These findings were hardly surprising, given that the 2009 Auditor General's report had already highlighted serious issues within the program. A 2009 CBC report quoted Auditor General Colin Younker stating, "There is an appearance that these individuals could have used their positions to gain approval under the program."[6]

Barely a year after his resignation in 2014, which had been seen as the early exit of a promising political figure, Robert Ghiz's reputation was seemingly in tatters due to the scandal, but he came out smelling like roses and never looked back. He currently works in Ottawa as President and CEO of the Canadian Telecommunications Association. The 2005–2008 iteration of the PNP had already collapsed years earlier, following federal intervention to shut down[7] what was perceived as a scheme devised by some of PEI's most prominent legal minds whose structure paid more to middlemen and the province in the form of the language and residency deposits than it did to business recipients. Nevertheless, a new version of the program was launched a year later, after only one new immigrant was processed in 2008.

Ghiz and his government faced a number of lawsuits, including the defamation claims (mentioned above) from the PNP whistleblowers and accusations of unlawfully disclosing private information, that will be explored more fully in the next chapter. A criminal suit also emerged, alleging the destruction of evidence and deletion of emails related to fraud within the PNP and an e-gaming fiasco.[8]

As the former premier struggled, the program itself spiralled downward. Weekly reports on major news networks detailed rampant spending, bribery, the acceptance of wanted criminals into the program, and a constant turnover of new Islanders. Hailed as a beacon for entrepreneurs upon its 2005 launch, the PNP had devolved into a gateway for exploitation.

Although they were required to stay a year, many immigrants only set foot on the Island for a few days and then moved on, despite forgoing their residency deposit of $25,000 if they did so. Some enterprising immigrants who wanted their money back attempted to maintain the illusion that they were living on the Island by claiming residence at the Sherwood Inn and

Hotel.⁹ The problem was, the hotel had about sixty rooms, but more than six hundred new Chinese immigrants were using it as their business address. Run by a Chinese family as a place for immigrants to receive mail, the Sherwood Inn and Hotel was thus fraudulently representing that those immigrants were living on the Island. This case will be explored later in the book.¹⁰ But in many more of the immigration cases, most of the program's beneficiaries headed west after their year on PEI was up. The government's own number suggests that less than one-third (33%) settled on the Island permanently, the lowest retention rate in Canada. The money was great while it flowed in, however, and landed in the bank accounts of the politically well-connected and of the many small businesses that accountants linked to middlemen had begged to apply for the PNP money, according to a number of businesspeople on the Island.

For a province that has so long featured immigrant success stories as a central part of its history, and has been such a hotbed of international tourism, the PNP scandal perverted a central pillar of Prince Edward Island's government and identity. But the public scandal was only the beginning. As the memory of the PNP begins to fade into an ever-moving national news cycle, PEI has tried its best to smooth over the scandal, launching the new *Here We Stay*¹¹ project to highlight the success stories of those few Chinese investors who decided to remain. The local Sunrise Group promises more Chinese-PEI success to come.

THE FOX GUARDING THE HENHOUSE: THE ARRIVAL OF FRANK ZHOU

Life moves on. On the surface, PEI is a culture set in stone: the beaches lined with colourful clapboard fishing towns and imitation boardwalk shacks, the main streets of Charlottetown an endless treasury of gift shops and Anne of Green Gables-themed merchandising. With that comes a sense of innocence, a quaint serenity more interested in the bustle of tourist season shopping than international malfeasance. But the innocence has been sold off. Under its picturesque, simple surface the fabric of PEI is being rewoven by global forces interested in using the Island as part of their global hegemonic ambitions. While the Provincial Nominee Program in its many incarnations was over by 2018 and new rules around immigration are emerging from Ottawa, that chapter is finished. But the legacy of the programs remains, and many in the past Liberal government and businesspeople will still credit these programs for the construction and investment boom that saw the Island's population grow by almost 20% over the past twenty years.

Thus, when Chinese immigrant and Simon Fraser University graduate Frank Zhou was apparently encouraged to come to PEI in the mid-2000s by Jean Chrétien, the prime minister was all in on investment and partnership with China. Since there were those within the Laurentian elite who saw immigration across the country as a primary goal for future growth, and getting well-to-do immigrants would be a boon for all of Canada, why not PEI too? It was a golden opportunity for both Frank and his wife, Sherry Huang, who formed a number of businesses on PEI. But it would be a small business partnership that Zhou entered into in 2011 —Anne of China Inc.—with former premier Wade MacLauchlan and his partner Duncan MacIntosh that saw Anne of Green Gables and her story being told in China in 2012. The *Anne of Green Gables* book and merchandise would be exposed to the Chinese market, which could bring additional revenue to the Island through tourism while providing profits to the partnership and royalties to the Lucy Maude Montgomery Foundation and the Anne of Green Gables Licensing Authority Inc. Duncan also sat on the board of the licensing authority.

Back then the deal was seen by Ottawa and many Islanders as a positive cultural exchange that would symbolize the strong partnership between Canada and China, like one of those true win-win arrangements that China under the leadership of the Chinese Communist Party had been promoting for more than a decade. MacLauchlan and his partner saw that this opportunity could lead to new business opportunities for Chinese investment capital and trade opportunities for Islanders. Little did they know then, but as has time has now demonstrated, these business opportunities are often part of a soft power strategy and are increasingly seen as a sharp power technique called "elite capture," which is a sophisticated trap used by the CCP throughout the world and documented in Canadian published books like *Claws of the Panda* (2019) *Hidden Hand* (2020), *Wilful Blindness* (2021), and *The Mosaic Effect (2023)*, as well as numerous documentaries, academic papers, and newspaper reports. One of the best academic papers written on the subject was a 2017 paper by the National Endowment for Democracy, interestingly titled "Sharp Power, Rising Authoritarian Influence." The hooks were in, [12] with the first critical pillar of the CCP's elite capture of key Islanders in place while the two unsuspecting politically and culturally invested Islanders who had formed Anne of China Inc. would enthusiastically promote cultural and business exchanges that would lead to more than a billion dollars being invested in this tiny province over the next decade.

As you will learn from this book, nothing is free or a win-win when it comes to dealing with today's Beijing, but Canada needed immigration and investment, which started with Brian Mulroney's Conservative government in the 1980s and has continued right up to today's Liberal government. So, when Canada and the world were all in on partnering with China, many just followed the leaders and saw the Chinese market as a great opportunity to diversify PEI's export markets and bring new immigrants to the province given that the aging of the population was leading to negative birth rates[13] on Prince Edward Island. Meanwhile immigrants were coming with lots of money to buy real estate, and that meant new jobs and new wealth for the Island.

Whatever the government's intentions, for Islanders, it was as if Anne of Green Gables, a symbol of the purity of rural life on the Island and her coming of age, had been sold out. Poor Anne's very soul and the innocence she represented had been sold to the most ruthless dictatorship and murderous regime the world has ever known, and this almost a decade before the brutal treatment of Hong Kongers and the exposure of the concentration camps in Xinjiang became known to the world. But in the provincial legislature. Wade MacLauchlan, rising to answer a question by then-opposition MLA Stephen Myers, spoke of how proud he was of the impact of Anne and his partnership in Anne of China Inc.[14] He also was quick to say he had resigned as a director of the company but his partner Duncan MacIntosh remained as a partner.

The intentions on our side were clear, and what better place to start than a place so peaceful that nobody could ever imagine anything being so offside. But as readers learn about Canada's tiniest province, they will come to understand it is also Canada's most corrupt and compromised.

Our forefathers are turning in their graves.

CHAPTER 2
GETTING TO THE ISLAND

When I received a LinkedIn message from someone I had never heard of but who referred to our just-released book *The Mosaic Effect* by Scott MacGregor and Ina Mitchell, I was intrigued. Optimum had just launched that book in October and then in Ottawa in early November we launched *Under Cover* by the former RCMP Superintendent of the Proceeds of Crime Division, Garry Clement, a career law-enforcement, undercover, and proceeds-of-crime expert who had learned about both books and had a keen interest in their findings.

The message I received was from Jan Matejcek, a Czechoslovakia-born Canadian lawyer whose family had endured the repression of the communists for decades. His family escaped to Canada when Russian troops invaded Czechoslovakia in 1968. Jan's father worked for the Canadian performing rights society and met many fine Maritime musicians, leading the family to spend many summers in PEI.

Jan married an Islander, Carolyn Cox, who had made her way out to Toronto in the '80s to work with Scotiabank. Jan was a young corporate lawyer who was headhunted by a large U.S. law firm to work in Europe as the markets of Central and Eastern Europe opened after the fall of the Soviet empire. He represented clients in business transactions throughout Europe, from as far East as Russia and Kazakhstan, to the Middle East and Africa. Although they eventually moved to London, Carolyn insisted that they retire to Prince Edward Island (PEI)—a quiet, idyllic island where time stood still and the people are kind, honest, and welcoming to all—a welcome change from the rough-and-tumble environment of emerging markets.

Soon after moving to PEI, Carolyn and Jan began hearing murmurs about a large Buddhist organization from Taiwan that was starting to purchase blocks of land and announcing plans to build large monasteries. Eventually, one of several groups of concerned Islanders met with Jan in 2023 and asked for his opinion of the true identity of the Buddhist organization and the end game being planned for the sleepy island.

After considerable research, it became clear that while the headquarters of the organization known as Bliss and Wisdom may have been in Taiwan it also appeared to have large operations in the People's Republic of China, and is a very substantial, multinational, fully integrated religious and business empire that is able to move hundreds of millions or even billions of dollars and hundreds of people internationally. The group realized that dealing with such an organization was beyond the capability of a few well-meaning citizens. Adding to the difficulty, they also recognized that neither the federal nor the PEI government had any will to review and investigate the organization's past and present activities.

After all, it had been green-lit and welcomed by successive Liberal governments under premiers Robert Ghiz and his successor, Wade MacLauchlan. While in opposition in 2018, now-Lands Minister Steven Myers seemingly had a lot to say about the premier's close ties to Frank Zhou and the People's Republic of China. The Conservatives had promised to clean up the Provincial Nominee Program mess and corruption and even investigate land acquisitions by the Bliss and Wisdom group. But after they formed the government under Premier Dennis King, they suddenly turned silent, and Islanders who wanted action were once again left holding the bag.

The group agreed that the best way forward was to bring in an expert in dealing with international influence operations and transnational organized crime to validate their concerns and build enough of a case to convince the federal and provincial authorities, which have the requisite investigative tools, to challenge Bliss and Wisdom's activities head-on.

After Jan reached out to me via LinkedIn, we got on the telephone. I explained that Optimum had plans to promote my authors' books: The *Mosaic Effect* that Jan was reading and *Under Cover: Inside the Shady World of Organized Crime and the RCMP* by Garry Clement. Jan agreed to help with the book launch on PEI and thought it would be good for Islanders to understand how PEI fits into all of this. So, I reluctantly agreed to come for a couple of days, but I didn't want to do the trip alone. I had a friend and colleague who I knew could help.

I called up my colleague, Michel Juneau-Katsuya, former Chief of the Asia-Pacific Desk for CSIS and former RCMP investigator, and asked if he would accompany me to hear about the Islanders' concerns. Michel had written a foreword for *The Mosaic Effect*[15] and knew all about the Chinese Communist Party's United Front operations in Canada. As a well-known media commentator about national security for more than two decades and the author of the infamous Sidewinder Report[16] that had made the connection between powerful Chinese triads (organized crime companies), the People's

Liberation Army (CCP), and our own elite politicians and corporate denizens, it didn't take too much effort to convince Michel that we should at least give the Islanders a hearing. So, a week later he got on a plane from Montreal and headed to Canada's island gem, Prince Edward Island, where I would be joining him from Toronto. I had called Garry Clement before I left and told him our plans, suggesting that I might need his expertise on organized crime and money laundering if our initial investigation turned up anything worth pursuing.

"Sure," he said, "but it's probably a long shot." I thought he might be right, but nothing ventured, nothing gained.

We had initially agreed to spend a day or two in PEI to assess the situation, but what we observed led us to stay for nearly a week and immediately launch a full journalistic investigation. Our first day would tell us a lot. My father, Michael Baxendale, had always taken the approach that you need to listen first, no matter how outlandish something might appear to be on the surface. If not, the hundreds of whistleblowers and witness accounts Optimum and other media outlets have published over fifty years or so would never have seen the light of day. When Optimum published *Who Killed Lynn Harper?* by Bill Trent and Steven Truscott, the latter was serving a life sentence for a murder he had not committed, and it would take twenty-five years after the book first hit store shelves for him to be vindicated. Michel as the seasoned RCMP and CSIS investigator and me as the publisher were now committed to giving some Islanders an audience to tell their truths.

We had no idea what we would hear when we got there, but that's why you listen, take notes, and then analyze what your witnesses had to say.

THE INVESTIGATION: THE ISLAND'S SECRETS

The house was quiet, almost too quiet. We had rented a cottage on the outskirts of the Island—an old New England-style house tucked away on a cliff overlooking the bay. It was the perfect setting for our investigation, the kind of place where you can feel the weight of history in every creaky floorboard, the salty air from the bay brushing against the windows. The view was breathtaking, with the water stretching out to the horizon and the sky blending into shades of blue and grey as the tide came in.

We never imagined that a place so peaceful would become the setting for something so intense.

Sitting across from me, Michel stared at the map covering the table, his gaze hard. The lines on his face seemed to deepen with every new revelation.

Sarah Willis (pseudonym), one of the government whistleblowers, sat at the other end, clearly unsettled but determined to speak her truth. She had been quiet for much of the first part of the meeting, but I could tell that she had seen far more than she was willing to admit at least at our first meeting—her experience inside the government department had given her a front-row seat to the manipulation of the Provincial Nominee Program (PNP), but she was currently doing research on the land holdings of Bliss and Wisdom to help out our second interviewee, who was also in the cottage with us.

The room was warm, the fire crackling softly in the hearth, the dim light from the windows casting long shadows across the room. The calmness of the setting didn't match the storm of questions swirling in my mind.

"Sarah," I began, trying to keep my voice even, despite the tension in the room, "you worked on the PNP applications during the rush to fill the government's apparent lust for cash in 2007. Tell us—what was it that first made you uneasy about the direction things were taking?"

Her eyes flickered nervously, but she met my gaze steadily. The silence stretched on for a moment before she spoke. "It wasn't just one thing," she said, the words slow, deliberate. "It was the way the applications were handled. People with questionable backgrounds are suddenly getting priority. Some of them hadn't even visited PEI, yet their applications were approved."

I glanced at Michel, who nodded, his eyes narrowing as he leaned forward. "What do you mean by 'questionable backgrounds'?"

"I mean," Sarah continued, her voice tightening, "people who had clear ties to business interests, people who were only coming for the land. They were getting pushed through faster than others who had been waiting for years. And then the night approvals started. Some were monks who clearly didn't seem to have a legitimate story or couldn't validate their income."

A chill crept through the room. The idea of night approvals—applications being approved when no one was around to monitor them and then colour-coding them for approval after they had been rejected. They were all getting bonuses to approve as many as possible in the short window left until the program would be shut down later in 2008 as mandated by the federal government.

"Night approvals?" I asked, leaning forward, the room suddenly feeling too small, the windows too far from where we were sitting. "Who was approving these? What was going on behind the scenes?"

Michel exchanged a glance with me, sensing the shift in the air. The house, once so full of light and space, suddenly felt constricting, the walls inching closer as Sarah spoke.

"It wasn't just the usual staff anymore," Sarah said, her hands gripping the edge of the table. "The 5th Floor—that's the Premier's office—was getting involved. They were pushing things through after hours. And I suspected Frank Zhou's hand was in on it, making sure certain people got through the system."

The name hit me like a punch to the gut. Frank Zhou had been Atlantic Canada's go-to-guy if you wanted to do business in China, and hearing his name pop up immediately was interesting, to say the least. The idea that he may have been pulling strings behind the scenes as far back as 2007 was of concern to both Michel and me. Frank Zhou had been identified in *The Mosaic Effect* and from other intelligence sources as a "Red Princeling" and part of the United Front Work Department.[17][18][19] The UFWD has been best described by both Mao and later Xi Jinping as China's magic weapon against the West, their apparent mortal enemy. For a long time, no one knew about the UFWD or understood its significance.[20]

"If the 5th Floor was involved," Michel pondered, his voice steady but tense, "this wasn't just the result of a few bad actors. The premier's office was helping this happen."

Sarah nodded, her face grim. "Exactly. It was orchestrated. And it wasn't about helping people. It was about controlling the land, making sure certain people with connections got what they needed and the premier and his friends wanted all the money that it would bring to the Island's coffers."

The silence in the room grew heavier. I could hear the distant sound of the waves crashing against the rocks outside, but it felt like the peaceful setting was mocking us. The house that had once felt so open and airy now seemed like a cage, closing in on all of us as we listened to her talk.

Once Sarah had finished her story, Jeff, who had been sitting in the corner listening, was ready to add his own deeply personal and connected experience. His appearance was quiet, unassuming, another Islander who had been living here his entire life. I knew he was here to provide the background and help us assemble a puzzle, the pieces of which were expanding almost by the minute. Jeff had worked with the nuns and monks of Bliss and Wisdom, and although he was never one to draw attention to himself, his knowledge of the inner workings of their operations was crucial to us better understanding what had gone on with the extensive land acquisitions through the PNP beginning around 2012 in the Three Rivers community centred on Montague.

"Jeff," I said, trying to steady my voice, "we've been hearing about the connections between the PNP and the premier's office. You've worked alongside these monks for years—what can you tell us about their operations? What are they really after?"

Jeff didn't waste any time. He sat down, his eyes shadowed with the weight of the truth he was about to reveal. "It's not just about the land. It's about power. Zhen-Ru may have come through the program legally, but the others—they're using the PNP as a front to acquire land. And now it's apparent to me and other Islanders that they're using that land to build influence. It's a long-term plan, and they've got powerful people helping them." I thought that was an incredibly astute observation, but then Jeff had an understanding few would have. He was there.

My eyebrows shot up. "Powerful people? Who's backing them?"

Jeff didn't flinch. "It's not just the monks. It's the people behind the scenes—businessmen, government officials, developers. The Back Room Boys.[21] They're all part of the same group that have controlled the Island for generations." According to many we spoke with, this group of politically well-connected Islanders have controlled the Island and who gets what for generations. When you hear that you think, it's just local folklore, but as we investigated more it seems that this group of Island elites did make a lot of critical decisions that we are sure were very well intentioned but on such a small island had a huge impact on many people.

So, the words hit like a bomb. Everything was connected, from the land deals to the political influence. We were dealing with a much deeper story that probably started out very innocently and then turned bad when the money was flowing and times were good.

I leaned back in my chair, staring at the window where the view of the bay had once seemed serene. Now, it felt distant, like we were too far removed from the calm to see it clearly. "So, this isn't just about the monks anymore. It's about a network—a web of influence that stretches from the 5th Floor to the business elite. It's a lot bigger than we thought."

Jeff's eyes hardened. "Exactly. And it's not going to be easy to unravel. But knowing what I know, if you follow the money, follow the land deals, you might find the truth." I was thinking about the irony of that statement because it was what Michel and Garry had been doing for all of their careers, and why would PEI play out any differently.

The silence in the room stretched on. The setting sun visible through the bay window was casting elongated shadows across the table. Each of us was lost in thought, but I could feel the pressure building. The peaceful bay view was now a mere illusion, masking the deeper storm that was gathering around us.

"So, what are we looking at here?" Michel's voice cut through the stillness, his words deliberate. "Are we dealing with a few bad players in the system, or is this a full-on conspiracy to reshape the land and politics of PEI?"

What was clear from the insights that had been revealed is that the monks and nuns have a plan, and the land acquisition is just one piece of it. The land deals, the political manoeuvring—they're all tied together. They've been building something massive here on the Island and at each turn when they were exposed as lying or not disclosing their real plans, they simply claimed they didn't know the culture or the legal environment on the Island. As we would discover later, that was hardly a supportable defence. The 5th Floor had no idea what they were unleashing back in 2006 through 2010 but were complicit in something they had no clue about. They were enabling money and influence, without asking questions as to why certain individuals were being processed when they were rejected by the very government employees who were paid to review the applications. Perhaps the money meant more to those in charge than actually getting citizens to the province that would stay and become solid members of the community. If they had so many applicants, why override the rejection of some applicants based on the criteria laid out by the immigration department for the Island? If it was truly about fixing an immigration and investment problem then there should have been no need for those on the 5th Floor to override the process, and yet they did.

I looked at Jan's map of PEI again and said "This has been a most interesting day of insights and information sharing. Thank you. I think we have only just begun this journey, and it's going to take a lot more work to uncover the many more pieces of the puzzle." Our guests left, but Jan stayed behind. Michel used his marker and began writing out single words from our day's findings on a large pad of paper mounted on an easel. We had identified a lot of key elements that suggested that the land deals, the political payouts for loyalty, and the connections to the 5th Floor meant this was going to be a complicated investigation. This isn't just a case of fraud or favouritism, it's a network of corruption that runs deep into the heart of government and business. It has been running for decades in the backrooms of the PEI elite, something ingrained in the Island's political culture, where the politicians promised the moon and the stars but often delivered far less. There was hope back in 2007 and 2008 that this time would be different, but as we would find out, it was just another day on the Island.

Jan, ever the pragmatic lawyer, spoke up. "I told you it would be enlightening, but of course you're going to need a lot more evidence. And we need to act quickly. The longer we wait, the more they'll get away with."

I crossed my arms, my eyes narrowing, and said "You're right, we need more than just speculation and conjecture. We need concrete data points and proof."

There were hundreds of reports on the PNP scandal and many reports detailing the activities of Bliss and Wisdom, along with its two representative companies, the Great Enlightenment Buddhist Institute Society (GEBIS)[22] and the Great Wisdom Buddhist Institute (GWBI).[23] It was clear that our job would be to research, validate, and sift through any hypothesis that might surface. I couldn't help but feel the weight of it all or even comprehend how the two stories might be connected to each other

What is sad and unfortunate is that Premier Ghiz had never been held to account for his actions, I thought, remembering that the only consequence—albeit a significant one—was Robert Ghiz's sudden and controversial resignation back in 2014. The damage, however, ran far deeper. Corruption had tainted the lives of so many Islanders—yet none more so than the two brave souls who had shared their truths with us that cold December day on the Island.

As we were about to conclude our first day of investigation, the room fell silent. For a moment, it seemed as though the weight of what we'd uncovered was settling in. The peaceful cottage with its sweeping view of the bay had felt like the perfect place to start our work. But now, the calmness of the setting began to feel like a mere façade. The investigation was no longer just a routine task—it had grown into something much more dangerous. Michel and I were in deep, entwined in a web of shadows spun over the years, and it was becoming impossible to ignore and yet so difficult to comprehend.

"We're on the right track," said Michel. Now we just have to stay focused and follow the truth, wherever it leads."

And with that, the choice was clear. We were committed. We couldn't back down now, not after the revelations we had uncovered. What had begun as a simple mission to promote books by authors I admired—Michel and Garry among them—was quickly spiralling into the need for a full-scale journalistic investigation. An investigation that would delve deep into political corruption, the CCP's United Front Work Department, Tibetan Buddhism, and even potential espionage.

It was almost too much to comprehend, especially in a place so beautiful and serene—a place where Anne of Green Gables once frolicked in the fields, untouched by the darker currents of the world. How could such a quaint, idyllic setting harbour such deep, hidden conflicts? Yet here I was, standing on the edge of something far bigger than I could have ever imagined. The investigation was only just beginning, and the truth was out there, waiting to be uncovered, no matter where it led.

CHAPTER 3

PARADISE PATTERNED

FROM HONIARA TO CHARLOTTETOWN

We realized after just ninety minutes on Prince Edward Island and hearing the first testimonies that this situation was not unique. Both Michel and I had seen this kind of operation in other parts of the country and in the world. What I was hoping was not to be true of PEI was unfolding quickly and was a deeply troubling case of political infiltration and elite capture in Canada's most romanticized province. In fact, it was a microcosm of the Chinese Communist Party's global campaign.

In 2023, I spent the summer with two political refugees—Daniel Suidani, the deposed premier of Malaita Province in the Solomon Islands, and Celsus Talifu, a courageous friend and policy advisor to successive prime ministers—confirmed what I had only begun to suspect: the CCP's playbook had been exercised far beyond our Atlantic shores. For those of you who don't know about the Solomon Islands, just watch *PT109*, the 1953 World War Two classic[24] that helped Americans get to know who Jack Kennedy was.

Daniel and Celsus had fled the Solomon Islands, a Pacific paradise under siege. They had refused to sell out their people for quick cash and shallow praise. Daniel's rejection of Beijing's diplomatic overtures made him a target. His removal from office came not from his constituents, but from political machinations backed by a foreign regime. When the two men arrived in Canada, they sought nothing more than temporary shelter and the safety to tell their story. In hosting them, I gained a frontline view into how the CCP's playbook operated—shrewd, methodical, and disturbingly familiar.[25]

What startled me most were the parallels between Prince Edward Island and Honiara province—two seemingly disconnected islands, both small, isolated, and steeped in colonial history. I flew to Washington on the invitation of my colleague, Cleo Pascal, who was a board member of the China Democracy Fund, of which I was honoured to be the CEO. Cleo, a Canadian by birth, had been working in and around Washington for some time and was currently advising on South Pacific policy matters and the QUAD. Officially the Quadrilateral Security Dialogue, the QUAD is a group of four countries: the United States, Australia, India, and Japan. Maritime cooperation [26] among them began after the Indian Ocean tsunami of 2004. But today the countries—all democracies and vibrant economies—work on a far broader agenda, which includes tackling security, economic, and health issues.

In both islands, the CCP exploited economic fragility, co-opted political elites, and deployed a soft power strategy that turned national pride into a currency of influence. I had witnessed this first-hand in PEI, where Chinese operatives used immigration pathways, real estate, and cultural symbols to embed themselves in the fabric of local governance. And I was now hearing it from men who had faced it, fought it, and lost their seats for resisting.

THE BLUEPRINT OF ELITE CAPTURE

The term "elite capture" as we have laid out previously, once sounded like academic jargon—something reserved for think tanks and white papers. Now I, along with Michel, was once again seeing it for what it was: a sophisticated assault on sovereignty, which both Michel and Garry had been warning successive governments about for decades. In the Solomon Islands, China used infrastructure investment (debt-trap diplomacy)[27] and political contributions to fracture the nation's democratic processes. The Belt and Road Initiative (BRI), pitched as a solution for underdevelopment, became a lever for control.

Daniel Suidani's refusal to engage diplomatically with Beijing made Malaita an outlier in a nation that had otherwise accepted China's overtures. The prime minister, trade minister, and finance minister were all in the pocket of Beijing, and they wanted to end Daniel's rebellious stand, which was based on ethical principles and the Rule of Law. But that refusal was short-lived. CCP-linked actors funded opposition campaigns, manipulated legislative votes, and bought influence until they had their desired outcome: Daniel's ousting. Celsus Talifu, another vocal critic of China's intentions, faced harassment, surveillance, and legal threats. The message was clear—oppose Beijing, and you will be removed. We can inform readers now that Daniel won his court case against the government's ouster of him and was awarded damages and back wages. It was a small victory, for democracy in the South Pacific for all of those involved. [28]

The tools of influence varied—some were financial, others cultural or spiritual—but the intent remained the same. In PEI, those tools were wielded by individuals like Frank Zhou and Sherry Huang, who operated as entrepreneurs and as agents of soft power. Their businesses, real estate deals, and philanthropic ventures acted as a front for United Front Work Department operations—a CCP network that blurs the lines between civilian, commercial, and governmental interests.

POLITICAL ACCESS IN PEI

One need look no further than Robert Ghiz, the former premier, to understand how elite capture operates in a Canadian context. During his tenure and beyond, Ghiz maintained a close relationship with Frank Zhou who would go on to become a godparent for one of his children. That level of intimacy speaks not just to personal friendship, but to a strategic alliance. Zhou purchased Ghiz's personal home according to the PEI land registry record that we obtained. The purchase on its face appears benign, but when examined in the context of land transfers and development privileges, perhaps reveals a deeper, more calculated exchange.

Adding complexity to the picture is developer Tim Banks, CEO of APM Group a local real estate developer was also involved with Zhou and the premier on the same property according to a land registry record. Banks has developed several major projects on PEI. This includes the controversial Blackbush project which the permit applications began in 2017 according to government records. In a October 24, PNI Atlantic Article Banks said, "It's only narrow-minded people that have an issue with it," Banks said bluntly. "Our community, which is extremely strong, are all in favour of the project because we employ 100 people. We have 55 working in our restaurant alone to make us the busiest restaurant on the north shore."

Had Bank's cozy relationship with Ghiz help pave the way for approvals when the Liberal government was still in power in 2017 that might have otherwise faced bureaucratic obstacles? It's a development, that has created new jobs and economic benefits to be sure but, is the process objective and transparent for all? In the seemingly opaque corridors of PEI's government and real estate approval process, sweetheart deals seem to the currency of power. These transactions may not breach legal boundaries, but they test the integrity of public office.

During the early 2000's PEI's vulnerability laid not in its leadership alone, but in seemingly structural dependence on foreign investment and capital programs like the Provincial Nominee Program (PNP), designed to attract investment and stimulate immigration. What began as an economic development tool as the record will indicate became a visa-for-influence scheme. Zhou and Huang, along with their ties to Beijing and extensive Chinese business connections, funnelled investors through the system, gaining not just financial leverage but political access and social status. They were the go-to couple if you wanted an opportunity in China, and the province and its politicians all lined up at the trough to gain access and build opportunities that would also benefit Islanders, but nobody calculated the long-term costs of aligning with an increasingly belligerent and authoritarian regime.

And then there was Anne of Green Gables—Canada's literary jewel, co-opted as a soft power symbol. Zhou founded Anne of China Inc., along with PEI insiders Duncan McIntosh and his partner Wade MacLauchlan, who at the time was chancellor of the University of Prince Edward Island. When it was formed in 2011, everyone painted the project as a cultural exchange and good for Canada/Beijing relations. With everyone on board, including the prime minister, who could blame them? In reality, and as we can now assess, it was an instrument of narrative warfare. By inserting Anne into the fabric of Canada–China relations, the project framed Chinese influence as wholesome, educational, and benign. The underlying truth—that the profits went mostly to private and foreign hands, and the Anne of Green Gables Foundation received paltry royalties—was conveniently hidden from public view. We contacted the Foundation, but they did not agree to our request for an interview.

TWO ISLANDS, ONE STRATEGY

As Daniel and Celsus made their story public, the symmetry became haunting. Like PEI, the Solomon Islands is a post-colonial democracy struggling with underdevelopment. It has a small population, limited infrastructure, and a deep reliance on foreign aid. This makes it a prime target for Beijing's United Front Work Department, which seeks out "soft targets" to establish geopolitical footholds.

The security agreement signed between the Solomon Islands and China in 2022 caused international alarm. It allowed for the possibility of Chinese military presence in the Pacific—just miles from strategic shipping lanes. The deal was shrouded in secrecy, approved without full parliamentary oversight, and criticized by transparency groups as a violation of democratic norms. It mirrored the backroom style of politics we had seen in Charlottetown, where land deals, business licences, and cultural programs were green-lit in silence.

Both islands fell prey to a colonial inversion—instead of European missionaries and traders, they now welcomed Beijing's billionaires, monks, and "philanthropists." But the methods of social control remained strikingly similar: control the narrative, capture the elite, marginalize dissent, and wrap it all in the flag of development.

MORAL COMPROMISE, POLITICAL CAPTURE

The story of Robert Ghiz is not an isolated scandal; it is a case study in political compromise. When Zhou purchased his home, was he buying property—or buying access? When Zhou and Huang stood as godparents to his child, was it an act of friendship—or a strategic relationship sealed in sentiment? When Anne of Green Gables was marketed to China with the help of Ghiz allies and former Canadian dignitaries, was it diplomacy—or the sale of national identity?

The answer lies in the cumulative effect of these actions. On their own, each transaction might seem legal, even innocuous. But taken together, they form a mosaic of elite capture. As premier, Ghiz oversaw the expansion of the Provincial Nominee Program that ultimately enriched his future business allies. As a private citizen, he benefited from transactions with individuals now widely reported to be part of CCP networks. His resignation under a cloud of silence in 2014, and the election of Wade MacLauchlan, a partner in Anne of China Inc. and then as premier, signalled to most: your secrets are safe with us and indicated to any public observer or analyst that it was going to be business as usual on PEI. But the mounting evidence that is presented throughout this book backed by already countless media stories highlights the a pattern of potential corruption and political skulduggery that seems to have existed for decades on the idyllic Island.

The cycle continues. Progressive Conservative MPP Steven Myers was seen hammering the premier about his relationship with Frank Zhou, speaking indirectly about sweet deals and elite capture, and made it known that he and Conservative Party leader Dennis King were going to make change and get to the bottom of the PNP land purchases by the Bliss and Wisdom group and the scandal of it all.

Of course, as history has played out Myers did nothing, and neither did Premier Dennis King, who may have had a walk in the snow like Trudeau, resigning on February 20, 2025. Many speculated about the troubles facing King, and hence the resignation. However, his reward was to be named ambassador to Ireland. The prime minister was still dealing with his proximity to Beijing and foreign interference, but he named King ambassador two weeks before giving up the reins of the Liberal Party to Mark Carney after he won the Liberal leadership race.

I hope the premier-turned-ambassador enjoys the Guinness and green countryside of Ireland. Ireland is used to former premiers, as King joins former premier Pat Binns, who also enjoyed this plum assignment after leaving office in 2007. One can only assume the political elite on the Island thought there was growing discontent amongst Islanders and needed a new horse to back. The premier had lots of opportunity to investigate endless numbers of scandals but chose not to, at the expense of all. His government had a great opportunity to look deeper into PEI's reliance on China when he came to power, and to set a new course. But a lot of good investment and money was flooding the Island, so why go down that route.

GLOBAL PLAYBOOK, LOCAL EXECUTION

China does not send tanks or troops. It sends cheques, charm, and Confucius Institutes. It embeds agents of influence within temples, real estate firms, tech incubators, and literary foundations. It whispers in the ears of vulnerable leaders and cloaks imperial ambition in the language of mutual growth.

Daniel and Celsus had seen this strategy tear apart their nation's democratic institutions. They watched friends take money, betray values, and rationalize their choices in the name of "partnership." They had fought back, paid the price, and were now seeking refuge in a country facing the same challenge from the same adversary.

Their courage helped clarify mine. What was happening in PEI wasn't a scandal—it was a symptom of a larger disease. From real estate transactions in Stratford to political purges in Malaita, the tactics were identical. Only the language, the packaging, and the geography changed.

ONE ISLAND IS A WARNING, TWO OR THREE OR MORE IS A PATTERN

Canada cannot afford to see PEI as an anomaly. It is the canary in the coal mine, just as the Solomon Islands were for the South Pacific or Antigua and Barbados were in the Caribbean, according to the U.S. State Department, which we contacted in April 2024 while attending a diplomatic event in Montreal. Following the event, we got on a conference call with U.S. State officials in late May to discuss the disturbing influence and control Beijing seemed to be exerting on the Island's politicians and academics and its economic future. They had seen the same strategy been deployed in the Caribbean islands and wanted to compare notes.

When we ignore the soft whispers of manipulation in small provinces, we invite louder consequences in larger ones.

China's strategy is not about one island. It's about proof of concept—if elite capture works in Charlottetown and Honiara, it can work in Ottawa, Wellington, and Washington. What we're witnessing is not just infiltration; it is the deliberate construction of an international order reshaped by silence, purchased loyalty, and cultural confusion.

As this book will show, PEI's story is not just about Anne, Buddhism, or immigration. It's about the soul of a country and the lines we draw to protect it. It is about revealing the CCP's strategy to covertly establish forward operating bases (FOB) with the intention to operate within our borders. And if the world is to learn anything from Daniel, Celsus, and the quiet deals in our own backyard, it must begin by naming the threat: elite capture, directed by a foreign regime, hiding in plain sight.

CHAPTER 4
THE UNITED FRONT
FROM BEIJING TO CHARLOTTETOWN

"Through its United Front work strategy, which Xi Jinping has called a "magic weapon," the Chinese Communist Party uses every tool at its disposal—whether legal or illicit—to influence the American people and interfere in democratic societies. Our bipartisan memo on United Front work will help the American people recognize and resist the CCP's malign influence."

MIKE GALLAGHER,
Former Chair, House Select Committee
on China, (US Congress)

THE UNITED FRONT AND THE EVOLUTION OF INFLUENCE OPERATIONS GLOBALLY

THE LONG MARCH OF INFLUENCE: FROM MAO TO XI

Mao Zedong once famously declared, "The United Front is a magic weapon for the victory of the revolution." This phrase was not merely rhetorical; it defined a strategy to shape the Chinese Communist Party's (CCP) approach to internal consolidation and foreign influence for nearly a century. From the early days of the CCP's struggle against Japan's imperial forces[29] to its modern-day global influence campaigns, the United Front strategy has remained a central pillar of Chinese foreign policy. Today, under Xi Jinping, this strategy has evolved into a complex, multifaceted network designed to infiltrate, manipulate, and control academic, religious, charitable, and government institutions worldwide.

In our respective fields, our team have spent years tracing the lines of influence stretching from Beijing to Western capitals, uncovering the mechanisms through which the CCP extends its reach. From Canada to the United Kingdom, from the United States to Germany, the same playbook appears time and time again—leveraging economic dependence, co-opting elites, embedding operatives within political circles, and using transnational repression to silence critics in the academic, diaspora, journalism, and human rights communities. As we begin to explore the CCP's United Front Work Department, all of this will become much clearer.

THE HISTORICAL FOUNDATIONS OF THE UNITED FRONT

The United Front Work Department was forged in the fires of ideological warfare and honed during China's civil war and its struggle against Japanese occupation. Mao understood the necessity of alliances—however temporary—to advance his revolution. He co-opted business leaders, scholars, and even rival political factions, weaving a complex web of loyalties and dependencies that ultimately served the CCP's ambitions. These tactics, perfected domestically, would later be adapted for international application, targeting foreign elites, politicians, and diaspora communities.

With Deng Xiaoping's economic reforms in the 1980s, the CCP found new avenues to advance its influence. No longer relying solely on ideological appeal, it wielded economic leverage to entangle foreign nations in its orbit. The Belt and Road Initiative (BRI), Confucius Institutes, and state-owned enterprises served as Trojan horses for the CCP's political agenda, embedding its interests within the institutions of its global partners. Rather than taking you down the academic path, we have assembled some case studies with citations that best illustrate anecdotally how this works in Canada and worldwide. We have investigated, researched, and published papers, articles, and books on elite influence and capture in Canada and have seen how easily individuals can be captured, often without even understanding that they have become a tool for foreign government influence.

WHAT IS THE UNITED FRONT AND WHY DOES IT MATTER?

The United Front Work Department (UFWD) is a key organ of the Chinese Communist Party (CCP), responsible for managing relations with various groups and individuals both domestically and internationally to advance the

CCP's interests. As of 2019, the UFWD was reported to have more than 40,000 personnel and an estimated budget exceeding $2.6 billion, surpassing the funding allocated to China's Ministry of Foreign Affairs.

Under Xi Jinping's leadership, the UFWD[30] has expanded significantly. Reports indicate that the department has doubled in size since 2015, reflecting its elevated role in the CCP's strategic operations globally. Internationally, the UFWD operates through an extensive network of organizations and individuals aimed at influencing foreign societies and governments. For instance, a 2020 investigation identified nearly 600 groups linked with the United Front in the United States, and a more recent database compiled by Nic Eftimiades,[31] professor at Penn State and former CIA official, has identified close to 900 groups. In Europe, a 2024 study uncovered 233 individuals across the continent connected to the United Front system, and in Canada we have close to 100 UFWD affiliated organizations, including on Prince Edward Island. These affiliates engage in various activities: political lobbying, cultural exchanges, and business collaborations, all designed to promote Beijing's interests abroad.

The UFWD's global reach and influence have raised concerns among several governments and organizations about foreign interference and the covert promotion of CCP agendas.[32]

CASE STUDIES IN CCP INFLUENCE OPERATIONS

UNITED STATES: COVERT POLITICAL INFLUENCE AND ELECTORAL MEDDLING

Infiltration of American political institutions has long been a CCP objective. Her relationships with U.S. politicians, including infiltration of American political institutions, has long been a CCP objective. The case of Fang Fang, a suspected Chinese intelligence operative who embedded herself in California's Democratic circles, is a textbook example of elite capture tactics. Her relationships with U.S. politicians, including Representative Eric Swalwell, raised alarms within the intelligence community about Beijing's ability to cultivate assets within the American political system. The exposure of this operation was only the tip ...

Meanwhile, technology has provided another vector for CCP interference. TikTok and Huawei have become battlegrounds in a larger struggle to control digital infrastructure and data sovereignty. According to the U.S. Council on Foreign Relations,[33] Huawei's expansion into Western 5G networks was curtailed after intelligence agencies in the United States and allied nations identified backdoor access risks that could allow Beijing to conduct espionage and cyber operations on an unprecedented scale.

In September 2024, Linda Sun, a former aide to New York governors Andrew Cuomo and Kathy Hochul, was arrested alongside her husband, Chris Hu, on charges of acting as an illegal agent for the People's Republic of China (PRC) and money laundering.[34] Federal prosecutors allege that Sun leveraged her influential positions within the New York State government to covertly advance Beijing's interests, including obstructing Taiwanese representatives' access to state officials and modifying official communications to align with PRC objectives.

Sun's deepening ties with Chinese officials were further evidenced by her attendance at the 70th anniversary of the Chinese People's Political Consultative Conference (CPPCC) in 2019, held at Beijing's Great Hall of the People. This event convenes overseas Chinese elites and is a platform for the CCP's United Front Work Department to engage influential individuals in promoting its global agenda. Sherry Huang and Frank Zhou, known for their involvement in fostering China–Canada relations, were in attendance as well demonstrating they are part of China's United Front.[35]

The case of Linda Sun underscores the PRC's strategy of elite capture, wherein individuals in key positions are co-opted to further foreign interests within domestic institutions. By embedding operatives like Sun within the U.S. political framework, the Chinese government effectively manipulated policy discussions and access at the state level. By this infiltration, the integrity of New York's governance was severely compromised. This case exemplified a broader pattern of foreign interference aimed at undermining democratic processes from within.

The Department of Justice (DOJ) was able to lay charges against Sun using its *Foreign Agents Registration Act* (FARA), passed in 1938. It was enacted to require individuals acting on behalf of foreign entities in the United States to register with the Department of Justice and disclose their activities, relationships, and funding. FARA was originally intended to combat the spread of Nazi propaganda during the pre–Second World War period.

CANADA: ELITE CAPTURE AND ECONOMIC LEVERAGE

Canada has emerged as a key target for CCP influence operations, particularly in political and economic circles. The case of Michael Chan, a former Ontario cabinet minister and now the deputy mayor of Markham, illustrates the depth of elite capture. Intelligence sources flagged Chan for his close ties to Beijing, raising concerns about the CCP's ability to shape Canadian policy through proxy actors embedded in government structures.

Michael Chan has been investigated and has been the subject of multiple Canadian Security Intelligence Service (CSIS) inquiries. However, in the 2021 election cycle, Bill Blair, then Ontario Minister of Public Safety, delayed signing the warrant for surveillance by fifty-three days. This delay was first reported by the *Globe and Mail* and further investigated by journalist Sam Cooper, who noted that top-level CSIS officials had briefed the minister in advance as well as during testimony in the House of Commons in 2023.

The entire episode had the hallmarks of high-level political interference designed to protect a friend and colleague—Michael Chan (former MPP and minister in the Wynne and McGuinty governments)—from being investigated during the 2021 election. Chan had been a key fundraiser within the so-called "Mandarin Class" elite for both the provincial and federal Liberal parties for decades. It seems, for some, national security should not interfere with the political influence and operational latitude of the PRC's consulates and United Front actors in Ontario.

The Michael Chan affair illustrates a sobering reality: candidates aligned with the interests of the CCP can be directly voted into public office and exert influence over decisions that affect Canada's national and economic security. Unlike other democracies, Canada lacks legislation requiring foreign agents to register their activities. This absence has contributed to a national security vulnerability that has persisted for decades.

By 2024, the Foreign Interference Commission, led by Justice Hogue, was fully under way. While exploring foreign influence operations by hostile states and their proxies, the need for legislative action had become obvious. Despite repeated promises, the federal Liberal government continued to stall on enacting a Foreign Influence Transparency Registry. This contrasted starkly with jurisdictions like the United States, where individuals suspected of acting as foreign agents can be prosecuted.

Recognizing this legislative void, activists Gloria Fung and Marcus Kolga established the Canadian Coalition for a Foreign Influence Transparency Registry. The coalition, composed of more than thirty multicultural, human rights, and policy organizations, was granted standing at the Hogue Commission. Their objective was clear: to pressure the government to enact long-overdue legislation.

Gloria Fung (Podium), Marcus Kolga (far right). From left, Liberal MPs Sameer Zuberi, Ali Ehsassi, and John McKay; René Villemure, The Bloc (centre left); Jenny Kwan, NDP, behind Gloria Fung (podium); Uyghur activist, Raziya Mahmut; and Conservative MP Tom Kmiec.

On 30 April 2024, Fung and Kolga organized a press conference on Parliament Hill to draw attention to the lack of a federal registry. Although only Robert Fife from the *Globe and Mail* and I attended in person, the event was livestreamed and viewed widely. Politicians from every major party, including Green Party leader Elizabeth May, NDP MP Jenny Kwan, Liberal MP Sameer Zuberi, and Bloc Québécois MP René Villemure, voiced their support for immediate legislative action.

Fung stood at the podium and declared: "The government has been talking about creating [a registry] since 2021. There has been extensive consultation. The only thing lacking is the political will to get it done. If the legislation is not in place before the next election, the interference we saw in 2019 and 2021 will repeat itself."

During the Q&A session, Robert Fife posed the first question and I posed two questions, the first to MP Jenny Kwan: "Since you have been a target of foreign interference, and whistleblowers have been critical to these hearings, how will you protect journalists and whistleblowers who have come forward?"

Her response was candid: "Thank you for that excellent question. Journalists and whistleblowers have been targeted as well. Much of the information we've learned about foreign interference came from leaks and whistleblowers. We must undertake measures to protect them. We hope the [Hogue] commission will protect the diaspora community and use every tool we have to protect all Canadians. Bloc MP René Villemure added, "We have legislation that we're going to table during this session. It will be strong and ensure that everyone is protected. We went outside the box—something quite different, but effective."

That wouldn't become necessary, as the press conference marked a watershed moment in forcing the government's hand. With media pressure mounting and political consensus forming, the government tabled Bill C-70, the *Countering Foreign Interference Act*. It received its first reading on 6 May 2024. The legislation passed committee with several strengthened provisions and was given Royal Assent[36] on 20 June. However, despite its passage, no commissioner had been appointed by April 2025, and thus the registry remains non-operational.

At a subsequent press conference in February 2025, Fung, Kolga, and other human rights advocates again demanded implementation. Gloria told me in an interview on 17 April 2025, "There is still no political will. Without a commissioner, the registry cannot be enforced."

In the midst of this, the United Front Work Department continued its activity, about which all who attended the press conference in Ottawa said without equivocation: This is going to happen in the next federal election—and it did. During the 2025 federal election, its proxies showed strong bias in favour of the Liberal Party under new Prime Minister Mark Carney,[37] who had recently won the party leadership.

The controversy intensified in March, when Liberal MP Paul Chiang[38] was forced to resign as the candidate for Markham–Unionville following revelations that he had encouraged the public to locate his Conservative rival, Joe Tay, and deliver him to the Chinese consulate to collect a $1 million Hong Kong bounty. Tay, a pro-democracy Hong Kong activist and operator of the YouTube channel Hong Konger Station, was among dozens of diaspora figures targeted by Beijing. Two of the original eight wanted activists, Nathan Law and Finn Lau, both known to our team, have also written forewords for recent titles published by Optimum in which they participated as sources and writers.

After a long weekend with many calls for the Liberal leader to remove Chiang from the ballot, Prime Minister Carney stated on Monday, 30 March, that he had confidence in Chiang. The PM initially continued to defend Chiang's comments as a "teachable moment" and allowed him to remain on the ballot. However, with mounting pressure, Chiang eventually resigned just after midnight on Tuesday.

But as soon as that controversy was over, the PM chose another candidate with an equally troubling background and closeness to Beijing. Peter Yuen, the new Liberal candidate, had also been linked to United Front groups and had reportedly attended a military parade in Beijing hosted by Xi Jinping in 2015.[39]

Yuen's name appears as an honorary director of the Jiangsu Commerce Council of Canada (JCCC), an organization based in Toronto with longstanding ties to the United Front. Had the Liberals been paying attention—or better still, taken foreign interference seriously—perhaps they would have chosen a more pro-democracy diaspora citizen to represent the riding.

Whether in British Columbia or Prince Edward Island, the CCP has consistently demonstrated an enduring interest in influencing Canadian politicians and business leaders nationwide, and our provincial and federal leaders seem to keep welcoming the incursion.

THE REAL ESTATE CONNECTION

Simultaneously, Canada's real estate market has been used as a conduit for Chinese capital flight and money laundering. The "Vancouver Model," which involves underground banking networks and illicit financial flows, has allowed billions of dollars to move through Canadian financial institutions—some directly linked to United Front operatives and transnational organized crime.

As you will discover in Chapter 17, "Evidence of Money Laundering," this same network was used to purchase properties worth hundreds of millions of dollars on Prince Edward Island. I want to emphasize that not all of the money being invested in businesses or real estate is money from criminals. Often, individuals would simply use this underground bank to move money into place in various jurisdictions and deposit their personal or business money in the bank accounts of the organized crime groups, netting a 3 to 5% commission on the proceeds now in Canada or other jurisdictions.

UNITED KINGDOM: THE CCP'S INFLUENCE IN ACADEMIA AND POLITICS

The United Kingdom has faced significant CCP infiltration efforts, particularly in its academic institutions and political system. Confucius Institutes, ostensibly cultural and language centres, have been used as tools of influence, silencing discussions critical of Beijing's policies on Taiwan and Tibet, and human rights abuses in Xinjiang. [(UK Parliament Foreign Affairs Committee, 2021)].

Perhaps the most glaring case of political interference in the United Kingdom is that of Christine Lee, a lawyer identified by MI5 as an agent of the UFWD. Through strategic political donations and legal consultancy, Lee gained access to British politicians, influencing parliamentary debates and policy discussions on China. [(MI5 Intelligence Report, 2022)].

GERMANY: INDUSTRIAL ESPIONAGE AND ECONOMIC DEPENDENCE

As Europe's largest economy, Germany has found itself in a precarious position due to its economic dependence on China. Volkswagen's continued operations in Xinjiang, despite overwhelming evidence of human rights abuses, exemplify the CCP's ability to pressure Western corporations into complicity. The German auto industry's reliance on Chinese markets has created vulnerabilities that Beijing has exploited to advance its geopolitical interests.[40]

In addition, intelligence failures have exposed Germany's vulnerability to CCP espionage. The arrest of Klaus L., a former German intelligence officer caught spying for China, underscored the extent to which Beijing had penetrated European security agencies in 2022, according to the German Federal Office for the Protection of the Constitution.

THE 2049 STRATEGY: THE CCP'S LONG-TERM OBJECTIVES

As China moves towards its 2049 centennial goal—intended to mark its full emergence as the world's dominant power—its foreign influence operations will continue expanding. The CCP's approach, honed over decades, seeks to systematically weaken democratic institutions, control global narratives, and erode the resilience of Western societies.

Through a combination of elite capture, technological dominance, economic entanglement, and transnational repression, Beijing has positioned itself as a formidable force in shaping global governance. The challenge for democratic nations is clear: recognizing these threats and developing coordinated strategies to counteract them.

As for Prince Edward Island, there is more than enough open-source intelligence that clearly documents China's interest in the Birthplace of Confederation and, as the next section lays out, the more pragmatic case for elite capture and the United Front's influence on the Island.

THE UNITED FRONT

PRINCE EDWARD ISLAND: THE SOFTEST TARGET

At first glance, Prince Edward Island seems an unlikely theatre in a global influence campaign. Canada's smallest province by population and GDP lacks the diplomatic weight of Ottawa, the economic pull of Toronto, and the multicultural complexity of Vancouver. And yet, it is precisely this combination—small scale, limited scrutiny, and outsized political access—that made PEI a perfect target for elite capture.

The CCP understands that influence doesn't always require hard power. Sometimes, all it takes is a handshake, a dinner, and the promise of investment. PEI's leadership was all in. The red carpet was rolled out for Chinese delegations. Memoranda of understanding flowed. Trade missions were treated like diplomatic breakthroughs. The Island, once imagined by Lucy Maud Montgomery as a pastoral refuge, was now an entry point for a broader geopolitical strategy. The Island's first United Front operatives arrived in the 1990s, but most of them, according to Alan MacPhee, tried to recruit.

Nowhere is this more vividly captured than in the story of Anne of China Inc. (2011),[41] involving Frank Zhou, a Canada-wide entrepreneur, Wade MacLauchlan, who at the time was president of the University of Prince Edward Island but became the premier of PEI in 2014, and his partner, Duncan MacIntosh, the artistic director of the Charlottetown Festival. The initiative aimed to export Anne of Green Gables—the Island's most iconic cultural brand—to China, thus transforming a beloved Canadian literary figure into a vehicle for soft power diplomacy.

Of course, it served as a conduit for tourism and investment by Chinese people unfamiliar with the tiny idyllic Island so as not to diminish its more utilitarian purpose. At the time, we believe both countries considered this a win-win scenario as it fit the prevailing position of Global Affairs and the government that further investment and integration with China was good for PEI and Canada. Once MacLauchlan became a candidate in 2014, he resigned from the company, but there was no mention that his partner resigned or whether he dissolved the corporation.

The Anne of China project, which will be explored later in this book, was more than just cultural exchange. It was a strategic move. It symbolized how deep the ties had grown between PEI's political leadership and actors with direct or indirect connections to Beijing's influence networks. What began as tourism and trade soon evolved into more sophisticated partnerships—business development zones, real estate ventures, agricultural collaborations. In many cases, transparency was lacking, scrutiny absent, and resistance muted.

A source familiar with the Island's political scene put it bluntly: "PEI offered Beijing a boutique showroom for its influence model. Small enough to control. Big enough to matter."

It wasn't just about what China wanted. It was about what Canada—especially in places like PEI—was willing to give.

In October 2025, I attended an event to which my colleague Nury Turkel (Senior Fellow, the Hudson Institute) had invited me to in October 2024. He introduced me to Mike Gallagher, the once very powerful Chair of the U.S. House Select Committee on the Chinese Communist Party (CCP) from its establishment on January 10, 2023, until he resigned from Congress on April 24, 2024.

After the event, we briefly discussed *The Mosaic Effect*, which he was aware of through the DC network of staffers on the Hill. We got onto the United Front and espionage by the CCP in America and Canada. I brought up PEI and how Anne of Green Gables became the perfect tool for benign reciprocity between PEI and Beijing. Gallagher[42] shook his head. "You know, Canada needs to wake up and quick. Thanks for publishing the books you do."

Mike had recently joined Palantir Technologies, a defence organization leveraging AI to streamline and deliver more cost-effective solutions to the U.S. military, and spoke about the need for the Pentagon to also get its head out of the sand as we are not able to build out its military infrastructure (ships, planes, tanks) fast enough to meet the emerging and significant threat posed by America's number one enemy, China.

With PEI once having China as its second-largest trading partner and Canada needing to choose who it will align itself with, PEI and Canada are faced with some tough choices until the Communist regime makes the necessary changes that so we can engage with a partner not an authoritarian and repressive China.

Like many politicians across Canada, the Island's political leadership was eager to court the Chinese and Hong Kong capital. It bought into the myth of benign investment and mutual gain. But behind the red envelopes and friendly optics was a system designed to build loyalty, extract influence, and shape political outcomes. This was elite capture at its most subtle—and most dangerous.

And PEI wasn't alone. It was just the easiest entry point.

The struggle against Chinese Communist Party (CCP) foreign interference is not merely a geopolitical concern—it is a battle for the preservation of democratic values and national sovereignty. Governments must move swiftly to implement robust foreign influence transparency laws, reinforce counterintelligence capabilities, and build economic resilience against Beijing's increasingly coercive tactics.

It was unanimously agreed in 2024 that Canada would introduce a Foreign Agent Registration Act, Bill C-70. Yet, as Canadians have now voted in the 2025 federal election, no such legislation has been enacted, no commissioner selected for the process. The delay is not only troubling—it is dangerous.

As a group who has spent years investigating, writing, and publishing about these influence operations, we have witnessed first-hand the scale, reach, and sophistication of the CCP's strategy. But I have also seen how exposure, vigilance, and coordinated resistance can blunt its advance. The fight is far from over, and the actions taken—or not taken—today will shape the balance of global power for decades to come.

The world now stands at a critical crossroads. Whether democratic nations can mount a sustained defence against CCP subversion will define, in no uncertain terms, the geopolitical balance of the twenty-first century.

Prince Edward Island became an easy target. Jean Chrétien helped introduce Frank Zhou to the province, and both Robert Ghiz and Wade MacLauchlan, seemingly elite-captured, maintained close relationships with Zhou and Sherry Huang. They were portrayed as innovative entrepreneurs, an immigration success story and they are, but beneath that surface lay deeper connections—connections shaped, if not directed, by interests in Beijing. What unfolded on the Island was not unique; rather, it is a microcosm of what this book will continue to explore.

The next chapter will take you on a somewhat disturbing journey of discovery as to how this influence led to the destruction of people's lives and how, once again, PEI always tries to bury its secrets.

CHAPTER 5
PRINCE EDWARD ISLAND'S ENGAGEMENT WITH THE PEOPLE'S REPUBLIC OF CHINA
(2000-2020)

INTEGRATING THE TRUDEAU GOVERNMENT'S STRATEGIC VISION AND THE BELT AND ROAD INITIATIVE

To better understand how the book unfolds, it is best that we all revisit our past. As China was gaining acceptance around the world and was busy modernizing its nation, every democracy had a role to play. In Canada our politicians fully believed that by engaging in cultural and trade missions we could start to wean ourselves from our dependency on North American trade, create growth, and target immigration from the People's Republic of China (PRC) and other Asian nations.

From 2000 to 2020, PEI embarked on a journey to strengthen its cultural, educational, and business ties with the PRC. This period coincided with significant national efforts under Prime Minister Justin Trudeau's administration to enhance Canada's relationship with China, aligning with China's Belt and Road Initiative (BRI) and the vision of "shared values for the common destiny of humankind." This chapter explores PEI's multifaceted engagement with China, set against the backdrop of national strategies and global initiatives. Since 2020 both interaction and engagement with the PRC has slowed due to the lingering effects of both the Covid-19 pandemic and the "two Michaels" affair.[43]

We also explore how PEI and Canada are caught between a superpower rivalry that already resembles the preamble to World War Two. In the CCP's hybrid warfare strategies, you can't win the Art of War (not a single shot to be fired) without people-to-people engagement and relationships. The

Chinese government and people are a patient lot, and while we look at four-year election cycles, they work on 100-year plans, and the 2049 plan speaks to those ambitions. Understanding the interests of Canada and hence of Atlantic Canada and PEI will be better viewed during the period from 2000 to the pandemic in 2020.

In the early 2000s Prime Minister Jean Chrétien and the Liberals were falling all over themselves to build a stronger relationship with China and were anxious to also help PEI get its fair share. Frank Zhou and Sherry Huang, the power couple from China who were about to open the doors for trade and commerce for PEI and other eastern provinces, had spent some time in Ottawa and were introduced to key political figures linked to the federal Liberals. They included Robert Ghiz and Wade MacLauchlan (pictured below with the Prime Minister and Zhou and Huang), as well as business entrepreneurs on the right side of Canada's ambition to develop opportunities with the PRC.

Making friends: Robert Ghiz, Lawrence MacAulay, Frank Zhou, Sherry Huang, and Former Prime Minister Jean Chrétien.

CULTURAL AND EDUCATIONAL ENGAGEMENTS

PEI's educational institutions have been at the forefront of fostering cultural and educational exchanges with China. Holland College, for instance, established joint ventures to deliver programs such as International Hospitality Management and Computer Networking Technology in China. These collaborations not only provided Chinese students with access to quality education but also enriched PEI's academic environment with diverse perspectives.

EDUCATIONAL INITIATIVES WITH CHINA (2000-2020)

Holland College Educational Joint Ventures (2000–2001): Holland College signed several Educational Joint Venture (EJV) agreements with partner colleges and institutes across China. These ventures aimed to share educational methodologies and create opportunities for students in both China and Canada. The programs were structured over three years, with the first year focusing on English-language preparation and subsequent years dedicated to delivering Holland College diploma programs in English. This allowed students to earn a Canadian credential without leaving China.

Jinling High School Affiliated Program (2015): In September 2015, an affiliated school agreement was established with Jinling High School in Nanjing, China. The school offers the PEI public school curriculum for grades 10 to 12. In the 2020–2021 academic year, the program had an enrollment of 159 students.

Ganzhou School PEI Curriculum Program: A school in Ganzhou, China, offers the PEI curriculum to students in grades 10 and 11. Students who successfully complete these courses attend school in PEI for grade 12 and, if successful, are granted a PEI high school certificate. In the 2020–2021 school year, the program had 24 students.

Holland College Service Agreement (2018): During the Atlantic Growth Strategy mission to China in 2018, Holland College signed a service agreement to promote and explore the potential of its international study program in designated areas in China.

Study Abroad Partnership (2018): A partnership agreement was established to increase the number of Chinese students in Atlantic Canada, enhancing cultural exchange and educational diversity.

In 2018, during the Atlantic Growth Strategy mission to China, Holland College signed multiple agreements to expand its educational offerings. These included delivering programs in Accounting Technology, Business Administration, and Marketing and Advertising Management.

Such initiatives underscore PEI's commitment to educational excellence and cultural exchange.

Premier Wade MacLauchlan highlighted the significance of these partnerships, stating, "This is great news for a great PEI organization. I offer my congratulations to Holland College and its employees, all of whom are playing a part in growing the Atlantic economy by creating more exports."

BUSINESS AND TRADE RELATIONS

The period from 2015 onwards marked a pivotal phase in PEI's trade relations with China, influenced by national policies aimed at diversifying trade partnerships. The Trudeau government's emphasis on engaging with China as a key trade partner resonated with PEI's strategic objectives. In 2018, during the Atlantic Growth Strategy mission, several PEI-based companies secured significant agreements with Chinese counterparts, collectively valued at approximately $321.6 million. Notable among these was Sunrise Group's partnership to promote Canadian brands on Chinese e-commerce platforms, reflecting the growing importance of digital trade channels.

Minister of Agriculture and Agri-Food Lawrence MacAulay emphasized the quality of Atlantic Canadian products, stating, "Atlantic Canadian products have a universal appeal and are known for their quality." This sentiment was echoed by Scott Brison, President of the Treasury Board, who remarked, "Atlantic Canada is home to many innovative companies that are creating growth and well-paying jobs by moving into new export opportunities in growing markets."

TOURISM DEVELOPMENT

The designation of 2018 as the Canada-China Year of Tourism highlighted the mutual interest in promoting travel between the two countries. PEI capitalized on this momentum by showcasing its unique cultural heritage and natural beauty to attract Chinese tourists. Initiatives included collaborations with Chinese travel agencies and participation in tourism expos to position PEI as a premier destination for Chinese travellers.

ALIGNMENT WITH THE BELT AND ROAD INITIATIVE

China's Belt and Road Initiative (BRI), announced by President Xi Jinping in 2013, aimed to enhance global trade connectivity and foster economic cooperation. PEI's proactive engagement with China during this period can be viewed as a regional alignment with the broader objectives of the BRI. By strengthening infrastructure, expanding trade routes, and enhancing people-to-people ties, PEI contributed to the vision of shared prosperity and mutual development.

CHINA: TRADE AND DIPLOMATIC STRATEGIC VISION UNDER TRUDEAU'S LIBERALS

The Trudeau government's approach to China was built on a vision of deep economic ties, framed by the belief that trade and diplomacy could strengthen Canada's long-term prosperity. Ministers spoke in sweeping terms of opportunity, progress, and the value of collaboration. Business leaders were courted, deals were made, and press releases heralded the dawn of a new era in Sino-Canadian relations.

One of the most significant expressions of this vision came in 2018, when the Atlantic Growth Strategy mission to China took place. Federal ministers and Atlantic premiers led delegations to Beijing, showcasing what Canada had to offer. Businesses, educational institutions, and regional stakeholders saw the trip as a chance to expand their reach into a market of over 1.4 billion people. Deals were signed, partnerships announced, and the trip was deemed a success—at least on the surface.

Premier Dwight Ball of Newfoundland and Labrador reflected on the mission's outcomes, highlighting the enthusiasm that permeated the delegation's efforts.

> "This Atlantic Growth Strategy trade mission to China has provided valuable opportunities . . . to focus on building more markets for our quality goods and services, attract investment, and create more jobs."

His words spoke to the carefully cultivated optimism of the time. The vision was clear: Canada would step boldly into a future defined by trade, investment, and cooperation with China.

Yet, behind this optimism lurked a more complicated reality—one that the Trudeau government seemed either blind to or wilfully dismissive of.

At the time, Trudeau was still chasing the elusive prize of a free trade agreement with China. His government operated under the assumption that China viewed Canada as a valued trade partner, an essential player in a mutually beneficial economic relationship. This assumption was not just flawed—it was dangerously naive.

China's interest in Canada was never about balanced trade or mutual prosperity. It was about control and influence. Beijing's true priorities were far more strategic: access to the United States for espionage and covert operations, securing Canada's critical minerals, and gaining a foothold in the nation's vast oil and gas reserves.

The Trans Mountain Pipeline, a project that had been a point of contention in domestic politics, was, in reality, part of a broader international equation. It fulfilled a promise originally made by the Harper government, serving both Canada's economic interests and China's energy security objectives.

Trudeau and his delegation may have walked into negotiations with hopes of a fair trade deal, but Beijing's position was clear.

Xi Jinping flatly rejected the idea. The Chinese leader had no interest in negotiating a trade agreement on Canada's terms. For Trudeau, who had staked both political capital and economic strategy on this outcome, the rejection was a bitter pill to swallow. His backers—many of whom saw deepened ties with China as a lucrative opportunity—were undoubtedly just as disappointed.

And then there was the fly.

According to one source, a subtle but unmistakable message may have been delivered to Trudeau during his diplomatic engagements in China. His limousine was discovered with a single fly inside. Was this mere coincidence? A harmless detail? Or was it a deliberate act of psychological statecraft, a carefully placed warning from Beijing's shadowy political operatives?

If the latter, it was a tame gesture compared to what Jason Kenney experienced years earlier during a trip to Beijing in 2012.

During his tenure as Immigration Minister in the Harper administration, Kenney and Ambassador David Mulroney travelled to Beijing for official trade and immigration discussions. The trip prior to their arrival for the official meetings had been routine—until, suddenly, it wasn't.

Their car's engine started to smoke, then burst into flames. Forced to evacuate, they stood on the roadside, watching as the vehicle was engulfed in fire. A new car was summoned, and they arrived safe, but a bit shaken at the Great Hall. They were greeted by then-President Hu Jintao, who said "I trust your journey here was uneventful!"

Kenney, recalling the event in a conversation in London this past March, was blunt about its significance:

"They were sending me a message because I had shown my unwavering support for His Holiness, Tibet, and religious freedom in China."

Kenney and former Conservative Senator Consiglio Di Nino had played a central role in ensuring Prime Minister Harper met with the Dalai Lama—a gesture that had sent Beijing into a diplomatic rage. The contrast with the attitude of previous Liberal governments was stark.

Former Prime Minister Paul Martin had taken a much more deferential approach. When he agreed to meet the Tibetan spiritual leader, it was not in an official capacity or a dignified government setting. Instead, the meeting took place in a church basement, without cameras or fanfare, and without formal acknowledgement of the Dalai Lama's status as the exiled leader of an oppressed people. According to Liberal insiders, this was done specifically to avoid offending Beijing.

Kenney, by contrast, had never played that game. He knew exactly who he was dealing with. And yet, under Trudeau, the Liberals had seemingly fully embraced Beijing's influence.

BEIJING'S UNITED FRONT AND THE LIBERALS' FINANCIAL TIES

By 2015–2016, the financial links between the Trudeau Liberals and Beijing's influence networks were impossible to ignore.

The Papineau Federal Liberal Association, representing Trudeau's own Montreal riding, had become a magnet for substantial donations from British Columbia—an unusual trend, given the geographical distance.

On July 6 and 7, 2016, nearly $63,000 flowed into the riding's campaign coffers from forty-one donors in Vancouver, Richmond, West Vancouver, and Delta, BC. Most of these donations were for $1,500 each, the maximum allowable contribution. Among the donors were directors of Tiger Arms Ltd., a gun shop in Port Coquitlam, including Rongxiang "Tiger" Yuan, Ke Xiao, and Peiran Yang.[44]

Between October 2014 and September 2016, a staggering $224,000 in British Columbia-based donations flowed into Trudeau's re-election fund, with $118,774.55 coming from just eighty-two donors in the crucial months before the 2015 election.

The RCMP's E-Pirate investigation into money laundering would later identify Rongxiang "Tiger" Yuan, an individual deeply entangled in transnational crime networks, as Suspect No. 3.

As Juneau-Katsuya's *Sidewinder Report* and Operation Dragon Lord have long illustrated for anyone interested in taking the lessons, the United

Front's influence operations are designed to blur the lines between political donations, legitimate business, and state-backed criminal enterprises.

Between 2000 and 2020, Prince Edward Island's engagement with China seemed like an economic success story—a small island province leveraging a rising superpower's economic might. The partnerships, educational exchanges, and trade deals all painted a picture of prosperity. The Island's economy has grown, immigration has grown, and property values have doubled and even tripled over the past fifteen years, all signs that successive governments were on the right track with their economic development programs, suggesting that as we look to 2025 and beyond people on the Island should have no concern about how that growth was achieved. But that is the point. If you don't really understand where the money is from or why it is on the Island, it will, as readers will see lead to tensions, disputes and a battle over who controls the lands on the Island.

As global tensions rise, PEI may find itself trapped between two superpowers, with its economic prospects for trade and economic expansion hanging in the balance.

While the tariffs from both China and the United States might be short-term, market access is shrinking at this time. Therefore, sales and hence profits are dwindling. And nowhere is this being felt more acutely than on PEI—where China officially remains the province's fourth-largest international trading partner, despite being an ocean away.

Perhaps PEI's former premiers knew exactly what they were doing, catering to the Beijing elite's taste for Atlantic lobster, mussels, and rare eels, but in a global conflict having control of the ownership of your resources and future business opportunities should be job one of any government whose mandate is to protect the Island's economy.

For now, it looks like Islanders are truly caught between a rock—and a lobster.

CHAPTER 6
ELITE CAPTURE AND THE WHISTLEBLOWER
SUSAN HOLMES AND THE PEI PROVINCIAL NOMINEE PROGRAM SCANDAL

Susan Holmes believed in fairness. She believed in good governance, in doing what was right, and in upholding the integrity of the public service. But in 2010, she found herself caught in the machinery of a system that had little regard for any of those things. What started as a standard government contract-bidding process quickly spiralled into a political scandal that would destroy her career, threaten her safety, and expose deep-seated corruption at the highest levels of Prince Edward Island's government.

It all began with an English as a Second Language training contract—one that was supposed to be awarded fairly but was, in reality, already spoken for. And the price for not playing along? The total destruction of Susan Holmes's career and reputation.

Holmes was the manager of the Population Secretariat[45] in the provincial government, overseeing immigration and settlement, retention, and attraction programs. Part of her job was managing and ensuring that government contracts were awarded based on merit. When the province put out a call for proposals for an English as a Second Language (ESL) training program for new immigrants, two major contenders stepped forward: Holland College, a well-respected public institution, and Study Abroad Canada, a private company owned by Frank Zhou and Sherry Huang.

Frank and Sherry were smooth operators working as the go-to immigration and business opportunity consultants. They organized numerous "Team Eastern Canada" trade missions to China, as they were close to the regime in Beijing, with Sherry's mom being a senior Communist Party official in the Ministry of Health. They have been identified in intelligence files as being part of China's elite United Front Work Department team of foreign agents. This was highlighted in Chapter 9 of *The Mosaic Effect*. In August

2024, after some of the new revelations I called up Michel and said "I am going to call Sherry Huang and ask for comment on her being identified as part of Beijing's United Front." Michel thought it was a worthy exercise but said it would be fruitless. She declared during that call that she was on PEI to bring up her daughter and had nothing to do with the United Front Work Department. He was right yet again.

Frank and Sherry weren't just business owners—they were fixtures in the province's immigration and investment circles, showing up in government offices regularly, greeting officials with warm smiles and small talk, as if they were colleagues rather than contractors. They embodied what the government was eager to promote: the integration of visible minorities into PEI's business community and the economic benefits of investment from Mainland China. And it was working—at least on paper. Immigration numbers were rising, foreign capital was flowing in, and PEI was held up as a model of small-province global engagement.

Yet beneath the surface, the reality was more complicated. Despite the influx of capital, only about one in three immigrants stayed on the Island. Many simply used the program as a gateway to larger Canadian cities, while others engaged in speculative investments that benefited a select few. Frank and Sherry were at the heart of it all, leveraging their relationships and influence to shape policy, secure contracts, and ensure that government decisions aligned with their interests. Were they responsible for the shenanigans in the PNP? Of course not, but government officials were totally aware of the situation, and Frank and Sherry were gladly benefiting from it.

They weren't just winning contracts—they were influencing immigration policy itself. The Provincial Nominee Program (PNP), originally designed to attract skilled labour and investment, had become a tool for the well-connected. Applications were fast-tracked, sometimes without meeting criteria. Investment requirements were often overlooked if the right names were attached.

From the beginning, Susan Holmes took every measure to ensure the contract-selection process was transparent. She and her team assembled a panel of adjudicators—seasoned government officials with no vested interest in the outcome—to review the proposals.

"It (the ESL contract) was a unanimous decision," Holmes recalled. "Holland College presented a superior proposal—comprehensive, cost-effective (in fact cheaper per student), and designed to meet government standards."

That should have been the end of it. But it wasn't.

When Holmes submitted the results to her director, Jane Mallard, she met an unexpected and aggressive response. "This is not the outcome we were looking for," Mallard said, her voice sharp, her expression unreadable.

Then came the demand: Change the results. Make it look like Study Abroad Canada matched Holland College's score.

Holmes refused. "I told them I couldn't do it." She told Mallard that the decision was unanimous, and she would not betray the committee's trust. "If they wanted the results changed, they'd have to find someone else to do it."

That act of defiance sealed her fate. She was accused of insubordination. All this paradoxical harassment (for simply wanting to have the results of the adjudication process amongst staff and experts honoured) was done verbally in her director's office.

Jane Mallard made Holmes's life unbearable. Workloads tripled overnight. Tasks meant for an entire team were suddenly hers alone. She was excluded from meetings and frozen out of decision-making processes. It was workplace bullying at its most calculated level—designed to break her, to make her leave of her own accord. A colleague in the federal government recommended to Susan that she collect all the records she could, as "they might be helpful down the road."

Holmes was repeatedly called into closed-door meetings where Mallard would berate her, raising her voice and demanding compliance. "She yelled at me, called me difficult, accused me of being disloyal," Holmes recalled. "But I knew what they were asking was wrong."

Before the contract was awarded, Frank and Sherry continued to make their presence known, casually stopping by the department, chatting with officials, and reinforcing their close ties with the government. They had the confidence of people who knew they were untouchable.

The connection between government officials and elite business figures like Frank and Sherry wasn't just about friendship—it was about influence. Holmes would later come to understand this as a form of elite capture, where powerful individuals manipulated government institutions for personal or political gain. What was happening in PEI wasn't unique; it was part of a broader trend seen in small jurisdictions where a few well-connected figures could exert outsized control over economic and political decisions.

But Holmes didn't quit. She kept showing up.

So, they didn't renew her contract. No explanation. No severance. Not even a letter of reference except from Ottawa (who knew her work from federal-provincial-territorial [FPT] committees) and her executive director, who had since left his position with the Population Secretariat, also in difficulty with Mallard.

Her name was blacklisted. No one in PEI would hire her, and few outside the province would hire her without a recommendation from her employer, which

Mallard and the deputy minister, Mayne, both refused to provide, even though her performance review prior to the ESL RFQ process had been exemplary.

However, a senior-level manager at the Government of Canada, Angela Connidis, who was co-chair of the FPT Settlement Working Group (Canada) at Immigration Canada, had only glowing things to say about her interactions with Susan and expressed those directly to the deputy minister, who refused to acknowledge the communication. I reached out to Mallard for comment on the letter and spoke with her in person, but she said she could not recall the incident. We asked for comment in writing, but she has yet to respond.

EXHIBIT 1

Reference Letter: Susan Holmes

Dear Dr. Mayne,

As a co-chair of the FPT Settlement Working group, I would like to take this opportunity to express my appreciation and acknowledgement of the contribution of Prince Edward Island's representative, Susan Holmes, to the work of this committee over the last year. As you know, over the past several months all jurisdictions have been collaborating to define national settlement and integration outcomes. This work has brought together many different perspectives across the country on how to define Canada's success as a nation in settling and integrating the many immigrants we welcome to our country.

Susan has brought valuable insight and analysis to our discussions, both at the full committee and as a member of the subcommittees.

Sincerely,
Angela Arnet Connidis,
Co-chair, FPT Settlement Working Group, (Canada)

Her contract review interview and report prior to the incident said the same....

For the full letter, see Exhibit 1 on p.206.

But this letter was no help so, desperate for employment, Susan ultimately was ready to pack and move anywhere to get a job so she could pay her mounting bills. But where could she go?

This was her reward for doing what was best for taxpayers and those taking the courses. Susan later went on to say this was not going to cut it on the 5th Floor.[46]

"The premier called our allegations crazy," Holmes said. "That set the tone for how we were treated. We were ridiculed, discredited, and harassed."

Even before she left the province the intimidation began.

"A black SUV started appearing at the end of my driveway. Then one day, it drove up to my house. A man got out, slammed the door, and said, 'I know who you are.'"

She began receiving anonymous phone calls. Some were silent. Others carried veiled threats. "You don't know what you're getting yourself into, " one voice had said before hanging up. "Maybe it's time to move on." She already knew that there was only one course at the time, and these kinds of threats only reinforced her decision to get out as soon as she could.

As the scandal unfolded, and with an election in full swing in September 2011, the government turned to more insidious tactics to discredit Holmes and two of her colleagues, Cora Plourd Nicholson and Svetlana Tenetko, and to distance themselves from the scandal. Personal information about them was leaked to the media by Spencer Campbell, the Liberal Party president and a lawyer at Stewart McKelvey,[47] who in 2022 was named president of the Law Society of Prince Edward Island. The women's personnel files were splashed across the pages of the local newspaper.

"They wanted to smear us," said Holmes, "to make us look unreliable." The attacks escalated after Holmes, along with her colleagues, went public with their concerns after being introduced to each other by Martie Murphy, who was running for office to become an MLA. Murphy told us in an interview that she was tired and fed up with the corruption on the Island and provided us with her scrapbook of more than 250 articles and documents related to the PNP and other political scandals.

Although their story was about approving immigration applications for the PNP, and Susan's was about the tender involving the premier's friend Frank Zhou and his wife's company, you will discover later how it all intersects.

By 2012 Susan was becoming desperate for employment after the government had ostensibly blackballed her in the province. Her mounting bills and obligation to her contractor meant she had a lot of sleepless nights. "I had no choice but to leave," she told me, "so I took a job in the Yukon. I was in the middle of building a home in PEI, but I had no way to stay."

She headed to the Yukon where they were desperate for good educators and were less concerned with her contract being renewed. Several years later, things would begin to turn for the better. A report published by the CBC[48] on February 2, 2018, detailed how Holmes and the two other whistleblowers had their personnel files leaked to the Liberal Party during the 2011 election. The documents contained private employment records, internal emails, and even confidential details about a human rights complaint. It was an orchestrated attack, designed to paint them as politically motivated troublemakers rather than dedicated public servants trying to expose corruption.

She would return that year to the province she loved and seek a meeting with then-premier Wade MacLauchlan. He refused to see her. "I came forward with an outstretched palm and he did not take my hand," she told the CBC. Ultimately, Wade probably knew where most of the bodies were buried, and he knew Susan and the other whistleblowers' accounts were leading to bad poll numbers and a lack of confidence in his tired government, who were being exposed for their nepotism, corruption, and deals that would benefit a select few with some trickle down to the citizens of PEI.

Susan shared a document with us, which we read and found deeply unsettling. The source was a government contractor responsible for IT services, including the archiving of all government emails. He was closely connected to the inner circle of decision-makers, informally referred to as the "Backroom Boys." During a phone conversation, Susan transcribed his comments as he revealed them.

This contractor, Serge Serviant, had intimate knowledge of Prince Edward Island's political and technological infrastructure. As someone tasked with maintaining the government's digital communications, he had both access and insight. In a conversation with Susan, he relayed what officials had explained to him regarding the province's Provincial Nominee Program (PNP). According to Serviant, Robert Ghiz's intentions behind the PNP were, in his words, "that the PNP was designed to enlarge the circle of elites and keep Islanders poor." See Exhibit 2 on p. 208.

With no other recourse, Holmes, Nicholson, and Tenetko filed a lawsuit against the PEI government.[49]

Susan further recounted, "Once the privacy commissioner ruled that our rights had been violated, just before the statute of limitations would run out the government settled the case."

But even winning in court couldn't undo the damage done to Susan, Cora, and Svetlana. After years of legal battles, being fired and shunned by friends and former work colleagues because they had chosen to do the right thing, the only thing they were left with was a meagre sum of less than $175,000 (CAD).

They had exhausted their financial resources but won the court battle, which came as little consolation for their pain and suffering. In a *W5* documentary[50] and in a telephone call with us, Cora Nicholson expressed pain and grief and said, "No financial reward can give me back the time I had to live under relentless stress and pain because I decided to blow the whistle on corruption." She recently moved away from the Island and headed West to get as far away from the rot and corruption as she could. Tenetko had already moved to British Columbia years ago, where she is undergoing treatment for cancer.

"We were financially ruined," Holmes admitted. "I lost over a decade of income. The settlement didn't make up for that." She finally returned to the Island, vindicated by the settlement and the *W5* documentary. You can never reclaim the lost years, the pain, the suffering, or the financial loss, but she was back.

Holmes's story isn't just about corruption—it's about power, influence, and the cost of integrity in a system designed to serve the elite. We have to ask: How many others saw what she saw and chose to remain silent? Our investigations suggest dozens and dozens, but on an Island where everybody knows your name and everybody knows your secrets, few speak out, because there is nowhere to hide on lil'ol Prince Edward Island.

CHAPTER 7

THE ISLAND AWAKENS

When Jan reached out to me in November 2023, I told him my main goal was to do a book launch for *The Mosaic Effect* and *Under Cover*. It's what publishers do, and I wasn't going to be denied. But this book launch would turn out to be much more than that.

We had rented one room with a capacity for 300 people—and within minutes, we realized we had underestimated the hunger for this conversation. The room was packed to the walls, the aisles jammed, people standing shoulder to shoulder. The buzz in the air was unmistakable, a mixture of curiosity, concern and, I dare say, quiet rebellion. We scrambled to open the second room, sliding back the partition, rolling in chairs, making space as more Islanders poured in. By the time I took the microphone, I was standing before a sea of faces—farmers, teachers, business owners, students, journalists, retired civil servants, and community elders.

It was St. Patrick's Day on Prince Edward Island. Green scarves and shamrock pins dotted the crowd, but this was no ordinary holiday gathering. We had come together under the banner of *Canada Under Siege* to talk about a threat few on this Island had ever been asked to confront: the Chinese Communist Party's global operations, its infiltration into democracies, and its quiet entanglement with this beautiful, unassuming province on Canada's East Coast.

As a publisher (Optimum Publishing International), I had spent decades investing in the accounts of countless journalists, academics, and whistleblowers who had tracked Beijing's expanding influence. Michel and Garry had been sounding the alarm since the late '90s, and now we were gathered in front of a crowd that was desperate for information—some even wanted blood. And this time, I wasn't just a publisher—I was a messenger, but I was also part of the investigation. I welcomed the crowd and introduced our panel: David Weale, a beloved Island historian and public thinker; Garry Clement, a former RCMP investigator with decades of experience in transnational organized crime; Michel Juneau-Katsuya, a former CSIS Asia-Pacific bureau chief and one of Canada's foremost experts on Chinese espionage; Dominic Cardy,[51] a politician from New Brunswick who had gone head-to-head with Beijing's soft power in his own province; and me, Dean Baxendale, who would be acting as host.

PEI ON THE FRONTLINE

www.opibooks.com @opibooks

CANADA UNDER SIEGE!

Exposing the Chinese Communist Party's hybrid war on Canada as described in 'The Mosaic Effect' and 'Under Cover'

**BOOK LAUNCH PRESENTED BY
OPTIMUM PUBLISHING INTERNTATIONAL**

AGENDA

WELCOME & INTRODUCTION
DEAN BAXENDALE, *President, Optimum Publishing*

FOREIGN INFLUENCE OPERATIONS
MICHEL JUNEAU-KATSUYA, *former Chief of Asia Pacific Operations, CSIS*

MONEY LAUNDERING IN CANADA
GARY CLEMENT, *former National Director RCMP (Proceeds of Crime Division)*

CCP ELITE CAPTURE IN NEW BRUNSWICK
DOMINIC CARDY, *MLA New Brunswick*

PANEL DISCUSSION AND Q&A — PEI ON THE FRONTLINE
David Weale, Dean Baxendale, Michel Juneau-Katsuya, Gary Clement, and Dominic Cardy

CLOSING REMARKS
ALAN MACPHEE, *IM4Democracy*

Sunday, March 17, 2024. Starting at 2:00 pm

Delta Prince Edward Hotel
18 Queen St, Charlottetown, PEI

**INAUGRAL EVENT FROM
I AM FOR DEMOCRACY CANADA INC**
An advocate for democracy and accountable government

EVENT DETAILS ON OUR WEBSITE
www.optimumpublishinginternational.com/events-1

Hosted and sponsored by

 OPTIMUM PUBLISHING INTERNATIONAL
LONDON | MONTRÉAL | TORONTO

The energy in the room was electric, and not without tension. We had come to challenge old assumptions, to break open difficult conversations, and to ask Islanders to take a hard look at the political, financial, and cultural currents reshaping their home.

David Weale took the podium first.

"Well, well, well," he said, letting the words settle over the crowd. "Look at you. Look at you." The crowd rose and gave him a standing ovation that lasted for well over a minute. He had been a champion for those who had asked questions, but those who demanded a shift in the Island's culture and financial makeup had made David out to be a villain, calling him out as a racist. He wasn't, and I knew that was an issue we could use to reach out to the other crowd. But today would be his moment, one he could certainly be proud of.

He smiled, and the room softened. David had a way of connecting with people that no outsider could match. "You are a beautiful sight to see," he said, "Islanders who care about their place, who are committed to change."

He told the story of his friend, George, a man from Little Sands who, years ago, had taken him for a drive around the Island, pointing to parcels of land being sold off. "David," George had said, "there's more going on here than you and I know about." That sentence, David said, had lodged in his mind like an anchor in wet sand.

This gathering, he told the audience, was about surfacing what had remained hidden, about turning ignorance into understanding, and understanding into action. "Sometimes," he warned, "when you're too close to a thing, you can't see how big it really is." He then emphasized why we were here. "That's why these guys are here. They are going to help us understand what is going on at that level. . . . There are few in the country that have the collective knowledge of these gents. They're going o tell us how big it is or, to quote George, 'They'll help us understand what is going on that we don't know about.'"

When it was my turn to speak, I thanked David for his wonderful introduction to set up this panel. I introduced my colleagues and laid out the program and how hybrid warfare had rolled up right to Charlottetown, PEI. I then reminded the audience that none of us had landed on this Island by accident. A concerned Islander had reached out to me after reading *The Mosaic Effect*, and that phone call had sparked a five-month-long journalistic investigation. We had followed trails from PEI to British Columbia, from Washington to Munich, talking to more than two dozen individuals—insiders, whistleblowers, human rights activists, religious leaders. What we uncovered was not just a local story, but a global one: the CCP's hybrid warfare, elite capture, religious infiltration, and use of business as a tool of statecraft.

Frank Zhou, Duncan MacIntosh, Wade MacLauchlan. Those names surfaced again and again, along with organizations like Bliss and Wisdom, with their shadowy influence. And through it all, the same pattern: financial inducements, access to political leaders, and the quiet reshaping of communities.

Michel Juneau-Katsuya took the microphone next. His message was blunt. "Every prime minister of this country," he said, "from Brian Mulroney on, has been compromised by agents of influence." The room fell into a stunned silence. Michel was not offering conspiracy theories; he was delivering the hard truths of someone who had spent his life in intelligence, watching Canada's political class look the other way. He reminded the audience that

PEI's small size made it an ideal laboratory for influence operations: it was a place where a little money, a few handshakes, and a handful of connections could open doors that led straight to the heart of government.

He called for foreign interference laws modelled on Australia's, warned about the long game of the United Front, and underlined a crucial distinction: "We are not talking about the Chinese people," he said. "We are talking about the Chinese government. The Chinese people are victims, just like we are."

Then came Garry Clement, a man with fire in his belly from decades of experience investigating just this type of crime. "Shame on the politicians," he declared. "Shame on the lawyers." Garry laid bare the grim machinery of organized crime: the fentanyl flooding into Canada, the money-laundering operations that run through real estate, the triads working in tandem with political elites.

"I've seen it first-hand as a career undercover cop and as someone responsible for the Proceeds of Crime division within the RCMP/Money Laundering section," he told the room.

He praised the courage of Islanders who had come forward, who had risked careers, reputations, and relationships to expose what was happening. And he didn't spare anyone and especially the politicians and officials who seemingly for almost two decades never cleaned up the Island even when confronted by very angry citizens.

Dominic Cardy, the final speaker, delivered a chilling account of political infiltration. As New Brunswick's education minister, he had fought to expel Confucius Institutes from public schools, only to face pressure not just from local politicians but from Chinese diplomats. He told the audience how he had been invited for "coffee" with former premier Shawn Graham and a Chinese private school executive, offered gifts, and urged to soften his stance.

When that failed, the Chinese vice-consul himself arrived in Fredericton, warning that the province's lobster sales to China were at risk. The audience gasped. This was not abstract geopolitics; this was local, immediate, and personal.

Cardy reminded us that the most dangerous lie we had told ourselves was that democracy was a permanent feature of our lives, something encoded in the Canadian DNA. "It's not," he warned. "It's fragile. It must be defended."

During the Q&A, the tension in the room cracked open into urgency. A woman raised her hand, her voice trembling. "What about the Buddhist groups here? What about Tibetan Buddhism?"

Another man stood up. "I've seen the properties," he said. "I've seen the money. It doesn't add up."

We explained what we could: how religious organizations, including Bliss and Wisdom, sometimes became conduits for soft power, how faith itself could be weaponized for political ends. And we spoke of the Tibetan community—of their long struggle, their displacement, and their ongoing surveillance by the Chinese state.

The questions kept coming—about land sales, foreign donations, local politicians, and global stakes. The hunger for answers was palpable.

In answer to a question Garry stated, "In my opinion there is ample evidence to start a police investigation." That was a powerful statement that was not lost on anyone in the audience.

As the afternoon drew to a close, we rolled the final slide. In stark black letters, it read:

Are you part of the problem, or part of the solution?

I stood at the podium, looking out over the crowd. There was a hush, the kind that only comes when people are absorbing something far bigger than they expected.

I told them what I believed: that PEI was not just a target, but also a potential model. That if Islanders chose to stand together, if they demanded accountability, if they refused to look the other way, they could push back—and they could win. Then Michel, Garry, and Dominic summarized some key points on next steps.

ENOUGH IS ENOUGH!

TODAY ISLANDERS WE NEED SERIOUS ACTION FROM YOU

ARE YOU PART OF THE SOLUTION OR PART OF THE PROBLEM?

If you have information and evidence to share
Please call us at
647-970-1973

As we packed up that day, and as people lined up to buy books, to share their stories, to whisper their own quiet fears and long-held suspicions, I knew that something had shifted. One lady came to me crying and telling me how thankful she was for us coming to inform Islanders. I was naturally taken aback by her outpouring of emotion, but it was something, I had become accustomed to over the past few years, given the books we were presenting to the world.

We hadn't just informed an audience; we had sparked a movement. Alan MacPhee, a well-known figure in PEI, closed the event with some comments about democracy and his new organization "I Am for Democracy Canada." He was looking for those who were all in. MacPhee mentioned we had invited all of the provincial politicians and the local media. No politician or media person had shown up other than Avery Haines from *W5*, who had flown from Ottawa to Halifax and then to the Island, and with her cameraman made the 2.5 hour drive to Charlottetown to tape the entire event. We were hoping that *W5* would be a partner and do a serious story on foreign influence and the land grab.

We left that day knowing that we were in a battle for Canada's soul, not to mention our real estate and our way of life. And this is where it would be fought, not just in Ottawa or Toronto or Vancouver, but right here, in Charlottetown, in Little Sands, in rooms like this one, where ordinary people gathered to decide what to do next.

And as we walked out into the cold March evening, we knew the Island had awakened. But would they continue to help us get to the bottom of the story? On an Island of secrets where everyone knows your name, where you are one rumour away from being ostracized or sometimes a hero, would people be willing to act?

Would they continue to be part of the problem or be part of the solution?

CHAPTER 8
VOICES OF DEVOTION
THE JOURNEY OF THE GREAT WISDOM BUDDHIST INSTITUTE

"I think when people all over the world come to this charming countryside, all their troubles disappear. Although they haven't dealt with their situations back home—but by looking at the trees, looking out at nature, looking at the skies—it's as if their hearts have taken flight."

TEACHER ZHEN-RHU

A PATH TO ENLIGHTENMENT: WHY CHOOSE THE MONASTIC LIFE?

It was March 19, just two days after our book launch on the Island, which had drawn the biggest audience ever for a non-fiction book launch in Eastern Canada. With over six hundred slanders showing up, including some nuns and monks, we were intrigued by what we would encounter when we met Joanna, Jingli, Heather, and Sabrina.

Our intention was to meet with the nuns to give them a fair chance to answer some questions, but also to present their side of the story. Our intentions were cordial, not hostile. This was not Michel's first rodeo or scenario where he had been confronted with people who tried to hide the truth. We came with an open mind, but already the evidence we had collected would make it hard for them to steer us in the wrong direction. But again, in all fairness, we needed to hear their story directly from them.

We drove up to their tiny temple and teaching facility, which had a chain across the road to bar entry by strangers. After one of the nuns unlocked it, we drove into the compound, and they locked the gate behind us. Three smiling and happy nuns greeted us and ushered us into their sanctuary.

Initial introductions took place at the door, and then we accompanied them into their hall, where three tables were set up in a U-shape. We faced a television screen where we would later watch some video and PowerPoint presentations on the work performed by and the community engagement the nuns on Prince Edward Island were part of. With candles and incense burning, it was a bright and warm atmosphere.

The nuns asked if we would like a tour of their prayer room, and we enthusiastically accepted. Jingli pointed out her ordination picture with His Holiness in the background. She had travelled back to India in 2023 to have the official ceremony after it was delayed due to Covid-19. A small 8"x 10" picture of the ceremony with His Holiness in the background was set among the various religious artifacts for us to observe.

We were both struck by the fact that no larger picture of His Holiness was present. Having attended many Buddhist sanctuaries and homes, we know that a picture of His Holiness is a mainstay in Tibetan Buddhist temples, except of course in Tibet or anywhere in China. He is often featured prominently and certainly has a conspicuous place in the Toronto temple at the Tibetan Community Centre in Etobicoke. Benedict Rogers (who wrote *The China Nexus*), former Senator Consiglio Di Nino, and I visited the temple in 2023 for a presentation to the Tibetan community.

My two new friends from the Solomon Islands, Daniel Suidani and Celsus Talifu, who had become political refugees due to the CCP attacking them in their state-controlled press and banning Suidani from office, had also come with us. The CCP's elite capture techniques, including direct payments to politicians to support then-Prime Minister Sogavare to officially recognize China over Taiwan, had been clearly on display, as you read earlier in the book.

It got me thinking about how our event on Saturday (the book launch) was a watershed in many ways, and now we were meeting the local management of the Great Wisdom Buddhist Institute, generally referred to as GWBI, on the Island. The group known as Bliss and Wisdom has been the subject of much local opposition and protest by many Islanders after an initial period of peace and tranquillity in the mid-2010s.

When they arrived, they gave the appearance they had little to no possessions and purchased a run-down motel called the Lobster Shanty. Over the next two decades, however, they built a fairly sizable empire, partly using donations from Taiwan and a religious exemption that provides tax-free income for the group, according to the rules of the Canada Revenue Agency regarding religious organizations operating in Canada. Their spiritual and business leader, Master Zhen-Ru (also known as Mary Jin), came to visit in 2007 and was accepted as an immigrant business investor under the heralded Provincial Nominee Program (PNP) supported by Premier Ghiz but later shut down by the federal government due to its problematic structure. Mary Jin claimed to be the owner of a lamp manufacturing company, according to our confidential source. His company had handled her immigration file and introduced her to the charms of the Island. As you will read later in more detail, she never told the immigration consultant she was the leader of a Buddhist monastic group based out of Taiwan.

For the sake of the investigation, we also needed to touch on their connection with His Holiness the Dalai Lama and the Buddhist world. The monastic activities and the devout belief in and promotion of Tibetan Buddhism and the concept of dharma would be what we would discover through our meeting, or so we hoped. One thing was certain, this time the gentle nuns were not talking to people without knowledge of the Buddhist faith and monastic life, or the international politics surrounding them.

Bliss and Wisdom has its roots in Taipei, Taiwan, also known as the Republic of China (ROC). Still, as you are discovering in this book, the People's Republic of China) PRC and the Chinese Communist Party have played a significant role in the development of Bliss and Wisdom and its operational success as a business entity. The nuns we were about to meet were from the United States, Singapore, and Taiwan. Bliss and Wisdom practitioners from China are also living on the Island, but our hosts made it clear they were separate and that they dared not even mention the Chinese Communist Party for fear of reprisal of some sort or another.

Our hosts offered us tea and cookies as we were about to start our three-hour interview, which was about to get off to an informative start. Both Michel and I were most interested in discovering why the women chose to renounce the conventional world and enter a Buddhist monastery, as it is a profound and deeply personal journey. Each nun's journey is unique, shaped by individual experiences, intellectual pursuits, and an inner calling towards a life of devotion.

As we sat around the table with our new friends in their serene prayer hall at the Great Wisdom Buddhist Institute on PEI, Michel launched straight into that first question. It was clear that his training as a former RCMP member and career CSIS officer had set him up to be direct but charming at the same time.

"What makes a person decide to become a Buddhist nun?"

They took turns answering the question, and we have captured each of their journeys on the next few pages. What won't be in doubt is the nuns' seemingly profound commitment to Buddhism: no one should doubt that their belief is a tenet of their physical and spiritual journey here on earth.

SABRINA'S STORY: FROM CLINICAL PSYCHOLOGY TO SPIRITUAL FULFILMENT

Sabrina, a former University of California, San Diego psychology student, reflected on her path. "I really love people and observing what makes them happy or sad. Initially, I wanted to become a clinical psychologist to help others. But then something changed," she said. "Buddhism showed me how to truly understand the workings of the mind. Behind every emotion, there's a thought, and by working with these thoughts, you can actually cultivate happiness—not just for yourself but for others too."

Her transition to monastic life was not just an academic curiosity but a deep personal transformation prompted by an encounter with the Dalai Lama. "I attended a lecture by His Holiness at UC Irvine over ten years ago, and something clicked. I realized that instead of just studying the mind in a clinical setting, I wanted to experience and embody the teachings of Buddhism. That's when I decided to dedicate my life to this path."

JINGLI'S JOURNEY: FROM WALL STREET TO THE MONASTERY

Another nun, Jingli, had a strikingly different trajectory before joining the monastery. "I was born in Singapore, studied at the Wharton School of Business, and worked on Wall Street for a decade. Materially, life was perfect—everything was paid for, I didn't have to work weekends—but I felt an emptiness inside."

She recounted a moment of clarity. "One day, a colleague told me: 'You should really think about what makes you happy—not just the job, but what you're doing with your life.' That resonated with me. I realized I wanted to contribute to the world in a meaningful way."

Jingli initially explored entrepreneurship. "I started a business making organic almond milk pudding. It was through selling my product in New York's organic stores that I met members of the Buddhist community. What struck me was not just their knowledge but their kindness and wisdom. They weren't just successful—they were fulfilled. That's when I knew this was the life I wanted." She was doing well, making lots of money but decided to pursue a monastic path and was now, along with her colleagues, running GWBI.

VOICES OF DEVOTION

HEATHER'S AWAKENING: A SCHOLAR'S PERSPECTIVE ON BUDDHISM

Born and raised in Taiwan, Heather had an academic inclination before entering monastic life. "I studied sociology in France and was deeply interested in social structures and human freedom. I was particularly fascinated by Marxist theories of freedom and what it meant to be truly free."

She said her turning point came from a conversation with a Buddhist mentor. "I asked him, 'Why is it that in Buddhism, everyone becomes a Buddha? Do we really have freedom of choice?' He responded, 'Do you believe you are truly free now, in this society, under the influence of media and cultural expectations?' That question stayed with me."

It is a question many of us wrestle with as we toil with bringing up a family, or going to church or our local club, or living every day in our wild world.

Buddhism, in Heather's words, was providing her with intellectual rigour and spiritual fulfillment. "I love that Buddhism encourages critical thinking. When I have doubts, I can ask questions, read what Buddha said, discuss with friends, and find my own understanding. That's why I committed to this life." It is a noble life; weathering the long cold PEI nights is a mission in and of itself. We admired their commitment to their monastic life, but was there something else lurking beneath the surface?

JOANNA'S DECISION: FROM THE UNITED STATES TO ORDINATION IN INDIA

Joanna, originally from Massachusetts, had a different journey. She spent much of her life in the United States before being ordained in India. "For me, becoming a nun was about discipline and wisdom. I wanted to develop clarity of mind, and I knew that the best way to do that was through a monastic life." It is a path many devout Buddhist practitioners have followed.

She described the experience of being ordained. "We travelled to Dharamshala, but His Holiness was unable to perform the ceremony due to health reasons. We later went to Bodh Gaya, where I was finally ordained. It was a life-changing moment. I remember feeling pure joy, and my friend had to remind me to calm down afterward!"

Her path had not been easy, but she felt a deep sense of belonging in the monastery. "I feel that here, surrounded by others walking the same path, I can focus entirely on my spiritual growth."

Teacher Zhen-Ru has a special gift: the ability to clearly explain the Buddhist teachings in a way that inspires and allows her students to easily apply the teachings to their everyday lives. Teacher Zhen-Ru's students have seen improvements to their relationships with others and in their overall quality of life after applying these Buddhist teachings. As such, Teacher Zhen-Ru's students from all over the world wanted her to settle in their hometowns so they could readily learn from her.

BUILDING THEIR HOME ON PRINCE EDWARD ISLAND

After recounting their personal experience, they showed us a PowerPoint presentation about their faith, monastic life, and mission. It was well produced but felt more like a lengthy television commercial than a genuine source of information. The presentation took a long time, and at the end, Michel politely remarked that most of this was already well known to us.

He then launched into some key questions. Why did the Great Wisdom Buddhist Institute choose PEI as their sanctuary? Why leave Taiwan and the United States for a small Canadian province?

"We wanted to create a peaceful environment to study and practise Buddhism without external distractions," one of the nuns explained. "PEI offered that space."

According to Islanders and the numerous articles about them that are available, when they first came to the Island and started building, many locals met their arrival with curiosity, and some with scepticism, but for the most part, they were welcomed to become part of the community. Michel asked his next question, "We understand that when a large group of Buddhist nuns and monks move into a small community, people have questions." Sabrina replied, "Some people welcomed us warmly, while others had concerns. But in Buddhism, we approach everything with patience and understanding."

During their two-hour presentation, the nuns presented several slides and a short video about how Bliss and Wisdom acquired a set of ancient scriptures from India. They showed Master Zhen-Ru accompanying the scripture back to PEI. Given my time in Dharamshala and meeting with the archival team, whose job is to document and preserve Tibetan history, language, and culture, I was immediately interested in this new development. Michel and I had discussed this prior to going in, and he led by asking those questions although we were both knowledgeable about the CCP's efforts to dominate Tibet and Tibetan Buddhism in China and around the world.

According to Jingli, "much of the monastery's work involves translating Tibetan Buddhist texts into Traditional Chinese. This effort stems from a crucial issue: the decline of the Tibetan language."

I asked, "Who is overseeing the translation of these ancient scriptures? Is there anyone from Dharamshala involved in the process?"

Jingli, who with her colleagues has been instrumental in the monastery's educational structure, responded. "Yes, we directly connect with Buddhist masters in South India who oversee the translations. Every book we translate goes through a rigorous review by scholars deeply trained in Tibetan Buddhist scriptures."

Another nun elaborated, "The process isn't just about language—it's about faithfulness to the original teachings. We don't just translate word for word; we consult with Tibetan Buddhist masters to ensure that the core meanings and interpretations remain intact. This is a responsibility we take very seriously." This raised an alarm for both of us. Michel had been investigating and witnessing this practice for decades, and I had already published a few books that dealt with the subject. By translating the text, a person or group could ultimately influence its meaning. This tells us there is a subjective aspect to the translation, (Sinicization of its content),[52] and we know from the Buddhist Association of China that if Master Zhen-Ru is influenced by Beijing, they would certainly have a hand in actively monitoring and rewriting passages to comply with party doctrine.

GWBI has flatly rejected the notion that Beijing or the CCP has any control or influence over them or their monk brothers at GEBIS. At the time of our interview, we did not have any proof that they purposely altered the scriptures when translating them into Traditional Chinese, but it was a risk, and we both knew it. Once again, this may all be in line with Tibetan Buddhism without the influence of Beijing but given the rebirth of Zhen-Ru as a Master Guru when she was inside China (as she claims), one has to be somewhat sceptical. But we pressed on with more questions.

Wanting further clarity, I persisted, "So, do Tibetan Buddhist scholars from Dharamshala actively verify your work?"

The nuns explained, "While we engage with scholars and experts in Buddhist philosophy, our primary focus is on internal verification within the monastery. We also consulted with some monastic scholars in South India. But do they speak Traditional Chinese? To ensure accuracy, we study extensively and consult senior members with deep knowledge of the scriptures."

This sent alarm bells ringing in my head, and I could see Michel thinking the same, given our extensive understanding of the Sinicization of Tibetan

Buddhism and the influence and takeover of Buddhist organizations in Taiwan by the Chinese Communist Party.

The nuns nodded. "Yes, we send completed manuscripts for final review. Some of our texts have received feedback and adjustments from monastic scholars in South India. The goal is to ensure that these teachings remain as close as possible to their interpretation." Their responses underscored the monastery's commitment to a Chinese translation that would preserve the authenticity of the original Tibetan text. They tried to emphasize that their important work bridges the past and the future, ensuring that Tibetan Buddhist wisdom remains accessible despite the declining number of native Tibetan readers and speakers.

Back to our education, learning session, and interview.

Now, the number of people who can fluently read and understand Tibetan is shrinking, especially due to the pressures inside Tibet itself," said Joanna. If we don't translate these teachings, they could be lost. It was apparent that these Bliss and Wisdom nuns truly believed they are on a mission from their Guru Zhen-Ru and that they are carrying out the wishes of His Holiness. They stated, "Our goal is to make them accessible in Traditional Chinese while still training younger generations in Tibetan." None of them speaks Tibetan fluently, but they want to learn more.

During the interview, Michel shifted the discussion towards the nuns' discretion in their work, particularly regarding their translations and the potential political sensitivities surrounding Tibetan Buddhism.

"With the work that you're doing—preserving Tibetan Buddhism—do you think the Chinese Communist Party would have an interest in it?" Michel asked, leaning forward. One of the nuns responded carefully. "The Chinese Communist Party does not support Tibetan Buddhism at all."[53] To me, this was a very odd statement, given that anyone dedicated to Tibetan Buddhism is aware of the CCP's extensive infiltration of Tibetan Buddhism and the Buddhist Association of China, which you will learn a lot more about in the coming pages. In fact, its very survival in China, according to Lobsang Sangay, the former Sikyong—elected leader—of the Central Tibetan Administration (the formal name of the Tibetan government-in-exile) in India, depends on the Buddhist Association of China and its co-optation of Taiwanese Buddhists to teach Tibetan Buddhism. We can assume the nuns were simply unaware of this fact, given their open devotion to the belief they are doing His Holiness's work on PEI.

But Michel and I both sensed the caution in their voices. One nun nodded and added, "That's why His Holiness is in exile."

Michel followed up, pressing the point further. "I see. So does that affect how you handle your work?"

There was a brief pause before Jingli again spoke. "We keep a low profile for many reasons. In December 2023, we were in Bodhgaya, and during an event at the International Sangha Forum, one of our community members was on stage with His Holiness. Hours later, that same person became involved in a concerning situation."

She let the weight of those words settle before continuing. "That's one of the reasons we don't publicize everything we do."

Michel nodded, taking in the response. Then he asked another pressing question. "You have a portion of your community that comes from Mainland China. How do they make it here, given the political climate?"

Sabrina responded with a measured tone. "Yes, some of our community members are from Mainland China. We don't discuss specifics about their journeys, but it's not unusual for people to seek out Buddhist teachings, even in difficult circumstances."

It was clear that while the nuns were open about their mission, they were cautious in protecting individuals who sought refuge in their monastery. They led us to believe their work was not just about translating scriptures and community engagement or building new facilities but about preserving Tibetan Buddhism while carefully navigating political realities. There is one slight problem: Where are the Tibetans in the management group in either the nuns' or monks' organizations? There are none that we were made aware of.

THE THOUSAND-YEAR MONASTERY: A LEGACY FOR FUTURE GENERATIONS

As we delved deeper into their vision for the monastery, the nuns spoke with quiet conviction about their long-term aspirations. "For me, legacy is ensuring that Buddhist teachings survive and remain accessible to future generations," Sabrina said. "It's about preserving Tibetan Buddhist wisdom while making it available to a global audience."

They were not just building "a monastery on PEI" but creating a 1,000-year monastery dedicated to preserving Buddhist teachings and philosophy that would endure across generations. "We are training young people," Joanna added. "Every year, students come to the monastery to study Tibetan and Buddhist philosophy. Our goal is to create a bridge between the past and the future."

Joanna elaborated, "We are structuring this monastery in a way that ensures its longevity. We are documenting Buddhist scriptures, training new teachers, and creating a sustainable environment where these teachings can be passed down for centuries."

Another emphasized the broader purpose of their mission. "We are not just here to preserve knowledge for ourselves. Our mission is to share wisdom with the world, engage with scholars, and provide a space for deep spiritual practice. This monastery is to be a centre of learning, meditation, and translation for generations to come."

Their dedication and devotion were evident, not just in their words but in their actions over the past decade. They had already begun laying the groundwork—training new nuns, translating ancient texts, and creating an environment where Buddhist philosophy could flourish well beyond their lifetimes. They truly believe.

"A thousand years from now, we want this monastery to still be a sanctuary of wisdom, peace, and learning," Jingli said. "That is our vision. That is our legacy."

GOING TO THE SOURCE FOR CLARITY

After a few hours, as we drove away from our engagement with this impressive and well-educated group of nuns, we were awestruck by it all. Why invest hundreds of millions in this far-flung province that isn't easy to get to on a direct flight from anywhere outside Toronto, Montreal, Ottawa, or Beijing?

If you square it from the dedicated nuns' perspective, who made it clear they were afraid of the CCP and its tentacles, then perhaps being so remote was part of their plan. But we both had a nagging sense there was a lot more to their presentation than met the eye.

What was also evident by their presentation and answers—or lack of them in some cases—was that they are "middle management." Not at the top and in the know about the big picture. They were adamant that Master Zhen-Ru was travelling a lot and did not seem to be interacting with the nuns very much. As a matter of fact, she had her own place during the summer with her own group of special monks to take care of her. By itself, in the context of the Buddhist monastic environment, the fact that men were serving a woman, even a guru, did not fit. Shouldn't she have nuns taking care of her?

After we left that meeting, we both expressed our concern and decided it was imperative to get in touch with some Tibetan authorities in Washington to gain further insights. Dean contacted representatives from the Central Tibetan

Administration. He wanted to confirm whether this relationship existed formally or informally, or if it existed at all. He was told in fairly direct language that Bliss and Wisdom has no administrative ties with Dharamshala. Yes, they send monastics to study in India like every other Buddhist monastic group. Still, neither the religious side nor the government-in-exile had anything to do with Bliss and Wisdom as promoters of Tibetan Buddhism.

This confirmation was another very important part of the puzzle. Contrary to the testimonies of the nice nuns, Bliss and Wisdom has no connection or formal relationship with his Holiness. As we discovered on Dean's trip to Taiwan, Bliss and Wisdom was actually, from the Taiwanese government, subject of investigations and suspicions for being somehow "assets" of the CCP and UFWD.

If you square what we learned from our interview with the nuns' perspective, who made it clear they were afraid of the CCP and its tentacles, then coming to PEI to get away from Beijing seems like a logical plan. But we both had more than a nagging sense that there was a lot more to their presentation than met the eye.

Optimum reached out to the nuns at GWBI on several occasions and we sought their response prior to publication. In fairness to the nuns, we have published the entirety of our exchange so that the reader can understand their position. The email is reproduced in its entirety in Exhibit 3 on p. 210.

CHAPTER 9
TIBETAN BUDDHISM UNDER SIEGE
THE PANCHEN LAMA AND TAIWAN'S ROLE, A FAITH UNDER OCCUPATION

THE EXPANSION OF INFLUENCE: CANADA AND PRINCE EDWARD ISLAND

Canada, home to a significant Tibetan exile community, has long been a stronghold for Tibetan cultural and religious preservation. However, concerns have emerged that Chinese influence operations may be extending into Tibetan Buddhist institutions in Canada—particularly through organizations like Bliss and Wisdom in Prince Edward Island.

Bliss and Wisdom, one of the largest Buddhist organizations in Canada, has historical ties to Taiwanese Buddhist networks that have increasingly fallen under Beijing's influence. The organization's founder, Master Jih-Chang, initially emphasized traditional Tibetan Buddhist teachings, but after his death, the movement shifted towards a more Beijing-aligned perspective.

Concerns have emerged that:

- Chinese funding may be influencing the organization's leadership and direction.
- Bliss and Wisdom's connections with CCP-friendly Taiwanese Buddhist groups suggest an attempt to integrate Chinese influence into Canada's religious sphere.
- The silencing of Tibet-related activism within Buddhist institutions could be a sign of growing political interference.

If Chinese influence can shape Buddhist discourse within Canada, it could ultimately reshape the global perception of Tibet—not through force, but through narrative control.

ERASING TIBETAN IDENTITY: THE WEAPONIZATION OF RELIGION

Tibetan Buddhism has long been a pillar of resistance against external domination. As Barbara Demick illustrates in *Eat the Buddha*,[54] monasteries historically served as centres of political thought, cultural preservation, and nationalist sentiment. However, Beijing recognizes that Tibetan identity cannot be fully suppressed without controlling Tibetan Buddhism itself.

The destruction of monasteries, forced political indoctrination of monks, and surveillance of religious activity are all part of a larger effort to erase Tibetan resistance through religious control. The Tibet Policy Institute has further warned that state-controlled religious institutions serve as tools of political suppression, ensuring that Buddhist teachings do not contradict CCP ideology.[55]

Now, this same strategy is being exported abroad. As Barry Sautman[56] argues in *Cultural Genocide and Asian State Peripheries*, China's efforts to manipulate Tibetan Buddhism fall under the broader framework of cultural genocide—a deliberate attempt to dilute and assimilate Tibetan identity so that opposition to Chinese rule fades over time.

The implications of this cannot be overstated. If China succeeds in controlling Tibetan Buddhism globally, it will be able to:

1. Install a CCP-friendly Dalai Lama without opposition.
2. Convince the world that Tibetans accept Chinese rule.
3. Suppress future Tibetan independence movements by removing religious institutions as centres of resistance.

THE URGENT FIGHT TO PROTECT TIBETAN BUDDHISM

The struggle for Tibet is no longer fought only on the plateaus of Lhasa—it is being fought in the monasteries of Taiwan, the Buddhist centres of Canada, and the religious institutions of the West. China's influence operations extend far beyond its borders, and its covert infiltration of Tibetan Buddhist organizations represents a sophisticated front in its campaign for control that has spanned the past four decades.

If Tibetan Buddhism is allowed to be co-opted by Beijing, the consequences will be profound:

- The Dalai Lama's succession will be hijacked, ensuring that Tibetans remain under Chinese rule.
- The global community will lose one of its strongest moral voices against China's human rights abuses.
- Future generations of Tibetans may never know an untainted version of their faith.

Governments must scrutinize CCP-linked funding in Buddhist institutions, empower Tibetan exile communities, and support genuine Tibetan-led religious organizations. The fate of Tibetan Buddhism should not be decided in Beijing; it should be decided by the Tibetans themselves.

The struggle over the succession of the Dalai Lama epitomizes the broader conflict between Tibetan spiritual traditions and the Chinese Communist Party's (CCP) political objectives. Central to this dispute is the role of the Panchen Lama, traditionally responsible for recognizing the reincarnation of the Dalai Lama. The CCP's influence over Tibetan Buddhist institutions, both within and beyond China's borders, further complicates this issue.

THE PANCHEN LAMA CONTROVERSY AND THE DALAI LAMA SUCCESSION

In 1995, the 14th Dalai Lama identified Gedhun Choekyi Nyima as the 11th Panchen Lama. Shortly thereafter, Chinese authorities detained the young boy, who has not been seen publicly since. In his place, the CCP appointed Gyaincain Norbu as the Panchen Lama, a move widely rejected by the Tibetan community. This act underscores China's intent to control the selection of Tibetan spiritual leaders, thereby influencing the future recognition of the Dalai Lama's reincarnation and highlights the lengths to which the Chinese government will go to assert its authority.

The CCP asserts its authority over the reincarnation process through regulatory measures. In 2007, China's State Administration for Religious Affairs issued Order No. 5, stipulating that all reincarnations of Tibetan lamas must receive government approval. This policy aims to legitimize the CCP's role in the selection of the next Dalai Lama, ensuring the appointee aligns with state interests. As Zhu Weiqun, chairman of the ethnic and religious affairs committee of China's top advisory body, stated, "The central government has never given up, and will never give up, the right to decide the reincarnation affairs of the Dalai Lama."

Since his abduction, Gedhun Choekyi Nyima has not been seen in public, leading to international outcry and demands for his release. Despite these calls, Chinese officials maintain tight control over information regarding his whereabouts, claiming he leads an everyday life without providing verifiable evidence. This situation exemplifies China's broader strategy of religious suppression and cultural assimilation in Tibet, raising serious concerns about the future of Tibetan spiritual and religious traditions and the preservation of their cultural heritage.

The Panchen Lama holds a position of immense spiritual significance in Tibetan Buddhism, second only to the Dalai Lama. Traditionally, the Panchen Lama plays a crucial role in identifying the reincarnation of the Dalai Lama, and vice versa. By installing their own candidate, the Chinese government aims to control the selection process of future Dalai Lamas, thereby tightening their grip on Tibetan religious affairs. This manipulation of spiritual traditions for political gain not only violates the religious rights of Tibetans but also threatens the very fabric of Tibetan Buddhism. The international community continues to advocate for the release of Gedhun Choekyi Nyima and respect for the religious autonomy of the Tibetan people, emphasizing that genuine religious leaders cannot be manufactured by state decree.

The disappearance of the Panchen Lama is not an isolated incident but part of a broader pattern of repression in Tibet. Reports indicate that Chinese authorities have systematically targeted Tibetan religious institutions, imposing strict surveillance, and detaining those who resist state interference. Monasteries are subjected to political indoctrination, and monks and nuns are forced to denounce the Dalai Lama. These actions are designed to erode Tibetan cultural identity and assimilate Tibetans into the dominant Han Chinese culture.

In recent years, the Chinese government's narrative surrounding the Panchen Lama has shifted. Officials now claim that Gedhun Choekyi Nyima is leading a normal life and does not wish to be disturbed. However, without independent verification, these assertions lack credibility. The refusal to allow access to Gedhun Choekyi Nyima fuels suspicions that he remains under state control and deprived of his religious role and personal freedom. This situation raises critical questions about China's adherence to international human rights standards and its respect for religious freedom. The continued detention of the Panchen Lama symbolizes the broader struggle for religious and cultural rights in Tibet, highlighting the urgent need for international intervention and advocacy.

The controversy surrounding the Panchen Lama is emblematic of the Chinese government's broader strategy to control and assimilate minority cultures within its borders. By interfering in the selection of religious leaders and suppressing traditional practices, China aims to weaken Tibetan cultural identity and quell any aspirations for autonomy. This approach has led to widespread resentment among Tibetans and has drawn criticism from the global community. The case of the Panchen Lama serves as a stark reminder of the ongoing struggle for cultural preservation and religious freedom in the face of state-sponsored repression. It underscores the importance of sustained international pressure to hold China accountable for its actions and to support the rights of the Tibetan people.

Tibetan Buddhism has long been the spiritual and cultural cornerstone of Tibet, shaping its identity, governance, and resistance to external control. Since China's occupation of Tibet, Beijing has sought not only to dominate its land but to control its faith—co-opting religious institutions, manipulating leadership appointments, and undermining Tibetan Buddhist autonomy worldwide.

Let's further examine this important narrative in the context of this story and the 11th Panchen Lama controversy and the impending succession of the 14th Dalai Lama. If beneath the surface lies a systematic campaign to infiltrate Tibetan Buddhist institutions, particularly in Taiwan, the United States, Australia, and Canada, using them as tools to reshape global perceptions of Tibet and erode resistance to China's rule seems to be part of the strategy.

If China is able to **co**-opt Buddhist institutions abroad, will it succeed in erasing Tibetan identity not just in Lhasa but in exile communities as well? It is a good question, and if Bliss and Wisdom has fallen prey to the United Front's plans for controlling all religious institutions in China and beyond, then we must alert the public and followers to just what is at stake.

CO-OPTING TIBETAN BUDDHISM: THE TAIWAN EXPERIMENT

As we have already outlined, Beijing's strategy to control Tibetan Buddhism extends beyond Tibet's borders, and nowhere is this more apparent than in Taiwan, which is the genesis of the story surrounding Bliss and Wisdom as a monastic organization. Although Taiwan has long been a refuge for religious freedoms suppressed on the mainland, reports for decades have suggested that the CCP continues to infiltrate Tibetan Buddhist organizations in the country, aligning them with its broader political goals.

According to the International Campaign for Tibet (ICT), China has strategically funded and supported Tibetan Buddhist groups in Taiwan that promote a Beijing-approved version of Tibetan Buddhism—one that downplays Tibetan autonomy, supports CCP narratives, and undermines the legitimacy of the Dalai Lama. The Tibet Policy Institute (TPI) further documents how China has provided direct financial and political backing to Buddhist temples and monasteries in Taiwan, ensuring that only clergy sympathetic to the Party's rule receive institutional support should be footnote.

What is the goal?

- Legitimizing China's role in Tibetan Buddhism: By controlling Tibetan Buddhist institutions abroad, China can assert that it—not the Dalai Lama—is the true authority on Tibetan Buddhism. This will be crucial when the CCP eventually tries to install its own China-appointed Dalai Lama.
- Silencing international support for Tibetan independence: Pro-Tibetan activism in Taiwan is being systematically undermined as Beijing-friendly Buddhist organizations suppress narratives that challenge China's occupation of Tibet.

Taiwan's support of Buddhism and proximity to China made it a natural target for the larger "Sinicization of religion" strategy currently being carried out by the CCP globally. Taiwan is on the front line of this battle, just as it will be when China invades it. If China can manipulate Buddhist institutions in Taiwan, what prevents it from doing the same in North America and Europe? Nothing, because it already has.

Are Bliss and Wisdom, the Great Wisdom Buddhist Institute (GWBI, for nuns) and the Great Enlightenment Buddhist Institute Society (GEBIS, for monks) infiltrated organizations, or are they dedicated to His Holiness's monastic Buddhist teaching and caught up in a geopolitical battlefield? Perhaps they are simply navigating their ties with China. We hope readers will certainly find out more in this book. This is not idle speculation but part of a legacy of academic works on this subject by noted scholars such as Michael Van Velt van Pratt, whose work I have referenced extensively in the writing of this chapter. This pattern has repeated itself worldwide.

Chinese influence operations do not announce themselves with fanfare; they unfold methodically, reshaping discourse before anyone realizes the shift. If Canadian institutions—governmental, academic, and religious—fail to recognize the risk, they will become complicit in China's broader ambitions.

The question is no longer whether China will attempt to rewrite Tibet's history beyond its borders—it already is. The real question is whether Canada and the global community will recognize the threat before it is too late. The struggle for Tibet's future does not rest solely in Lhasa or Dharamshala. It is being fought in Taipei, in Ottawa, and even on the peaceful shores of Prince Edward Island. If the world fails to act, Tibet's legacy may not be one of resistance and resilience but of a people erased from history while the world stood by and watched.

BUDDHIST ASSOCIATION OF CHINA (BAC)[57]

The Buddhist Association of China (中国佛教协会, BAC) was established in 1953 as the official state-sanctioned organization to oversee Buddhist activities and promote Buddhism in China. It operates under the supervision of the United Front Work Department (UFWD) of the Communist Party of China (CCP), which managed religious affairs alongside the State Administration for Religious Affairs (SARA) (until it was absorbed into the UFWD in 2018). The BAC's leadership structure includes a President (or Chairperson), Vice Presidents, Secretary-General, and other officials.

Since its inception, the BAC has been led by several prominent monastic figures. Here is a list of its presidents and their respective terms in office:

1. **Yuan Ying (1953-1956):** The first president of the BAC, Yuan Ying played a foundational role in organizing and leading the association during its early years.
2. **Zhao Puchu (1980-2000):** Serving for two decades, Zhao Puchu was instrumental in revitalizing Chinese Buddhism post-Cultural Revolution. He was also renowned for his calligraphy and efforts to promote interfaith dialogue. After him, no one assumed the role until Yicheng took over in 2002.
3. **Yicheng (2002-2010):** Under Yicheng's leadership, the BAC continued its efforts to promote Buddhist teachings and practices across China.

4. **Chuan Yin (2010-2015):** Chuan Yin's tenure focused on strengthening the organizational structure of the BAC and enhancing its outreach.
5. **Xuecheng (2015-2018):** Xuecheng was known for embracing modern technology to disseminate Buddhist teachings. However, his term ended amid controversies.
6. **Yanjue (2018-present):** The current president, Yanjue, continues to lead the association, focusing on the development and propagation of Buddhism in contemporary Chinese society.

Based on questions the authors submitted to Zhen-Ru just before the book was completed, they confirm that Bliss and Wisdom's Master Jih-Chang provided Lamrim teachings but seem to deny any relationship between Zhen-Ru and Xuecheng prior to his death. Their response confirms she does not have a relationship today, but it is clear she was from China and was with the group for at least six years, working directly in China. And if she was involved with Tibetan Buddhism in China she had to work through the Buddhist Association of China as all religion is controlled by the BAC under the United Front Work Department as highlighted in this chapter.

Our question to the nuns was about BAC President, Xuecheng (2015–2018): He was a key figure during the 1999–2007 period prior to Mary Jin arriving on PEI via Mainland China. What was their relationship?

Nuns' response: Prior to 2004 (when the late Master Jih-Chang passed away), Lamrim teachings were given to Ven Xuecheng. Teacher Zhen-Ru does not have a relationship with Ven Xuecheng.

Known Leaders of the Buddhist Association of China (BAC, 1995-2010) include:

- **President (Chairman):**[58]
  - **1993-2002: Zhao Puchu (赵朴初)** — A key figure in modern Chinese Buddhism, Zhao Puchu was a strong advocate for Buddhism's role within the framework of the Chinese state.
  - **2002-2010: Ding Guangquan (一诚法师, Yi Cheng)** — A highly respected monk, Yi Cheng focused on promoting Buddhism under CCP policies.
- **Vice Presidents:**

- During this period, the BAC had several Vice Presidents (Vice Chairs), but their names are not always well-documented in English-language sources. Some notable figures included:
  - **Ding Guangquan (Yi Cheng)** before becoming President was he Yi Cheng before becoming president?
  - **Xuecheng (学诚法师)**, who became BAC President in 2015
  - **Tong Hui (通慧法师)**
  - **Jue Xing (觉醒法师)**
- **Secretary-General:**
  - This role was responsible for administrative and policy-related functions within the BAC. Likely officials in this role included **Duan Zhengcheng** (段正城), but further verification is needed.

CHAPTER 10
CUSTODIANS OF THE FLAME

"If you drink from the waters of the land, you must abide by the Laws of the Land."

HIS HOLINESS, THE DALAI LAMA

Before departing for DC, Michel, Garry, and I produced a report for His Holiness's team, but since I had the contact, and given the sensitivity and nature of the inquiry, Michel and Garry thought it best that I secure the meeting and head to DC to gauge their reaction to our preliminary findings and conclusions. So, I flew down to Washington prior to our presentation to the Island to have a conversation about Bliss and Wisdom.

I met with His Holiness's representative, Namgyal Choedup.[59] We had been introduced to each other at the book launch for Benedict Roger's book *The China Nexus*. I had called him a week or so before arriving to present the brief from our team on what we had learned about this organization and its claims to be a Tibetan monastic group in Taiwan headed by a former Chinese national and citizen, Mary Jin, aka Master Zhen-Ru. We discussed many things about our findings, which at this, our first meeting about Bliss and Wisdom, were very new to him.

When I showed him the video featuring the venerable monk Fan Yin meeting in Dharamshala with His Holiness, he remembered the incident but knew very little about it. We then discussed the brief our team had compiled for him. He was not surprised by some of our conclusions but would need time to further research and validate some of our concerns. This would lead to more meetings and an opportunity to meet with Penpa Tsering, the Sikyong (elected leader) of the Central Tibetan Administration, when he was travelling in Canada later in May. My close colleague and mentor on understanding Tibet and China is former Conservative Senator Consiglio Di Nino,[60] who was with me. He had known Penpa for more than two decades. The Senator had been instrumental in his support of the Tibetan peoples in Parliament and had served on numerous parliamentary "Friends of Committees"[61] related to the Chinese diaspora communities. He had even helped to financially support the community centre in the '90s when they were struggling to secure a mortgage.

Over the next couple of hours, we talked about Tibet, his leadership, the Senator's contributions to Tibet in Canada, and of course, spent a great deal of time on our investigation. He was quite concerned about our findings and agreed to help where he could. He also took the time to explain that His Holiness's Middle Way[62] had guided the Tibetan people and their engagement with the People's Republic of China for close to half a century, but with the PRC's aggressive position on claiming they had jurisdiction over the Panchen Lama and the process for naming the next Dalai Lama the government-in-exile had separated from the spiritual side of His Holiness (since 2011). His patience for these claims was wearing thin. Our discussion centred on the influence of the Buddhist Association of China (BAC) infiltrating various influential Buddhist groups in Taiwan in order to execute on their plan to control Tibetan Buddhism and claim ownership. Of course, the irony is that an atheist party with no gods feels the need to control all religions in China. And those who practise them.

He explained to me that they were taking a new path to tell the story of Tibetans' claim to Tibet versus the CCP's claims that Tibet and Tibetans had always been part of China. As far as the CCP is concerned, if you can control the narrative, you can write whatever history you want and expect all of us to accept your specious claims over any and all lands. I would see him again in Munich in a few weeks at the World Uyghur Congress's annual meeting, where he would introduce me to some prominent Tibetans from Europe who would be helpful later to our team as we continued our investigation.

DOES THE CCP CONTROL TIBETAN BUDDHISM?

What we wish to do now is provide you, the reader, with a better understanding of what is at stake for Tibetan Buddhism and for those who lead Bliss and Wisdom if the CCP succeeds in its mission. So, as we lay out the rest of this chapter, let's take you to the serene hills of Dharamshala, the spiritual epicentre *of* Tibetan Buddhism in exile. A profound responsibility looms over the Tibetan community in 2025. His Holiness the 14th Dalai Lama, Tenzin Gyatso, has long been the beacon of hope and resilience for Tibetans worldwide. As he approaches the twilight of his life, the question of his reincarnation becomes increasingly pressing. The Dalai Lama has unequivocally stated that his successor will be born in a "free world," beyond the grasp of Chinese authorities, ensuring the preservation of the spiritual integrity of Tibetan Buddhism.

Central to this succession is the role of the Panchen Lama, traditionally responsible for identifying the reincarnation of the Dalai Lama. In 1995, the Dalai Lama recognized Gedhun Choekyi Nyima as the 11th Panchen Lama. However, shortly after this recognition, Gedhun Choekyi Nyima and his family were abducted by Chinese authorities, and his whereabouts remain unknown to this day. In his place, the Chinese government appointed Gyaincain Norbu, a move widely regarded by Tibetans and the international community as an attempt to exert control over Tibetan religious traditions.

The CCP, through the BAC, has systematically sought to dominate the narrative surrounding Tibetan Buddhism. By infiltrating religious institutions and imposing state-sanctioned doctrines, the CCP aims to reshape Tibetan Buddhism to align with the Party's ideological objectives. This strategy extends beyond Tibet to include efforts to influence Buddhist organizations in Taiwan, thereby consolidating control over the broader Buddhist discourse.

In response to these challenges, the Central Tibetan Administration (CTA) in Dharamshala has reaffirmed its commitment to preserving the authenticity of Tibetan Buddhist practices. The CTA emphasizes that the recognition of the next Dalai Lama will be conducted according to traditional religious procedures, free from external political interference. This stance is not only a defence of religious freedom but also a declaration of cultural sovereignty.

The role of the international community in this context is pivotal. Countries and organizations advocating for human rights and religious freedom are called upon to support the CTA's efforts and to challenge the CCP's attempts to politicize spiritual traditions. By standing in solidarity with the Tibetan people, the global community can help ensure that the flame of Tibetan Buddhism continues to burn brightly, untainted by political agendas.

As the world watches, the determination of the Tibetan community in exile serves as a testament to their unwavering commitment to their faith and heritage. The path ahead may be fraught with challenges, but with unity and international support, the sanctity of Tibetan Buddhism can be preserved for future generations.

As we think of the interests of the Buddhist Association of China and the links to Bliss and Wisdom in both China and Taiwan, His Holiness's emphatic stand should neutralize any suggestion that monastic groups outside of Tibet and Dharamshala will have any say over the reincarnation.

With that in mind, the passage reproduced below is from His Holiness's new book, given to me by Namgyal Choedup in Washington in late March 2025 during my final brief to him on Bliss and Wisdom and our findings. Given that His Holiness has never met Zehn-Ru or gone to their teaching facility in Taiwan (on one of his many trips), that should be taken as a sign.

The following is another sign that both the government-in-exile, its current Sikyong, Penpa Tsering, and the religious side of Dharamshala are no longer going to stand by as the CCP attempts to control and in fact eviscerate their traditions and culture in Tibet and control the narrative globally. We should all be guided by His Holiness's wise words and "abide by the laws of the land." As our team worked to uncover the truth about Bliss and Wisdom, we were guided by a simple process. Follow the facts and the journeys of others, and they will lead to the truth.

Whatever that truth might be.

In the meantime, let's let Dharamshala and His Holiness have the last word on who controls Tibetan Buddhism and the reincarnation of the next Dalai Lama, if it is to be.[63]

> People often ask me if there will be a next Dalai Lama. As early as the 1960s, I have expressed that whether the Dalai Lama institution should continue or not is a matter for the Tibetan people. So if the Tibetan people feel that the institution has served its purpose and there is now no longer any need for a Dalai Lama then the institution will cease. In which case I would be the last Dalai Lama, I've stated. I have also said that if there is a continued need then there will be the Fifteenth Dalai Lama. In particular, in 2011, I convened a gathering of the leaders of all major Tibetan religious traditions, and at the conclusion of this meeting, I issued a formal statement in which I stated that when I turn 90, I will consult the high lamas of the Tibetan religious traditions as well as the Tibetan public, and if there is a consensus that the Dalai Lama institution should continue then formal responsibility for the recognition of the Fifteenth Dalai Lama should rest with the Gaden Phodrang Trust (the office of the Dalai Lama). The Gaden Phodrang Trust should follow the procedures of search and recognition in accordance with past Tibetan Buddhist tradition, including, especially, consulting the oath-bound Dharma protectors[64] historically connected

to the lineage of the Dalai lamas as was followed carefully in my own case. On my part I have clearly written instructions on this. For more than a decade now, I have received numerous petitions and letters from a wide spectrum of Tibetan people—senior lamas from the various Tibetan traditions, Abbots of monasteries, diaspora Tibetan communities across the world, and many prominent and ordinary Tibetans inside Tibet—as well as Tibetan Buddhist communities from the Himalayas regions and Mongolia uniformly asking me to ensure that the Dalai Lama lineage be continued.

Now since the purpose of reincarnation is to carry on the work of the predecessor, the new Dalai Lama will be born in the free world so that the traditional mission of the Dalai Lama—that is, to be the voice for universal compassion, the spiritual leader of Tibetan Buddhism and the symbol of Tibet embodying the aspirations of the Tibetan people.[65]

The above excerpt is printed in *Brevity* in accordance with Chapter 15, "Situation Today and the Path Forward" from the book *Voice for the Voiceless*, in which His Holiness reflects on the current trials faced by Tibetans and lays out a vision of enduring peace, cultural preservation, and global solidarity. It is a fitting conclusion to the spiritual and political odyssey documented within this chapter and an important lesson for all those at Bliss and Wisdom who wish to follow in the path of His Holiness.

Perhaps it best to leave the last word on the matter to the government-in-exile.

This correspondence between myself and the Central Tibetan Administration emphasized to our team that there is no administrative link between them and Bliss and Wisdom or GEBIS and GWBI. They have always been concerned by Zhen-Ru's claims to be a "Guru" as she does not have the credentials to make that claim. This was a critical aspect to Michel, who was doing the significant research and analysis on who Zhen-Ru is, including her links to Tibetan Bhuddism and her origins in China as a claimed spiritual Guru.

Hi Dean,

It was a great pleasure to meet you in DC. Thank you for the follow up and as promised we did some preliminary inquiry into the matter. As far as we know, the original founder of *Bliss and Wisdom*, Master Jih-Chang (who passed away in 2004) received teachings from His Holiness the Dalai Lama. The organization was back then mostly engaged in reviving the practice of Buddhism in Taiwan and mainland China and therefore it was natural for the Master and many Chinese and Taiwanese followers to seek the teachings from His Holiness the Dalai Lama and Tibetan Buddhist teachers. In particular, the Tibetan monastic institute of Drepung (based in South India) did provide teachers for Bliss and Wisdom in Taiwan. However, none of the Tibetan teachers sent to teach at Bliss and Wisdom in Taiwan had any authority or formal position in the administrative/management including funding/financial matters.

His Holiness the Dalai Lama is highly revered and his guidance sought by many non-Tibetan Buddhist organizations. However, His Holiness has no say or control over how these Buddhist organizations conduct their practice, leave alone their administrative and management matters. His Holiness has always spoken out against the practice of conversion/proselytization and has always advised non-Tibetan followers to remain true to their original faiths/traditions. Furthermore, when it comes to abuse of authority and power in the Tibetan Buddhist community, he has always spoken on the side of justice and truth and advised the students to investigate thoroughly the moral conduct/practice of their spiritual teachers. He has always emphasized to the Tibetan followers the cardinal rule of following the law of the land by quoting the Tibetan saying "if you drink the water of the land, you must follow the law of the land."

In brief, we don't have any knowledge of the Buddhist organization run by one Master Zhenru on PEI and we totally understand the Canadian authorities and public wanting to make sure this Buddhist organization follows the law of the land.

We are more than happy to cooperate and answer any questions you have.

Best,
Namgyal

CHAPTER 11
SHADOWS ON THE ISLAND
AN IMMIGRATION CONSULTANT'S STORY

After our book launch in March, things were starting to break for us. Garry, Michel, and I had been collectively on the Island a dozen times by now, and people were beginning to trust us in telling their story, thinking that perhaps someone would provide Islanders with some hope that an investigation of any kind might come out of our work, since we were working towards publishing a book. Michel, as the career intelligence officer, thought to put up that slide suggesting Islanders could be part of the solution paying dividends. The *Canada Under Siege* event was one of the largest book launches ever and clearly demonstrated that Islanders wanted to know more, but first I felt we needed to lay the groundwork for our investigation. We didn't have all the answers, but we had a number of working hypotheses on the Provincial Nominee Program, elite capture, naive politicians, and what might be behind the leadership of the Bliss and Wisdom organization. But we were not ready to go public with that, and we needed the book launch to give Islanders a big global picture.

Avery Haines from CTV's *W5* had brought a cameraman to record the entire event. They wanted to do more on the story. We agreed to meet in mid-April at the CTV offices in Scarborough, a suburb of Toronto, to go over the next steps on how they might bring the story forward. I showed up in person, and Garry and Michel joined via video conference. They wanted to do something because they knew there was more to the story on PEI. However, W5 was going through a major reorganization as part of Bell Media's cost-cutting exercise. Another potential blow to investigative journalism in this country, but something being felt around the free world.

W5 had done an excellent job in exposing the PNP scandal through the three whistleblowers mentioned earlier in the book. The 15-minute news exposé titled, "Speaking Out Against a P.E.I. Immigration Scandal," highlighted Susan Holmes and Cora Nicholson and spoke about them being smeared and their names dragged through the unique red mud of the Island.

What they did not touch on was the links to China and the awarding of the English as a Second Language service contract that Susan had been fired over. In 2019 few dared touch anything that might have impeded our opportunities to repair our diplomatic relationship with China, given the two Michaels affair[66] that was known to most Canadians.

But Haines understood there was a lot more to the PNP scandal and its insidious links to Chinese immigration and investment on the tiny island. Our team was enthusiastic that they might do something big but by mid-May, with Avery's producer leaving for the CBC, this opportunity died quickly.

So, after we knew the CTV opportunity was dead, we planned for the next visit.

But, once again, you need people on the Island who are known and trusted, and Alan MacPhee, who spoke at the March event representing I Am for Democracy was very well connected on PEI. We let him know we were planning a trip to follow up on the leads coming out of our St. Patrick's Day book launch. So, during an early August trip to the Island, due to scheduling conflicts, I headed to PEI on my own. I asked if we could talk to George (a source) who had processed Mary Jin's (who eventually became Master Zhen-Ru) application back in 2007–08. Alan made the call. "I spoke with George last night," he said. "He's willing to speak. He's been in government since before Pat Bins (1996–2007) and he's got a memory like a vault."

MacPhee wasn't just arranging a conversation. He was orchestrating a meeting between history and revelation. "He knows all the bodies," Alan said, adding "he did the application for Zhen-Ru—the leader. He knew Frank Zhou. He even worked in financial security forty years ago. Said there was concern back then about spies coming into the country. He's not naïve."

It was Alan who arranged our breakfast meeting in downtown Charlottetown at one of the more popular restaurants. "He wants me to be there with you, just to ground the conversation. Tomorrow, Wednesday, at breakfast. He'll talk. He wants this out."

George didn't arrive like a man burdened by secrets. He arrived like a man used to them. As we sat in the bustling restaurant just to the right of the entrance way, it was a pleasant August morning with many tourists already walking Charlottetown's storied main street. They were brushing against the windows like whispers of the past. Over some strong coffee, the story began to emerge—not just of immigration, but of infiltration, hesitation, and the price of turning a blind eye.

George started in government before most of today's officials were even born. He'd come through economic development, dipped into trade, and eventually found himself shaping immigration policy for the Island. He wasn't trained in immigration—he learned on the job. What he didn't say with bravado he made up for in detail.

"We started the Provincial Nominee Program to save this place," he said. "No one was coming. No one cared. We figured if we got one out of ten to invest and stay, we were doing well." The feds had not been helping, and PEI needed an edge, so when they built out the 2005 version it resembled a hybrid between an immigration program and a scheme to line the pockets of the province. That will be discussed in another chapter.

He paused to stir his coffee. "Then they came. And then they kept coming."

But George wasn't unaware. Long before PEI was a talking point in Ottawa or being observed by Washington, he'd sensed something. "I worked in financial security in the '70s," he told us. "We had spies coming in then too. Quiet. Subtle. Not guns and espionage—just influence. Access. Buying silence."

It was against that backdrop that he met Zhen-Ru in 2007, the same year Robert Ghiz was swept into office and the Chrétien Liberals and the Island were all in on the hopes that China was going to be the solid partner and financial bonanza they had hoped it would be.

"She came in through the PNP," he said. "She looked perfect on paper. Net worth of $600,000. Five years in business. Clean. Smart. She said she ran a lamp company in China." Let's be clear, though—she was immigrating from Mainland China and not Taiwan. George and other consultants would normally introduce potential candidates for the Provincial Nomination Program to PEI by taking them on a historic and nostalgic trip of the Island. Confederation Hall, the northern shore, Anne of Green Gables Park, and a host of other landmarks.

He went on to recount his first encounter with Mary Jin, or Men Rong (her Chinese name) as she did not apply as Master Zhen-Ru.

"I was driving the van, taking a few applicants, including Mary Jin, as I knew her, around the Island. I had offered her the front seat. It was icy as I recall and cold. It was winter. And then I saw the black SUV in the rearview mirror, it was following us, so I pulled over and got out of my seat and approached the vehicle.

"Four Chinese nationals inside. Wired. They weren't tourists, and when I asked why they were following me, they simply pointed to the van and said we are with her." He said "ok" and went back to the van.

After the tour it was getting late, but one of the security guys asked if we could meet for the preliminary meeting that night. George said it was late, 9:20 as he recounted.

"They asked if they could do an interview late that night and I said that I was tired but Ok. So, there's a couch in my office and in come two of her security detail. One sits down on the right and one on the left. Then she came in and sat between the two of them. She was dressed in all red," George said, "and looked like someone who had just come from the slopes of Kitzbühel. Perfect makeup. Designer everything. She sat in the front of the interview room, flanked by two men." By this time George was getting the feeling she was special, and her security detail never spoke. They didn't need to.

The interview went flawlessly.

"She didn't blink," he said. Through an interpreter she answered all the questions. "Seemed to know every answer before I asked. Smooth. Polished. Rehearsed. She met every criterion."

As George viewed the landscape today, he had started to connect the dots that connected Bliss and Wisdom—her organization was something more than just monks and nuns. It was a business enterprise. As I described it to him based on the whistleblower and open source data, I suggested it could be something much bigger, or it could just be what they say it is. A monastic Buddhist group from Taiwan looking to relocate their global headquarters to Prince Edward Island and be the saviour of Tibetan Buddhism, or perhaps it was also a spiritual shell for a geopolitical goal.

It was then that I shared my side of the story.

"My authors and Optimum's research team have been tracking CCP operations globally," I told him. "From the Solomon Islands to British Columbia. We called it subnational state capture. And PEI—it was a soft underbelly. The perfect place to slip through."

George didn't look surprised.

"CSIS used to come to my office," he said. "One guy. Every few months. Never asked directly. Just listened. Took notes. Then left."

He knew the silence said more than questions.

George had been engaging with politicians on the Island since the '80s, and he brought up Mulroney and the Karlheinz Schreiber affair. The envelopes of cash. The lobbying denials. The lawsuits. "This," I said, "is the legacy of elite capture."

"When Mulroney got pulled into that mess," George said, "people here thought it was a one-off. But it wasn't. It was the first time the curtain got pulled back." I then recounted testimony that Michel had delivered to various committees looking into Chinese interference about how every prime minister since Brian Mulroney has been compromised by agents of influence.

And on PEI, that curtain hid more than just foreign interests.

"Frank Zhou was connected to everyone," George said. "Liberals, Conservatives. It didn't matter. He took every premier to China. Wine, dine, deals."

And then, the money.

"There were properties bought with cash," I added. This reminds our team of the Vancouver Model, which Sam Cooper had exposed in *Wilful Blindness* and his numerous reports for Global News. "Trusts. Shell companies. Linked to fentanyl labs in Vancouver feeding supply chains across North America and may well flow right through to the Island. We have seen the evidence of proxy owners. Empty houses. Cash paying for houses, contractors and suppliers and it looks like money is being laundered right under your feet."

George nodded. "I don't know anything about that. I just processed applications, but I did have one guy disappear with $100,000. Never saw him again." I didn't really understand how that fit in and I fell silent.

"You know, I wrote the application for Zhen-Ru," George said. "I was just doing my job. But I never forgot her face."

This was the reason I wanted this interview—George was the first person to encounter Mary Jin. But before he continued on about Mary Jin, the conversation began to wade into more stories about the Island and corruption, where another storm was forming behind the scenes—one that would give institutional weight to George's recollections and deepen the implications of what they had all been discussing with respect to the various Provincial Nomination Programs that brought countless, and many times faceless, immigrants to PEI.

On July 24, 2024, a week before I arrived GH Consultants received a formal request from Kathryn Dickson, Manager of the Access and Privacy Services Office with the Department of Justice and Public Safety. The letter, directed to George's consulting firm, invoked the Freedom of Information and Protection of Privacy Act (the "Act") and came with a warning: a large request had been filed asking for detailed historical records of the Business Impact Stream of the Provincial Nominee Program—spanning nearly a decade, from 2015 to 2024. He handed me his phone so I could see the letter.

The scope of the request was vast. Fourteen distinct queries asked for breakdowns of approvals, RFPs, nominee success rates, source countries, accounting firm involvements, and perhaps most significantly, a detailed listing of which Island agents had handled which cases—including George's own work under New Island Opportunities Inc.

Under Section 28 of the Act, George was informed that he was being consulted because the disclosure of these records could affect his business interests. The government was legally obligated to offer him an opportunity to respond. Under Section 14 of the Act, disclosure had to be refused if it met three specific legal thresholds. But if George didn't respond by August 13, the department could proceed with disclosure anyway.

Reading the email out loud at the table, George shook his head. "So, they're finally turning over the stones," he said. "And they're asking where all the footprints lead."

Alan and I fell into silence. Everything I had described—everything George had hinted at—was now being dragged from the periphery into full institutional daylight.

I looked across the table. "This is what we've been waiting for," I said. "Others are also looking at what has gone on behind the scenes because this is a big but mysterious story. Now they're going to see it. Not just the applications. Not just the approvals. But the architects, the lawyers, immigration consultants, and accountants who all made a lot of money from immigration from the early 2000s to 2009 in the fake business investment program that became the PNP scandal under the Ghiz government.[67]

I handed back his phone and he put it down. I asked him if he would share the request with me and he agreed to do so. Then he said, "Let's hope they know how to read the blueprint."

At the end of our breakfast, I opened my laptop and showed him the draft cover for the book. *Canada Under Siege: How PEI Became a Forward Operating Base for the Chinese Communist Party*. It was the interim title for the book

George read the title, then leaned back in the booth.

"That'll get people talking," he said.

I smiled. "That's the point."

George then shared the email with me and later shared one of the documents that he sent to the government. What is clear is that the government PNP was less about a balanced immigration program than it was about bringing people in from China. Over the three-year period in question 94% were from Mainland China, and none from Taiwan, where democracy was thriving. Could he just be an anomaly and that other immigration consultants were bringing in Bliss and Wisdom followers as the nuns and monks were suggesting?

I would meet with George once more, on August 10, after I left the Island to enjoy a little break in Nova Scotia, where I met up with a journalist colleague and author Stephen Maher. I had the opportunity to sail in my first long-haul maritime schooner race. It was an all-day affair culminating in stories and beers at the dock, as do most sailboat regattas that I have participated in.

If records are kept based on source country of nominations for applications submitted by each Island Agent, please provide a breakdown of nominations for each Island Agent since 2015.

Agent / PA Nationality	2015	2016	2017	2018	2019	2020	2021	2022	2023	2024	Grand Total
H.P. Consultants	41	38	36	2							117
China	41	36	33								110
Other (under 10)		1		1							2
India		1	1								2
Hong Kong			2								2
Vietnam				1							1

Brad provided all of the transactions over the past few years. All transactions were in cash with the explanation that they were donations.

I had lunch with George to confirm a number of key points and get answers to some of the questions we had about his interaction with Master Zhen-Ru. It was a great meeting, and I thanked him for his time and told him that his story was important for the book. He agreed to share any documents surrounding the FOIA request.

As I left the second meeting on that windy day at the Charlottetown Yacht club, I came away with a sense that all our hard work was beginning to pay off and we were uncovering important pieces of a complicated puzzle; this wasn't just George's small role in the story. This was a whole Island story. Canada's story.

The document was supplied by George's company to the FOIA office in late August of 2024 as part of the official request. Once again it clearly showed that even with the revamped immigration program that China was the predominant participant which of course did not surprise me, Garry, or Michel.

Wealthy Chinese and Hong Kong immigrants had been the target of the program from the beginning, and people like George, Frank Zhou, and others continued to follow the path of least resistance and the money.

CHAPTER 12
THE POOR GURU WHO WEARS PRADA
THE INTELLIGENCE ANALYSIS

To say she came in and made a big impression would be an understatement. As noted earlier, she arrived with four bodyguards, wearing designer shoes and dressed like she was coming out of a Paris fashion show. Her intention was clear: to leave China and to move permanently to the province. Welcome to Prince Edward Island's strangest case of spiritual politics.

For several years in the late '80s and early '90s, Brian Mulroney's federal government had put in place an immigration program to allow the provinces to attract investors. This program became very successful and was extended in various forms throughout the '90s and early 2000s. The provincial government of Prince Edward Island (PEI) built its own program, the most attractive in the country. Enticing foreign entrepreneurs and immigrants, it required them to invest $200,000 (CAD) and to stay in the province for two years. In return, their immigration applications would be processed quickly, and they would gain immediate permanent residency. It was a very good offer on all fronts for a rich and busy entrepreneur wannabe immigrant.

The idea was presented to the public as a form of new money investment that would stimulate local businesses and the economy and bring new talents into the province. In fact, the distribution of the investments revealed itself to be very complex, and very little of the proposed $200 000 investments ever reached local businesses. In general, the $200,000 was split between "fees" for handlers and middlemen, government and lawyers. At the end, all that was left was a handful of changes.

The immigrant investor was supposedly investing in a local PEI business, but in many cases these businesses were simply shell companies set up to receive the money and disappear shortly after. Businesses that qualified (anyone with a pulse) would receive much-needed investments, and depending on the business, some qualified for more than one unit ($25,000–$35,000).

Remember, the original goal was to attract investors and immigrants who wanted to invest in and build a life in PEI, yet less than two out of ten from the 2005 to 2007 program remain in the province today. In fact, the government knew that most investors did not stay in the province for more than seventy-two hours. Effectively, Canada received tens of thousands of rich immigrants who brought millions in investments, but the unintended (and unanticipated) side effects were loads of social and housing problems. For example, the housing market in some cities (Greater Vancouver and Greater Toronto) were quickly inflated to the point that houses that previously cost $500,000 to $750,000 are now selling for more than $1.5 million, and often more than $2 million, making it impossible for young buyers to even dream of owning a home in these urban centres.

Organized crime also saw the opportunity to come to Canada, and criminals could become citizens quickly. In short, blinded by the prospect of quick and easy money, Canadian politicians, both federal and provincial, sold our passport's good and valuable reputation for easy returns. In most cases, this benefited the business and political elites personally, and the security and police agencies were asked to remain quiet and on the sidelines. PEI is a fine example of what we have observed across Canada over the past forty years.

PRINCE EDWARD ISLAND AS A CASE STUDY

Right away it must be understood that PEI was no different from the rest of Canada when it came to making money from its immigration program. In fact, as the smallest province in the country and one very limited in natural resources and with almost no room to expand, it saw that facilitating the arrival of entrepreneurs/immigrants was an opportunity to bring some fresh money to its economy. It was Prime Minister Jean Chrétien who suggested the program to Premier Pat Binns who was visiting Ottawa. Chrétien even introduced a "personal friend," a young Chinese entrepreneur named Frank Zhou who would be able to help. As a young man born into a well-established communist family in China, where his grandfather was considered a hero of the Cultural Revolution (there is even a statue of him), Zhou was known as a "Red Princeling," a sobriquet given to children of ruling CCP members. With such connections, he became the focal point of many trips, business creations, and transfers of money between PEI and China.

So, PEI launched the Provincial Nominee Program (PNP) that would receive applications from various foreign entrepreneurs, assess the information, and accept or reject the application. A department was assembled, and with the assistance of immigration consultants, staff would receive applications and review them. There were some criteria to be met (but, hey, criteria are only there to show we have a process). In PEI, though, process can be bypassed as the leading party sees fit. This was established as a cultural practice in PEI way before the PNP program, and the general population has come to accept it, but with the PNP it would be abused way more than anything previously experienced.

MARY JIN'S FIRST VISIT

Mary Jin's arrival on Prince Edward Island in 2007 was unlike that of a typical investor-class immigrant. Her arrival was highly orchestrated and stood out immediately to those involved in her interview and immigration process. All the sources we interviewed regarding her application and interview expressed stupefaction and incredulity about how she arrived and was served by the system.

As part of the process for applicants visiting the Island, every immigration consultant was required to give them a tour. Potential candidates had to be charmed with the prospect of moving some assets to PEI and, who knows, keep them there and settle for good, although frankly, it was not the ultimate goal. It was the job of the consultants to enlist applicants into the PNP as soon as possible but to keep them here was not in the job description. Everybody was making very good money along the way for every file (immigrant investor) that used the PNP program to come to PEI.

Mary Jin, or Jin Meng Rong (金梦蓉), her real Chinese name, was initially treated like all potential applicants. Since Westerners have difficulty with Chinese names, it is customary for a Chinese person to choose a Western first name. In this case "Mary," the name of the virgin mother, was going to be suitable, as we will discover.

When Jin visited for the first time, it immediately attracted attention because she did not come alone. She had four bodyguards with her. She was meticulously dressed for the tour and looked like she had stepped out of a page of Vogue magazine. Not like a Buddhist nun or a guru. As a matter of fact, according to the sources, Buddhism was never mentioned at all during her first visit.

While driving Jin around for her tour of the Island, the consultant noticed that a car was following them. He stopped his vehicle and went to the car, which had pulled up behind them. Inside were four Asian men who explained they were "looking after her." The consultant noticed that all of the men had earpieces. In the mundane life of the Island, it was very unusual to see a potential immigrant arrive with four bodyguards.

A similar scenario surprised the source when Jin came for her interview. The meeting arrangements with her were handled with extra care. First, at Jin's request, she was to be interviewed late in the evening, around 9:30, which was atypical. Clearly, she, or those managing her presence, wanted discretion and control over the setting. It is common to try to accommodate a visitor's wishes regarding the timing of the interview, but this time it was evident that it was she who would control the process, and not the other way around, immediately establishing an understanding that forces were working in the background for her or were sufficiently confident that her "authority" was coming across. Either way, it worked.

During her interview Jin was flanked by two bodyguards, one seated on either side of her. As previously noted, she looked like she had just come from a Paris fashion show or the slopes of Kitzbühel. The message was clear: she was a person of importance and potentially at risk but certainly with money, lots of money. Her security detail was also unlike anything typically seen in the provincial immigration process.

Jin's appearance suggested someone who was either wealthy, politically connected, or both. Her manner was polished and composed, and although she required an interpreter, she spoke confidently and strategically, which suggested she was used to interacting with powerful individuals. This demeanour made a strong impression on the people present.

According to the source, Jin stated that she was coming to the Island alone and was not accompanied by children or a husband. All alone. By any metric, it was a great interview. She met all the criteria. She had a net worth of $600,000. She had been an entrepreneur for five years and said she was running some kind of lamp business. There was no mention of any Buddhist group, her role as a leader, the coming of monks and nuns, or the intention to move a small army of followers with her. Nothing of that!

She was a good catch! With Jin's application everything went smoothly and quickly—far faster than usual. According to our source, under the PNP, visas were issued about six weeks after arrival, but even within that timeframe, Jin's case stood out for how efficiently and quietly it was processed. It gave the impression that somebody in the government had been waiting for the paperwork and was able to accelerate the process with no questions being asked.

Even if the PNP program was designed to accelerate the immigration process, a minimum still needed to be done. The government had to demonstrate a certain "control" over the process. Normally that would mean multiple steps for investor immigrants, including investing in a business, presenting a business plan, moving to and to staying on the Island for a year to get their residency deposit back, and being issued their Permanent Residency Card almost immediately upon arriving in PEI.

But every immigrant consultant and government official knew that most applicants left after the first seventy-two hours, and nobody seriously really cared. The $200,000 investment mostly went to the same people for lawyers' fees, accountants' fees for the business plan that needed to be submitted, and other middlemen, like the brokers in China and the immigration consultants. In short, it was a phenomenal source of revenue not for the province but for the few privileged or chosen ones involved in the process. If the applicant left the Island, he or she would lose the money, which the vast majority did not claim.

THE PROVINCIAL NOMINEE PROGRAM

As mentioned, some businesses also received money. Most businesses would receive between $25,000 and $35,000 for each PNP unit, as they were known, but some got more, much more. Many companies were quickly registered to receive several units and closed soon after. Several of those companies were later identified as associated with or linked to family members, spouses, or friends of the government in power. Overall, more than three thousand people were accepted by the PNP program just for PEI.

In April 2008, the federal government announced it would be shutting down the PNP due to concerns about the abuses associated with the program and the quality of the applicants coming through. In other words, the federal government discovered that PEI did not really care about the quality of the applicants and did not even enforce the rules as prescribed by the PNP. The Robert Ghiz government was just interested in the money. When the news of closure came out, government employees were instructed to quickly process people and to accelerate their acceptance. In the last few months of the PNP, 1,750 applications were accepted. It seemed like there were few to no security background checks, no verification of their personal story, nothing. Sources within the PNP confirmed they received instruction to fast track the process so they could collect all the cash they could, and teams were sent to Hong Kong, Dubai, and other countries to meet with potential applicants and process their submissions on the spot.

JIN'S ARRIVAL IN PEI

The first monks and nuns to arrive in PEI came in 2007–08. They contacted the provincial government and explained that they intended to establish a small temple and school to study and practise Buddhism. Their first settlements were very humble and practical. Monks and nuns were living in separate locations and quarters. They first bought the old Lobster Shanty that was getting pretty run down, and they packed every man they could into that building.

Jin officially arrived in PEI in 2009. She immediately bought the large house of (name of the owner) with enough land to build adjacent buildings. Sources confirmed it was part official transaction and part extra cash. Multiple sources described to the investigators the setting for the home and the use of the various buildings built in support of it.

First there was the residence where Jin lives. It was bought with cash. It's not illegal to buy a house with cash, just unusual. It also minimizes supervision by the banks and federal authorities. We found some transactions involving cash and bank transfers, but this practice was adopted after the government and some real estate agents started asking questions.

The house was not fit for someone of Jin's status, so it was renovated to accommodate her. By then she started to be known on the Island as Master Zhen-Ru, her guru's name within the Bliss and Wisdom Buddhist sect. Although now known as the Master of the sect, she never lived among them. She remained apart from the rank-and-file monks and nuns already on the Island. It must be understood that according to Buddhist practices, men and women in Buddhist monasteries are to be kept separate.

Jin (aka: Zhen-Ru) has on-site, at her service, about twenty young male monks known as "Marco Monks." They are considered her personal close protection unit. According to various sources and confirmed by nuns we interviewed, Jin is in PEI for only part of the summer when the weather is nice and does not receive visitors often. During the winter, she goes to a private residence in the Caribbean surrounded by her Marco Monks. Her house is very sumptuous and has nothing to do with the humble, minimalist, and somewhat deprived life normal monks and nuns must experience. Already, the luxury of her living quarters and international destinations differs greatly from the image of a spiritual leader that most people imagine.

A second building was added to the complex, and according to several sources, it is full of computer desks with Marco Monks operating them. The building is secured, and access is restricted. Several high-end surveillance cameras have been installed, many more than for a normal house. A dedicated fibre optic line was installed at the cost of $2.1 million CAD (circa 2019) with strict instructions to Bell Canada that no other party from the community or elsewhere could be connected to it. Quite a strange approach for a group of enlightened and spiritual individuals preaching that they are here to help and to integrate with the community. But more importantly, from a national security angle, that begs the question: Why would a group of Buddhist monks need a very expensive, dedicated, and guarded fibre optic cable for themselves? Asking the question is partially answering it.

INITIALLY NOT A BLISS AND WISDOM PRACTITIONER

Jin was not always a follower of Bliss and Wisdom (BW), nor initially a Buddhist. She was first a devotee of Zhong Gong (中功). During the late 1980s and 1990s, there was a resurgence of interest among Chinese citizens in Qigong (氣功), an ancient practice combining physical movement and spiritual cultivation. This revival led to the emergence of various Qigong-based movements, including Zhong Gong, Falun Gong, and others. In the post-Mao era, the Chinese government, seeking to promote traditional Chinese culture, initially supported this revival and even established a national Qigong association.

Zhong Gong, founded in 1987 by Zhang Hongbao, quickly gained popularity in the early 1990s. It established numerous training centres, schools, and practice halls across China. Its rapid growth and national infrastructure eventually drew scrutiny from the authorities. On April 25, 1999, the political climate shifted when tens of thousands of Falun Gong practitioners protested in Beijing against negative portrayals of them in state-run media. Three months later, then-President Jiang Zemin labelled Falun Gong a threat to state stability and issued an arrest warrant for its founder, Li Hongzhi.

The government's response triggered a nationwide crackdown on spiritual and religious movements outside official control. Between October and December 1999, as the Chinese government tightened its laws, many groups—including Zhong Gong—were declared illegal. Leaders were either arrested or forced into exile. The crackdown also affected unregistered Buddhist and Christian house churches, which were swept up in the state's broader anti-*xie jiao* (邪教, "heterodox teachings") initiative. Although Zhong Gong was ideologically distinct from Falun Gong, it was nonetheless targeted as part of the state's effort to dismantle independent spiritual networks perceived as challenges to the authority of the Chinese Communist Party.

CHAPTER 13

THE FALL OF ZHONG GONG AND THE RISE OF MARY JIN

Since the late Ming Dynasty, Chinese authorities have used the designation *xie jiao*—often mistranslated in the West as "evil cults"—to classify religious or spiritual movements threatening political stability or ideological conformity. The term, more accurately rendered as "heterodox teachings," allowed the government to criminalize groups without clear evidence of wrongdoing. This practice was modernized under the Chinese Communist Party (CCP), most aggressively after the rise of the Falun Gong, as mentioned above. In the same period, Zhong Gong (中功), a rapidly growing Qigong-based movement founded by Zhang Hongbao, was also banned. Though Zhong Gong promoted physical wellness and mental discipline, its nationwide organizational reach and implicit ideological independence led to its proscription shortly after the crackdown on Falun Gong. The CCP dismantled Zhong Gong by early 2000, treating it as a structural and ideological threat to Party orthodoxy. Article 300 of China's Criminal Code,[68] which punishes involvement in a *xie jiao*[69] with up to life imprisonment, has since been widely applied to groups seen as challenging CCP control.

In the fall of 1999 and early 2000, several groups were declared illegal and banned. Leaders and several practitioners were arrested or issued warrants of arrest:

- **Falun Gong (法轮功):** The best-known case, officially banned on July 22, 1999, after large-scale demonstrations by its practitioners in Beijing.
- **True Buddha School (真佛宗, Zhenfo Zong):** An esoteric Buddhist school founded by Grand Master Luong, added to the list of banned xie jiao in December 1999.
- **Guanyin Famen (观音法门):** A Buddhist variant focused on devotion to the Bodhisattva Guanyin, also prohibited at the end of 1999.

- **Yuandun Famen (圆顿法门)**: A third esoteric Buddhist lineage targeted by the same wave of bans in December 1999.
- **Zhong Gong (中功)**: A sister Qigong movement, proscribed a few months later and dismantled in early 2000.

The CCP's aggressive posture hardened under Xi Jinping, especially with the expansion of "Sinicization" policies in 2017 that demanded all religions align with Party objectives. Independent or nonconforming faiths—like the underground Catholic Church, Protestant house churches, and The Church of Almighty God—risk immediate suppression and criminal prosecution. The latter, whose theology emerged from charismatic Christian revivalism and possibly shares historical roots with both the Shouters and Zhong Gong, has faced relentless targeting. While the CCP accuses it of serious crimes, independent investigations by Western scholars have shown many of these charges—like kidnapping and murder—to be unsubstantiated or based on false attribution. These scholars argue that the xie jiao label serves more as a political bludgeon than a legal or theological category, allowing China to suppress any group it deems inconvenient or threatening to Party control.

Beyond these five, the CCP Standing Committee's October 1999 resolution provided the legal basis to outlaw numerous smaller Qigong groups and local sects deemed xie jiao.[70] In the Marxist ideology, religions are the "opium of the people." After having let those groups emerge and prosper in the eighties and early nineties, the CCP was now considering it a mistake to let spiritual and other religious groups operate and grow without enough control. The numbers and commitment of its many followers that were now globally in the hundreds of millions together represented a threat to the Party's dominance. They had to be cracked down on and stopped immediately.

An arrest warrant was also issued for the founder of Zhong Gong. Zhang Hongbao first surfaced in American custody in February 2000,[71] when he and an associate landed in Guam without valid visas and immediately applied for political asylum at the U.S. immigration detention centre there. Although Beijing demanded his return, a U.S. federal immigration court in Guam ruled later that year that he could remain under "withholding of removal" status. On 13 June 2001, the U.S. Board of Immigration Appeals formally granted him protective residency—effectively asylum—overturning the earlier denial. He was supported by and involved with many Chinese pro-democracy groups. Zhang Hongbao died on 31 July 2006 in a traffic accident in Arizona. Although the official report classified the incident as a traffic accident, many of his followers supported the allegations of a mysterious death with possible involvement of the Chinese government. Nothing of that hypothesis was investigated or proven.[72]

THE FALL OF ZHONG GONG AND THE RISE OF MARY JIN

Jin may not have been so lucky. There were over 600 arrests of the group's leadership by the CCP who like the Falun Gong movement leaders were accused of terrorism and plotting against the state by the CCP. Bliss and Wisdom claim she was never part of this movement and whether she was arrested or not she found her way to Bliss and Wisdom. Abbott Fan Yin claims she was a Master in the Quiong Zhonggong group while claims on the internet suggest she was the number two person.

Immediately, knowing the brutality of the Chinese regime when it comes to eliminating "enemies of the state," it is interesting to see Jin within months of going from a leadership role in a suddenly outlawed organization to freely and openly walking into another spiritual sect to which she had no training in. But the intrigue does not stop there.

FROM SECT TO SECT, OR THE RISE OF A PHOENIX

When the Chinese government outlawed Zhong Gong in late 1999, Jin was among those redirected into a Beijing monastery where the departing leadership of Bliss and Wisdom—formerly based in Taiwan—was transferring its doctrinal expertise to the Buddhist Association of China (BAC). Her official involvement with Bliss and Wisdom began around that time, coinciding with the government's crackdown on Qigong groups, many of which were compelled to reorganize under state-sanctioned religious institutions.

Anyone familiar with the history of the People's Republic of China understands the severity of Communist Party repression. During the Great Leap Forward (1958–1962), Chairman Mao Zedong sought to transform China from an agrarian society into an industrial superpower, a campaign that led to widespread famine and the deaths of an estimated 15 to 55 million people. The subsequent Cultural Revolution (1966–1976) saw further devastation, with millions subjected to re-education, imprisonment, or death.

This pattern of ideological control and forced indoctrination remains evident in the Party's treatment of groups like the Tibetans and Uyghurs today. Given this history of suppression, it is striking that an individual with a leadership role in a once-outlawed Qigong group could navigate such repression without facing severe consequences.

However, it was not Jin's fate.

Now, let's remind ourselves she is not a Buddhist practitioner, she has not been ordained, and she is a woman going into an organization that only men have traditionally controlled. So how does a woman with no apparent credentials for the job within a few years become *the* spiritual leader of such an organization?

ORIGIN OF BLISS AND WISDOM

According to the Bliss and Wisdom (BW) website, the organization was established in 1992 by Venerable Master Jih-Chang (also known as Ri Chang), a Taiwanese monk who introduced his Buddhist practice to Mainland China in 1997. Master Jih aimed to promote Buddhism across the mainland, despite the CCP's longstanding suspicion of independent spiritual movements. To gain acceptance, he proposed a plan to the CCP-controlled Buddhist Association of China (BAC) to teach them how to organize and operate a profitable enterprise, leveraging his business success in Taiwan.

From an intelligence standpoint, the arrangement offered several advantages. It allowed the CCP to infiltrate a Taiwanese religious group with a substantial following—an asset in a country China eventually aims to control. The group could also help undermine the Dalai Lama's global legitimacy and extend Beijing's influence over Tibetan communities. Its financial success—through donations and commercial activities—meant the operation could be self-sustaining. For these reasons, BW was allowed to develop in China, though under strict surveillance. This understanding of BW's entry into and survival in China is supported by sources in Taiwan and various media accounts.

The BAC, founded in 1953 by the CCP to oversee Buddhist activities, was disbanded during the Cultural Revolution and reinstated after Mao's death. It has always operated under the United Front Work Department (UFWD),[73] the powerful CCP agency tasked with propaganda, infiltration, and the suppression of dissent. Western intelligence agencies regard the UFWD as a significant threat to democratic societies. After 2015, the UFWD underwent a major reorganization. That same year, the UFWD created a specific department to manage Buddhist affairs—underscoring the strategic value placed on religious influence.[74]

Given BW's years of collaboration with the BAC, the organization was likely influenced by—and may have received ongoing guidance from—the UFWD. In intelligence terms, a relationship with the UFWD is rarely temporary. In its 2025 report, Canada's public inquiry into foreign interference (the Hogue Commission) identified the UFWD as the principal organ of transnational repression and political interference.

JIN'S ARRIVAL AT BLISS AND WISDOM

In early 2000, a few months after the Zhong Gong sect was dissolved, Jin emerged within BW, rapidly becoming close to Master Jih-Chang. Her sudden rise was striking—she was neither ordained nor known as a Buddhist—yet she appeared to earn the founder's full trust. While some within the movement were uneasy, the Buddhist emphasis on obedience likely tempered dissent. Whether Master Jih saw something spiritually exceptional in her, felt personally drawn to her, or was advised by Chinese officials of her importance to the CCP, she quickly gained significant influence over him.

At that time, BW's relationship with the Chinese government was strong. Master Jih was training BCA officials on how to turn a spiritual organization into a highly profitable enterprise. This aligned with a CCP strategy often used against entities: "if cannot defeat, join them" . . . and assume control. By co-opting such organizations, the Party gains influence over both leadership and membership.

A few years later, during a visit to China, Master Jih became gravely ill and died on the night of October 15, 2004. According to social media sources, Jin was alone with him when he passed away. She emerged to announce both his death and that on his deathbed he had named her his successor—a claim never formally disputed by BW's leadership. Nevertheless, his sudden death prompted speculation among followers and senior members, with some alleging poisoning during medical treatment in Xiamen. While official records state that he died of natural causes, the abrupt leadership change caused significant upheaval within the sect. It is estimated that more than 40 percent of BW's followers left the organization in the aftermath.

IMPORTANT SOURCES CAME OUT PUBLICLY TO DENOUNCE BW

Many stories and denunciations can be found when searching for information about BW on the internet. Here, we choose only a few to demonstrate the kind of critique that can be found.

Among the first critics to come out publicly, Ven. Abbot Vanyin, the first abbot of Fengshan Temple, recorded a four-minute video in which he publicly apologized and expressed remorse for allowing Jin to manipulate the Bliss and Wisdom monastic community and legal entities, causing significant harm. His accounts will be tabled later in this book when Dean goes to Taiwan and finds him.

With the guidance and encouragement of His Holiness the Dalai Lama and the 102nd Ganden Tripa, Rizong Rinpoche, Vanyin finally undertook the responsibility to expose long-hidden truths.

In his message, he earnestly urged both Bliss and Wisdom's monastic and lay followers to summon their courage and conscience, confront the truth, and make righteous decisions. He implored them not to remain under Jin's control and deception. Was it simply bitterness or jealousy? We must point out that since his public statements, Ven. Abbot Vanyin has been missing.

Another witness came forward. Professor Chien Tuan-Liang specializes in ethics, philosophy, and Buddhist studies. He has been teaching at Yunlin

University of Science and Technology in Taiwan as a teaching project lecturer and continues to serve in this role.

Upon joining Yunlin University of Science and Technology in 2010, Professor Chien discovered that the institution was a key stronghold of the Bliss and Wisdom organization. Many university presidents and professors known for their strong academic backgrounds maintained close ties with Bliss and Wisdom. They actively promoted Humanistic Buddhism on campus, seeking to introduce religious teachings through life education while intentionally downplaying its Buddhist elements to attract younger participants. Bliss and Wisdom heavily promoted the "Lamrim Study Group" (廣論班) within Yunlin University of Science and Technology to expand its influence.

Between 2011 and 2012, Professor Chien began engaging with Lamrim study groups. He observed that Bliss and Wisdom established these groups within universities and actively promoted them in government agencies, corporate organizations, district prosecutors' offices, and courts. Through interviews with students, he discovered that many of the earliest followers of Master Jih-Chang had left the organization following the emergence of Jin (now Zhen-Ru). Internal disputes marked this period, and he confirmed that the monk Vanyin—a former monk of Bliss and Wisdom—had also left the group, further highlighting escalating tensions within the organization.

Professor Chien pointed out that Bliss and Wisdom deviated from the traditional Tibetan Buddhist lineage and operated under a structure centred around personal worship or guru worship. Within the organization, long-term members who gained favour with the leadership could be promoted to class leaders. Weekly group meetings encouraged members to share their personal lives, offering emotional support within a tightly knit and insular community. This structure fostered dependency, especially among members who were experiencing family conflicts or emotional struggles.

Professor Chien's experiences illustrate the deep infiltration and influence of Bliss and Wisdom in both academic institutions and broader society. Furthermore, the power structure and operational model of the organization remain highly controversial.

Another academic also studies the issues around Bliss and Wisdom. In 2017, Professor Chiang Tsan-Teng[75] publicly questioned and accused the Bliss and Wisdom organization in Facebook posts and television interviews, alleging that Jin first sought refuge within the group before manoeuvring to take control of its business operations. Professor Chien is a well-known academic in the field of Buddhist studies and the presence of the faith in Taiwan. He has published several books on the topic, and it is clear that Jin has covertly gained control of BW.

THE FALL OF ZHONG GONG AND THE RISE OF MARY JIN

"IF IT WALKS LIKE A DUCK AND QUACKS LIKE A DUCK, IT IS A..."

In the counterintelligence world, finding "smoking guns" is very difficult and sometimes impossible. After all, professional intelligence officers will do their best to cover their tracks and confuse their counterparts. But it does not mean we cannot find enough evidence to come to a solid conclusion. We have given a lot of attention to Jin's history. It is by all accounts troubling.

Let's recap what we found:

- Born and raised in China
- Both parents are CCP members
- She becomes the second in command at the religious sect, Zhong Gong.
- Her sect was declared illegal in October 1999 by the Chinese Communist Party.
- The same month, an arrest warrant is issued against its founder and leader Zhang Hongbao. He escapes China, reaches the USA and obtains asylum.
- Meanwhile, Jin, who could face an accusation of being an "enemy of the State," is able to reach and stay with Bliss and Wisdom in early 2000.
- Despite being a woman, not a Buddhist practitioner, not ordained, but believed to hold secret spiritual powers, she rapidly became close to the founder and Master of BW, Reverend Jih-Chang, according to many accounts and Venerable Abbott Fan Yin.
- On October 15, 2004, Reverend Master Jih-Chang died suddenly after a brief illness while staying in China.
- Jin is present that night and is the last person to see the Master alive. Upon exiting the room to announce his passing, she also tells the people present that on his deathbed, Master Jih chose her to become the next leader of BW.
- There is doubt and disbelief in the group about the Master's passing, and some of the monks, nuns, and laypeople leave.
- In 2007, Jin came to PEI under the PNP program and introduced herself as a wealthy and highly successful entrepreneur in the business of manufacturing of lamps. However, she does not mention Bliss and Wisdom at the time of the interview.

- Her application is processed and approved very quickly, as if somebody in PEI had been waiting for her arrival.
- According to several witnesses and a whistleblower who worked with BW, all land purchases in PEI are coordinated with Jin.[76]

INTELLIGENCE ASSESSMENT POINT OF VIEW

The Chinese Communist Party's infiltration of religious groups, especially Buddhist institutions, has long been a calculated strategy in its global influence operations. This approach has been thoroughly analyzed by both intelligence analysts, sinologist researchers and constitutional scholars. From Mongolia to Japan, and from Australia to Taiwan, extensive documentation demonstrates that the United Front Work Department (UFWD) systematically targets religious institutions to propagate CCP ideology and exert control beyond China's borders.[77]

One mechanism central to this approach is the Buddhist Association of China (BAC). In its 2022 paper, "The Buddhist Association of China and Constitutional Law" published by Cambridge University Press[78], Canadian Professor André Laliberté, explains that the association serves not simply as a religious organization, but as a constitutional tool through which the Chinese state enforces compliance and disseminates its ideological principles abroad. He details how international channels of influence are tightly controlled and structured.

In China's highly surveilled environment, any religious actor must operate under the auspices of the BAC. This body is managed by the State Administration of Religious Affairs (SARA, 国家宗教事务局), itself under the command of the UFWD. As Laliberté outlines, this structure ensures religious conformity and provides a framework for the CCP to export its ideology under the guise of religious practice. Refusing to cooperate often results in punitive action, while compliance is rewarded with opportunity.

This structural insight makes the case of Bliss and Wisdom, and its spiritual figure Zhen-Ru, particularly significant. Proponents of the organization maintain that her leadership ascension was organic. However, thorough our searches in both English and Mandarin have yielded no trace of her prior to her rise, no teachings, no record of monastic training, no history. This raises serious questions about how someone with no public footprint, no significant accomplishment, no acknowledgement from anybody could assume leadership of a high-profile religious body in a short period of time.

THE FALL OF ZHONG GONG AND THE RISE OF MARY JIN

Only one reference to her past appears publicly: a post dated March 21, 2012, on a Chinese forum titled "The Voice of a Propagator of Zhong Gong," under the name Jin Mengrong (金梦蓉). Whether this post represents a factual disclosure or a deliberate plant remains uncertain. Nevertheless, its existence is critical. In a state where digital records can be deleted or rewritten, where everything written is monitor by the State, the absence of corroborating evidence may reflect intent rather than coincidence.[79]

Alex Joske, in his 2020 research paper "The Party Speaks For You," describes how the UFWD constructs networks of loyalty by grooming individuals to become agents of influence. He emphasizes that individuals tied to banned movements, like Zhong Gong, can be repositioned as state-sanctioned figures if they are deemed useful to Party goals. Joske's analysis supports the theory that Zhen-Ru's rapid rise and spotless official record are indicative of coordinated narrative control and strategic positioning.[80]

The strategic silence around Jin Mengrong's origins and her integration into Bliss and Wisdom align with both Joske's and Laliberté's findings.[81] Their work suggests not only a pattern of identity obfuscation and loyalty engineering, but also the legal and institutional mechanisms by which this is accomplished.

Communist Party tasked with controlling diaspora communities and religious institutions abroad. Our analysis has cited her unusually swift immigration file, her transition from a banned sect (Zhong Gong) to a state-sponsored religious organization (Bliss and Wisdom); all are hallmarks of engagement with the United Front Work Department in China. In her defense, the original association to BAC was established by Master Jih-Chang himself and simply enhanced by Mary Jin's takeover of the organization and has been established in the previous chapters.

Today, Canada is no longer blind to the risks posed by transnational repression, covert religious influence operations, and foreign infiltration of civic infrastructure. Legislative reforms, Canadian Security Intelligence Service (CSIS) warnings, and judicial inquiries, most Commission have awakened Canadians most notably through the 2025 Hogue report. These have ushered in a move towards a more vigilant national security posture. Still, the legacy of programs like PEI's PNP and the latitude once afforded to foreign actors under the guise of economic immigration should serve as a waring to all in our country.

In the world of counterintelligence, certainty is rare but patterns are revealing. We can see that Teacher Zhen-Ru and Bliss and Wisdom's corporate interests inside China are patterns that can no longer be ignored.[82]

But a question remains: Why did the RCMP and CSIS not pay more attention to Jin and Bliss and Wisdom?

CHAPTER 14
THE KING GOVERNMENT
PART OF THE SOLUTION OR THE PROBLEM?

"The price good men pay for indifference to public affairs is to be ruled by evil men."

PLATO

I had just hung up the phone after arranging to meet my next interview when Dean arrived. I told him that this new contact had worked in Dennis King's government in Prince Edward Island (PEI), and that I wanted to evaluate if that government would be a suitable authority to listen and to fix the situation. It was obvious to us by now that major corruption had prevailed in the two previous governments, and hundreds of millions of dollars had been misdirected into the pockets of a few privileged individuals. There was no doubt anymore on that front. In our limited capacity as "private" investigators but with collectively close to one hundred years of experience, we had found enough evidence to justify a major criminal and national security investigation. We had enough evidence to demonstrate "beyond a reasonable doubt," to use a familiar expression in criminal law, that several actions and people had intentionally defrauded the province of hundreds of millions of dollars. What we found will necessitate a formal investigation from both the government and the RCMP. However, the most important question has not been answered yet: Does the sitting government have the moral and ethical courage to fix the situation?

My new contact and I had agreed to meet in a somewhat less popular but trendy restaurant, one that was public enough, yet discreet. Sources, especially women, often prefer the first meeting to be in a public setting because meeting with a male investigator is often intimidating. I know it well. I have interviewed thousands of sources: witnesses, criminals, defectors, spies, even terrorists, during my career. The first meeting is always fraught with tension. It's like two wrestlers entering the ring. We need to size each other up. This time, I am not interviewing or interrogating a criminal. It is a concerned citizen coming forward voluntarily to share her story. The aim is to build a relationship, so meeting in a public, more neutral, setting, is ideal. Anyway, I am not here to intimidate with the power of a "shield" that I don't carry anymore, but to gain her trust and collaboration. A public space is a form of protection for both of us. We will meet tonight around seven, as she has family to deal with before meeting with me. I am already grateful for her availability at short notice. She had been told by another contact previously interviewed that it would be important to meet with me and to share her experience.

I arrive a good fifteen minutes before the meeting. I want to scope the place and set-up as much as possible. The employee at the door welcomes me and asks if I have come for a drink or to eat. I reply that I am coming for dinner, and that a friend will join me. I also ask for a quiet place if possible. We will discuss "business," and we need some privacy. It would be nice not to bring people near us if possible. The employee nicely acknowledges my request and guides me to a table, but I ask for another one that will allow me to sit with my back to the wall and face the entrance so I can see her coming—and everyone else who comes in, even during our interview. It's an old reflex learned many years ago as an investigator. Always try to control the odds as much as you can.

She is a bit late. I suspect finding parking was a bit of a challenge. I had to search for a moment too, which surprised me in Charlottetown. Finally, she arrives. I pay attention to her look. When you meet a source for the first time, all the details must be observed immediately at the first encounter. Time is of the essence, and with experience you develop a quick assessment process. In the rapid and subtle scope I make during the time it takes to welcome a person, to sit down, to adjust yourself at the table, I must be able to build a first impression and be able to say: Can this person be credible?

I must profile this person. The way a person dresses knowing she is meeting an investigator with police and a national security background will tell a bit about her predisposition towards it. Today, there is no worry on that front. She comes well dressed, a little more than casual but not overly so. Her hair is also well done without excessive effort. She is obviously a person who takes care of herself and knows how to be professional. We are off to a good start, but the game has just begun.

I stand up to welcome her and shake hands. Her handshake is also indicative of her personality. A person with a weak or too soft handshake is one who can be easily influenced and manipulated. This is something to take into consideration later, during the evaluation of her testimony. In her case, again, a very good grip, but not too much. I would again describe it as professional. I shake hands with a full grip, hoping to communicate an air of assurance, but I hold it a few seconds longer than usual. This is to demonstrate that I am leading. Barely noticeable for many at a conscious level, the gesture sends that first message in the rhythm of our meeting. It is very subtle and is registered at her subconscious level.

We sit down and I offer a drink. I ask if she is hungry because I haven't eaten and would be pleased if she could stay for dinner. I am inviting her tonight. The waiter comes, and she opts for a glass of white wine. My first assessment is good.

Most people will not pay attention to all the details I just shared. But for an investigator, this is part of your professional training, or something you acquire with time.

The early conversation is trivial. We talk about the weather and the difficulties finding a parking spot. That allows me to assess her tonality and personality. Is she a soft speaker, energetic, or almost extravagant? Again, in her case, her tone of voice is very well calibrated for the circumstances. A clear voice, not too loud, and yet I can hear determination. Obviously, this person is in control of herself and has a certain degree of natural leadership in her.

All those observations are necessary to an investigator meeting a source for the first time because not only do we assess the person, but we must also gauge the kind of approach we will have to employ. I learned decades ago as a criminal investigator that the credibility of the source is important. The more professional, educated, articulate, and "solid" my source is, the more credible—and hence valuable—will be the information she or he shares with me. But that is not always the case. Some very intelligent people try to manipulate me or to show off. Some trade workers or people with a less prestigious social position can actually be extremely useful and deliver gold nuggets of information. I once interviewed a hot dog vendor on a street corner and learned information that led to the identification and expulsion of a Russian spy. This is why as an investigator you must put aside cultural or societal prejudice and appreciate and respect any source that comes along until you are able to make your own assessment of what they shared or how they shared it. So far tonight, we are off to a good start, although I must still discover what she has to say and if it will be valuable. I will later discover that this was a gem of a meeting.

Sometimes I meet people who try to deceive me. That, too, is very important to detect rapidly. In my line of business, deception is often practised by some individuals. This time, the circumstances are less suitable for that kind of game. Nevertheless, seasoned investigators are always on guard for this.

Next, I must assess her motivation for agreeing to meet with me. She tells me she agreed to come because her friend who had already had a few meetings with us convinced her that it was important to meet and share her story. However, this new source is not totally clear in her mind how she can help our investigation. She knows that we are on the Island to investigate the land acquisitions by the Buddhist community and some of the wrongdoing of the government. No news there—everybody knew it for years. She believes too that the foreign community had exceeded the permitted limitations and had not been totally honest or transparent with the government or the Islanders. She believes there could even be some legal ramifications. That confirms my quick and early assessment of her. She is obviously an intelligent woman and needs to be approached professionally. I need to demonstrate respect for both her intellect and her leadership.

At this point, it is important to give her a chance to talk about herself. How much she reveals in that bit of conversation will tell me how much she is a willing contributor, or if she is guarded, if she brags or is honest in sharing her information. I ask if she grew up on the Island and she responds quickly with a brief description of her family history. She shares with me that she briefly left to study at university in Ontario, where she got a master's degree in urban planning and worked for several years as an urban planner for important consulting firms and can say for herself that she was good at it. But eventually, she came back, as many Islanders do, because there is a special attachment to this unique place. She has been in the same field for the past twenty years and even chaired the National Association of Urban Planners. No doubt her professional credentials are well established on that front.

By now, it is natural for me to explain who I am and my background. I need to convey that I am a seasoned investigator, both with the RCMP and CSIS, and to talk about my academic background. I have also completed post-grad studies, so we have now established that intellectually we are on an equal footing. I am not just a "gum-shoed copper." I have worked all around the world and led important files. I hope this way she will feel reassured that our investigation is very serious and rigorous.

The waiter comes with our drinks and asks if we are ready to order. With that business taken care of, we return to our discussion. From that point, we can engage in a more substantial conversation. By now, our team has been investigating on the Island for more than a year, and I share with her that we have found disturbing evidence and testimonies. I want to find out her motivation for speaking with me. This is a very important step in the interview process because, as an investigator, I must protect the integrity of the process. A person with an axe to grind or a strong ideological view, or even worse, a racist motivation, will not sit well in our search for the truth. So, I must ask questions without being too obvious yet remain quite clear in my mind what I need to find out.

In her case, although she has heard many stories and issues from other people, she has enough professional training to keep some reservation about all this. Yes, as an Islander and, in addition, as a professional and experienced urban planner, she understands what is at stake here, and that was the angle that led her to agree to speak with us. She had worked with the King government, and what she experienced there convinced her to get involved in provincial politics.

That was what interested me. Our investigative team had already formed a pretty clear picture of the previous government and even of the political culture on the Island. For generations, politics was embedded into the culture as a way of life. After all, the provincial government has been the biggest employer in the province, and every time a new government comes to power, it is generally accepted and even expected that a musical-chairs scenario of appointments and jobs will take place. Friends of the new government are appointed or given jobs, and the supporters of the old leave. It's ok. Nobody really takes offence at it. It's a fact of life.

But when Robert Ghiz, and after him, Wade H. MacLauchlan, ran the province, nepotism went to another level of corruption. Our team had already established that fact with ample evidence and testimonies. But my interest now is to discover if the current government led by Premier Dennis King is the same. Because at the end of the day, people on the Island wanted to see some changes. They wanted to believe that somebody would do the right thing to address the situation. King had run his election campaign as a person of integrity and a leader capable of driving change on the Island. Corruption from the previous governments was well known to everybody, and King promised to fix all that. Did he?

The meeting with this evening's source is important because she worked under King's government for several years. in fact, her inner knowledge of the government was crucial to assess if King would be true to his promises and initiate the necessary changes to mitigate the level of corruption.

She goes on to explain how she was hired to assess the planning and management of the land on the Island. She was also required to submit a report and recommendations on how to better protect the most precious resource in this tiny province, its land. As an Islander herself and given her attachment to PEI, this project was an opportunity for her to give back to the next generation and to protect the Island's way of life. Her professional experience had prepared her for that task, and she felt empowered to perform a very serious duty. She reviewed every single historical regulation, current applications of the law, and decisions made by the Cabinet. She was given access to all the archives to help her draft her report and recommendations. It took her months.

She quickly realized that the records were poorly kept. It was impossible to determine, for example, if Bliss and Wisdom, or anybody else for that matter, had exceeded the authorized number of acres purchased. Since she found many problems in various purchase applications that were often overturned by Cabinet ruling, she decided to find and study the rules and regulations guiding the Cabinet decision-making process.

To her complete surprise, in some cases, PEI has no policy, regulations, or guidelines governing land planning. A law existed, the Prince Edward Island Land Protection Act, introduced in 1982 to address concerns regarding land use and ownership on the Island. This legislation aimed to protect agricultural land from being converted to non-agricultural uses, thus preserving the Island's farming heritage and ensuring sustainable development. The Act restricts the amount of land that can be owned by non-residents and requires that any sale of land to non-residents be approved by the provincial government. Over the years, the Act has been amended to adapt to changing social and economic conditions, reflecting the ongoing debate about land use, environmental protection, and community sustainability. But when it came to land planning, the province had done nothing substantial. At the end, everything goes to Cabinet, and it is the Cabinet that decides the outcome of various applications.

This situation had to be corrected, and fast. A good part of the population was already alarmed. Without clear policies or guidelines, the province was mismanaging its most precious and non-renewable resource. It is not because PEI did not do its homework. The Land Use Task Force was created in 2013, producing its report in January 2014. In its first pages there is a quote from Edward MacDonald, a well-known municipal official in PEI:

> On a small island, it bears repeating, land is a finite and fragile resource. Most of us have yet to concede just how fragile. Whether it is labelled environmentalism, sustainable development, or stewardship, the need to protect the land and the waters that surround it can only grow in importance. In the process, it will pose difficult choices between freedom and regulation, employment and preservation, private gain and the public good. In many ways, those choices are already upon us.[83]

But in 2014, the appetite for land by Bliss and Wisdom was not an issue. Now moving forward to 2024, the land issue was on almost everybody's mind. Finding out the Cabinet had no rules, regulations, or guidance was a major issue. Everything goes to the Cabinet, which decides the fate of a specific issue or situation. Records can be found, including when and by whom a Cabinet decision was made, but you still have to look for it.

So, she took her quest directly to Premier King. The answer she got was absolutely unreal. She heard from the premier himself that having no rules means nobody can accuse them of breaking the rules! It has always been handled this way because it gives carte blanche to Cabinet members to decide whatever and for whomever they want. Because no policy or rules means nobody is breaking the rules. So, there was nothing new with this government. They were working the same way everyone has always worked.

In other words, the Cabinet has the power and the opportunity to reward or to punish as they see fit. With no rules, there is no accountability either. This challenged all solid principles of good governance. For the source who had worked and studied all her professional life on how to improve governance and optimize the use of public goods, the weight of Edward MacDonald's words came from that one utterance.

In her time in office, she found problems in various applications that were often overturned by Cabinet ruling. She knows that Bliss and Wisdom had applied for a permit but not if they exceeded the limit of land allowed by law to be purchased because she left before the application was completed.

In her eyes, the government, and especially the Cabinet, has demonstrated its total ethical and moral failure.

For our investigation, this interview was capital. We had to find whether other witnesses had had similar experiences and came to the same conclusion. But considering this opinion from a witness who, in our investigator's judgment, was a very professional, rigorous, and honest person, the King government was as much a part of the problem as the previous governments. It was obvious that they would not have the inclination or even the courage to tackle the problems and issues we had discovered. Not only were they part of the problem, they were not the solution. We could see there was an even greater task ahead of us. We would have to seek other avenues and the help of strong citizens to bring about the changes needed in Prince Edward Island.

CHAPTER 15
LAND GRAB AND NO ACCOUNTABILITY
THE LEGACY OF SEVERAL PREMIERS

If you haven't visited Prince Edward Island (PEI), you want to see it one day. You will be charmed by the colours of the sky that meets the ocean on a sunny day against the copper red of the land and the green of its beautiful fields. It's Canada's smallest province, with only 5,686 km2 (2,195 sq miles) of land. So, by all accounts, a very small province and therefore limited in what it can give away. Like anyone who grew up on an island, its residents have often been there for generations, and the estimated 180,000 souls hold on dearly to their identity and connection to the Island.

THE *LAND PROTECTION ACT*: A BEACON OF RESISTANCE

In the '70s, people saw foreigners, mainly rich Americans, coming to the Island and buying the best real estate by the seashore for a handful of change. The Island's most precious resource, its land, was rapidly being grabbed by people who only came for the summer and barely contributed to the local life and economy. Thus, in 1982, the provincial government under Premier J. Angus MacLean passed a unique piece of legislation in Canada, the Prince Edward Island *Lands Protection Act*[84] (LPA)[85] designed to regulate how much land could be owned by a single person or corporation.

This law has been protecting the Island and is very specific in its prescription. If you do not reside on the Island, you can only own aggregate land holdings not exceeding five (5) acres. If you are a resident of the Island, not exceeding 1,000 acres, and if you are a corporation on the Island, not exceeding 3,000 acres. Very clear, very definite. But appearances led observers to believe land ownership by the monks and nuns was collectively approaching 18,000 acres. Was it possible that government officials had been blind to this manoeuvre, or were complicit in it? Worse, is it possible that some officials from the provincial or local governments even benefited from those transactions?

The irony? The very man whose vigilance helped pass the LPA, David Weale, remains one of the few historical witnesses to this unfolding tragedy. A tireless defender of the Island's land and culture, Weale fought for decades to preserve the spirit of the law. Sadly, his legacy is now being threatened by a quiet, but systematic, dismantling of everything he fought for.

TOURING THE LAND

The initial reason that brought us to PEI was the concerns expressed by many residents about what appeared to be rapid and excessive purchases of land by the monks and nuns of the Great Wisdom Buddhist Institute (GWBI) and the Great Enlightenment Buddhist Institute Society (GEBIS). Lots of stories were flying around, and we had to understand the scope of those concerns.

Within hours of landing on PEI, we were taken for a tour of the Island by a resident who became an important source of information because he first helped the monks and nuns before realizing that a bigger project—taking over the Island—was at play. He showed us all the real estate purchased first by the organizations GEBIS and GWBI. It was obvious that many plots of lands were not in use at all. They were also not all adjacent to each other. Clearly, somebody had rushed to acquire lands quickly when the price was low, and in such a way that eventually they would have a large area. In many places some willful locals were not selling, but since they had obviously been isolated, it was just a matter of time before they too agreed to surrender their land.

Now that was already impressive, but as we travelled around, the source also pointed out properties and farms that were bought by individual monks and nuns. Again, as investigators seeking patterns and motivation, it stunned us to learn that monks and nuns had become landowners. The obvious question came to mind: how can it be that monks and nuns committed to a life of poverty, spiritual quest, and abandonment of materialistic goods would have the money to buy large properties like these, or even be so ambitious as to buy land? Other important observations jumped at us as clear evidence of a certain practice: houses were bought but not occupied. Some were bought in a row, securing an entire neighbourhood, but many individual houses were also purchased, with local residents in between. It was explained to us that not all owners or farmers agreed to sell to the monks or nuns, but when your neighbours have already sold their property and you're caught between Buddhist neighbours, it's just a question of time before you also decide to sell.

During the tour, we were told that many people had stories about monks or nuns coming to the door unsolicited and offering a price for their property. According to the source, many, if not all, of the properties were bought with cash and with no mortgage to the local banks. Now, buying a house with cash is not illegal, but it is not a usual practice. You need to have a substantial amount of money available. Buying several houses or lands rapidly is not common and needs to be explained.

We heard of deals done with one price paid for the official paperwork and an extra payment in cash. There were many more stories of people refusing to sell but eventually giving up and accepting the cash. After all, almost all the properties were bought at an irresistible price that was way above the market value. So, for many people, it was a lifetime opportunity to get a substantial return for what would be basically their retirement money—a good deal for the individual seller, but on such a large scale very bad for the real estate market. Bringing the price of housing artificially high can only destroy the market forces. The balance of supply and demand is totally disturbed and, eventually, people cannot find affordable housing.

That appeared to be the situation in PEI. In the 1990s, similar situations involving foreign buyers, mainly Chinese trying to prepare an escape route in anticipation of the return of Hong Kong to Mainland China in 1997, were happening in markets like Toronto and Vancouver. Canada paid a severe price for that sudden influx of immigration.

CONFIRMING THE STORIES

Now, good investigators work with facts, not stories or innuendos. However, stories are a starting point when you're looking for witnesses. You try to find the source of the story and you let the people talk. Along the way, you assess the witness and their testimony to discover what is true or what is false. In this situation, we needed to find people who sold to the monks and nuns to confirm the details of the sales or real estate brokers who had assisted in the deals. Fortunately, we found many sources who agreed to speak to us about their experience either as sellers or brokers.

One source told us how her ex-husband sold his house and land to the monks and told her that he had accepted cash on the side over and above the official price. The lawyers knew what was going on. We even got an email from a source telling us about a lawyer who warned the monks about a procedure that would break the law but told them not to worry because he knew how to get around it and make it look legal. We must confess that when we got that piece of evidence, we couldn't believe our luck. For criminal investigators, that's a smoking gun. You have to be a very stupid lawyer to do that in writing, but we would take it.

ON-THE-GROUND TESTIMONIES: THE INSIDER'S PERSPECTIVE

Shortly after landing on PEI, our investigative team connected with a long-time local resident who had once worked with the monastic group. His first-hand account painted a disturbing picture: "They were everywhere, knocking on every door, offering cash deals that no one could refuse. One by one, neighbours were convinced to sell. In some areas, once a cluster of homes was vacant, the pressure intensified until even the last holdouts capitulated."

This insider revealed that many of these properties were never occupied after they were sold; they had been purchased as strategic assets. Farms and houses seemingly abandoned post-sale were left to deteriorate under the new ownership. The pattern was unmistakable—a calculated plan to control large swaths of land by slowly absorbing local properties with one irresistible cash offer at a time.

UNRAVELLING FINANCIAL ANOMALIES: CASH, CONTRACTS, AND CORRUPTION

Many people explained to us that numerous complaints were made to provincial and municipal officials. The Island Regulatory and Appeals Commission (IRAC) even conducted an official inquiry, but no report was issued and no action seems to have been taken to stop or to rectify the rapid purchase of lands and property by the monks and nuns.[86] The project was very different than what had been originally proposed to the Islanders, yet nobody was officially doing anything.

So, our investigation needed to find somebody who had first-hand knowledge of the transactions that occurred when a property was sold. Eventually we were put in touch with a few real estate brokers willing to share their stories. One in particular was very useful because she had been involved for a substantial period and had helped with several purchases.

LAND GRAB AND NO ACCOUNTABILITY

Our source confirmed that she was retained by the nuns and instructed to go to various properties and try to persuade the owners to sell. A list of about twenty properties was given to her, and she would knock at the door and try to convince the owners to sell. It was what we call a "cold call". No house for sale, just a direct approach to try to get the owners to sell. As a persuader, she had an irresistible price to offer. As an example, she told us the story of Norma Millar who was not interested at first and was even angry about receiving an unsolicited visit by a real estate broker. Her house and land were valued at $175,000 and needed a lot of repairs. In the end, she accepted $400,000 to sell, way more than the market value. That sale took place in 2017 and was first reported in the *Globe and Mail*[87] in 2024, and, yet nobody in the government seems to have paid attention.

It's easy to predict when you have this kind of pattern that the market will soon be totally upset and will become a great problem for future buyers. Why the government did not act remains a mystery. Well, not totally, because we found also that some sitting ministers and elected officials did sell their properties with great margins in their favour. That again could be part of a criminal investigation.

The source told us that one of the leading monks who spoke very good English told her that buying and establishing a large Buddhist community was a "1,000-year plan." That story was similar and consistent with what we had heard from the nuns when we interviewed them. Another source shared documents and testified that the current plan was to bring around 85,000 Chinese followers to the Island permanently. The monks and nuns understood it would take a certain amount of time, but it was why they needed so much land.

Beyond the curious tactics of property acquisition, our investigation delved into the financial intricacies behind these transactions.

- **Cash-only deals:** Multiple properties were bought entirely with cash, bypassing conventional financing methods. While purchasing with cash isn't illegal, it is atypical—especially for high-value properties. This raised immediate questions about the source of the funds.
- **Dual pricing schemes:** Numerous sellers reported that the official sale price was significantly lower than the cash actually paid, hinting at under-the-table "kickers" that might be used to launder money or avoid taxation.
- **Legal loopholes:** In one chilling example, a lawyer's email candidly detailed methods to skirt LPA limits. As one source described it later, "It was like reading a recipe for breaking the law, and the fact that someone

would put this in writing suggests a disturbing level of institutional rot."

Such evidence points to potential violations of multiple legal regimes—money laundering, tax evasion, fraud, and even abuse of public trust.

THE MONASTIC INVASION: 18,000 ACRES UNDER SUSPICION

Eventually, rumours turned into hard evidence: GEBIS and GWBI, had quietly amassed what appears to be as much as 18,000 acres of PEI land. At first glance, the numbers defied common sense. However, investigators uncovered a systematic strategy. First the corporation bought some properties. Then some monks and nuns bought also properties but not to live into it. Finally, some laypeople bought too some properties without any occupancy. The modus operandi was clear:

- **Rapid acquisitions:** Land parcels were snapped up quickly when prices were low.
- **Geographical fragmentation:** The properties were not adjacent but dispersed—designed to ultimately coalesce into large, uninterrupted tracts.
- **Intrusive tactics:** Reports emerged of monks and nuns approaching local homeowners directly, offering irresistible cash deals even for properties not actively marketed.

These methods hinted at a meticulously orchestrated plan, one that embraced the "divide, isolate, and absorb" model typical of stealthy corporate takeovers—but executed by an organization with a religious veneer. Now another question came to the investigators mind: if we were able to find all the evidence and testimonies, how come government officials, especially IRAC did not find it? Why the RCMP had not been brought in earlier to investigate what seems to be clear and simple collusion and even fraud?

HOPETOWN PROJECT

If the plan described by the monks is to bring 85,000 people in few years, you need a big piece of land to build an entire residential complex. HopeTown was exactly that project, consisting of a large, aggregated piece of land of about 504 acres to build the future community. When this project came to the attention of the local authorities of Kings County, the monks were asked to come and publicly explain their project. Originally, only one person was to purchase all that land, but when they were told their land purchases would contravene the LPA, a new corporation, HopeTown Development Company, appeared and two of whose shareholders were not residents of the province. That group was approved. Agriculture Minister Bloyce Thompson was asked by Green Party critic Michele Beaton why this transaction was authorized and what the government knew about the corporation, but the minister did not have an answer for her.[88]

HOW TO AVOID PUBLIC ACCOUNTABILITY

Now, from a law enforcement point of view, if the province has a special law to protect its land, and many people have stories to tell, would it not be easy to have found evidence of wrongdoing by government officials?

It was explained to us that, yes, the government got pressured by concerned citizens. In 2016, after many complaints and negative media coverage, the MacLauchlan government tried to calm the public uproar by calling upon the Island Regulatory and Appeals Commission (IRAC)[89] to investigate. Formed in 1991, IRAC is responsible to protect the land. We read on its website:

> The Prince Edward Island Regulatory and Appeals Commission is an independent quasi-judicial tribunal with appellate, regulatory, and administrative responsibilities defined in the *Island Regulatory and Appeals Commission Act* and in a number of provincial statutes.[90]

The problem is that each Chair and Executive Officer named to lead IRAC has been friends of the government in place. So, the "independent" element promised on its website was never very strong. In 2018, after two years of hearing many witnesses and receiving documents, the inquiry came to a sudden stop without any explanation or public statement. The promised report was never presented, and the MacLauchlan government ignored demands for it. To this day, Islanders are bitter about this failed expectation. Now a new inquiry has been promised by former premier Dennis King. But who is now leading the ISAC? Mrs. Pamela Williams, KC, former chief of staff of Premier Dennis King . . . looks like déjà vu? The reality is IRAC is not capable of conducting the level of investigation that needs to take place.

VOICES FROM THE ISLAND: THE HUMAN TOLL AND A PANORAMA OF ALLEGED CRIMES

For local residents, this isn't merely about abstract legal violations or corrupt bureaucracies. It's an existential crisis:

- **Housing crisis:** As land prices artificially surge, long-time Islanders face the prospect of being priced out of their own communities. Affordable housing is vanishing under the weight of inflated market values.
- **Cultural erosion:** With entire neighbourhoods being systematically acquired by outsiders, the tight-knit fabric of PEI's communities is beginning to unravel. Every parcel of land surrendered is a small piece of cultural heritage lost.
- **Deep-seated distrust:** The failure of regulatory bodies and the apparent complicity of political leaders have left many residents disillusioned. They now view the government not as a protector, but as a bystander—or worse, a participant—in their ongoing dispossession.

We were called to come and provide an assessment of what was happing in PEI because we were outsiders with no connection to the government or political parties and because of our reputation as career investigators with the RCMP and CSIS. We were not there to play games or to protect some "old friends." What we found was one of the easiest investigations of our career. Quickly it became apparent, with substantial evidence, that people had been breaking the law. Yes, there was a national security element to it, but putting that aside, just the transactions around the land purchases and the transfer of money were sufficient to call for a criminal investigation.

The cumulative evidence points unmistakably to systemic legal and ethical breaches. Some of the main issues that emerged include the following:

- **Money laundering:** Cash-dominated transactions and dual-pricing schemes indicate that vast sums of money appeared to be channelled through dubious networks.
- **Tax evasion:** Under-declared sale prices and off-the-books payments suggest efforts to sidestep tax obligations.

- **Fraud and conspiracy:** The orchestration of land deals to defy LPA limits, combined with documented advice from corrupt lawyers, underscores a coordinated conspiracy.
- **Abuse of public office:** Elected officials and civil servants with personal stakes in these transactions raise serious concerns over conflicts of interest and failure of duty.
- **Violation of charitable status laws:** Given that religious institutions typically operate under strict financial constraints, their activities in PEI appear to have contravened the rules governing charitable organizations.

With every piece of new evidence, the picture becomes more disturbing—a deliberate subversion of public policy, executed in broad daylight yet cloaked in secrecy.

Why no criminal and official investigation has yet been launched remains a mystery, but one thing is certain: laws have been broken here, and many officials knew about it.

Prince Edward Island, once a symbol of steadfast community and resilient heritage, now stands at a crossroads. The land grab is not only a legal scandal or a regulatory loophole; it is a stark reminder of how a community's identity can be compromised by covert transactions and political favouritism.

The evidence we gathered paints a chilling portrait of:

- **An elaborate scheme** by monastic organizations determined to transform the island's demographic landscape.
- **A political and financial collusion** that has allowed these deals to bypass decades-old protective legislation.
- **The gradual erosion of public trust** in systems designed to safeguard not only property but the very soul of the community.

For Islanders, and indeed for all citizens who believe in the sanctity of local culture and democracy, the urgent question remains:

How long will it take for those responsible—whether corrupt officials, rogue financiers, or even clandestine religious leaders—to be held accountable?

In a province so small that every acre carries immense historical and emotional weight, the stakes are nothing less than the future itself. As new inquiries are launched and as the truth continues to unfold, one thing is clear: the fight for justice on Prince Edward Island is far from over.

CHAPTER 16
A CONVERSATION WITH WAYNE EASTER
FORMER SOLICITOR GENERAL OF CANADA (2002-2003)

INTERVIEW BETWEEN DEAN BAXENDALE AND WAYNE EASTER

Q: Wayne, we appreciate you taking the time to sit with me today. As I explained to you on the phone, Michel, Garry, and I are conducting this investigation, and we will turn it into a book because we feel it's just another chapter in a bigger discussion here in Canada around the infiltration and influence of foreign governments. The book, *Canada Under Siege*, is about exposing the foreign influence operations that have been embedded in our institutions, businesses, and government. In the case of Prince Edward Island, we see the elite and sub-state capture that has played out over twenty years on the Island. The title came from our presentation in March that drew close to 600 islanders. You've been at the forefront of some of these discussions, particularly with your role in national security and intelligence oversight, but more particularly, as part of the National New Farmer Coalition and your connections to one of the key industries in PEI, farming.

We have a number of questions that we need an Islander, a past MP, and Solicitor General to answer. You're the only guy we know who fits those criteria. He laughed, and so we began.

A: Yeah, well, it's an odyssey, really. And I've been around this stuff for a long time, as you know. I was heavily involved in setting up the National Security and Intelligence Committee of Parliamentarians. I was even asked to chair it, but I chose to stay in finance. If the government had listened to the 2019 report that came out in 2020, we wouldn't need a public inquiry now. Everything was in that report, yet nobody in senior levels of government seemed to take it seriously—not the Cabinet, Privy Council, or even our own caucus, except for a few of us.

Q: That's been one of the most shocking things for me—how much was known and how little was done. Let's talk about the USB stick. The one Floyd gave you that you then handed over to CSIS. That seems to be a critical moment in all of this.

A: Right. So, our whistleblower friend, who had been closely following all of this, handed me a USB stick packed with critical information. It contained documents, transaction details, connections—hard data that exposed what was going on with the nuns and monks, money laundering, real estate transactions, and even potential political ties. When he gave it to me, I knew it had to go to the right place.

Q: And that place was CSIS.

A: Correct. I handed it directly to CSIS. Now, whether they acted on it or not, I don't know. They can't tell me, and that's part of the problem. You can deliver intelligence, but whether it gets acted upon depends on who receives it and if they have the will to pursue it.

Q: That must be frustrating. You've been in a position of oversight, and you know how these agencies work, yet you're left wondering if something this serious was even investigated properly.

A: Absolutely. You give them intelligence, and you expect it to be handled. But here's the problem—CSIS, like any agency, has its internal challenges. You don't always know if the information makes it to the right person or gets buried because someone doesn't want to deal with it. And let's be honest, there's been political pressure in all of this.
No one in government wants to admit they were compromised by foreign actors.

Q: And yet, the consequences of inaction are enormous. The Chinese Communist Party has embedded itself into Canadian institutions, influencing key decision-makers. If we don't root this out, where does that leave us?

A: It leaves us vulnerable, plain and simple. And that's what infuriates me. When I was in caucus, I told Justin [Prime Minister Justin Trudeau], "If we don't take China seriously, the U.S. will kick us out of Five Eyes." That wasn't just some offhand comment. That was a real risk; I know the Americans were discussing it.

Q: And now we're seeing the fallout. Our intelligence community is compromised, our politicians are compromised, and our economy is being influenced by foreign players who don't have Canada's best interests at heart.

A: That's exactly it. And look, I don't want to paint every politician with the same brush, but when you have direct monetary influences, backdoor deals, and politicians with close ties to China, you have to start asking real questions. And this isn't just about China—India, Iran, and Russia are playing these games too. The difference is that China is playing a much longer game. We think in election cycles; they think in centuries.

Q: So where do we go from here? We discussed this, but you handed over the USB stick to CSIS and tried to push for accountability, but the inertia in the system is staggering.

A: We need a public inquiry. That's the only way. Without subpoena power and the ability to track bank records and compel testimony, this will remain in the shadows. I'll tell you, PEI's legal and political apparatus is so tightly knit, I have real concerns about whether we can even get a fair inquiry here. Too many people are connected, and too many have something to lose.

Q: But we can't afford not to pursue it. This isn't just about PEI; this is about national security. This is about Canada's sovereignty.

A: That's right. And that's why, despite the challenges, we keep pushing. If we don't, we're handing our country over to foreign interests without a fight. And I, for one, am not willing to do that.

SOME CLOSING THOUGHTS ON OUR INTERVIEW

The conversation with Wayne Easter underscores his deep concerns about foreign interference and the failure of Canadian institutions to respond adequately. The USB stick he handed to CSIS represents a critical piece of intelligence that should have sparked immediate and decisive action but did not, and CSIS as an agency has often decided to protect the political interests of various provincial and federal political parties and leaders while not fully assessing both the short- and long-term implications and ignoring political influence and elite capture. Many in the intelligence apparatus, including a long list of company men, may at times choose political expediency for their career over what is right for Canada. After all, people are people and have families and careers to protect, right? The lack of transparency and the politics of the Hogue Commission[91] still leave us all questioning whether any real steps will be taken to investigate the extent of foreign influence operations in PEI or Canada as a whole.

As you get the picture, our investigative team is laying out the web of corruption, political complacency, and outright negligence, something this interview with the former Solicitor General of Canada highlights. He is pretty emphatic about the need for a public inquiry in PEI but confided to me that an out-of-province judicial body must do this. PEI stands at a crossroads: acknowledge and confront the problem or continue down a path of wilful blindness that will only serve to further weaken our democracy and sovereignty at the expense of the everyday citizens of PEI and Canada.

Furthermore, suppose we continue not to investigate such low-hanging fruit. No matter what the result, how can our Five Eyes partners have any faith in Canada as serious partners now or ever?

CHAPTER 17
EVIDENCE OF MONEY LAUNDERING

For the reader to understand the basis of the opinions I will be expressing in this chapter, it is necessary to demonstrate that I have the requisite background and knowledge. I am a retired RCMP officer who was directly involved in the policing of financial crime and money laundering in Canada for several decades. I have direct knowledge of the nature, scope, and organization of how money laundering occurs in Canada. Accordingly, through our team's investigation and the information obtained from those individuals who came forward in Prince Edward Island (PEI), I have direct knowledge of the facts set out in this chapter, except where I have indicated that I am expressing opinions based on the available information. In those cases, I state the source of that knowledge and believe that information to be true.

ANTI-FRAUD INVESTIGATIVE EXPERIENCE

I have an extensive background in fraud, security, anti-money laundering, and investigations including starting my own company and serving as an advisor to governments and corporations on their security, legal, and regulatory concerns in these areas. Before that, in a career spanning thirty years, I was a serving police officer and later Chief of Police in Ontario and a member of the Royal Canadian Mounted Police (RCMP), achieving the rank of Superintendent. Throughout my policing career, I worked predominantly in the areas of organized crime, drug trafficking, international smuggling, and money laundering. As well, during my time with the RCMP I was part of its Foreign Service Directorate in Ottawa with responsibility for Asia, serving for three years as a liaison officer with the High Commission in Hong Kong. A considerable focus at this time was working with Citizenship and Immigration Canada reviewing files of suspected criminals and/or suspected organized crime individuals and/or associates who were seeking to immigrate to Canada. This responsibility afforded me an opportunity to gain considerable knowledge in the assessment of international files, primarily those in which there were circumstances requiring the need for enhanced due diligence Currently I am both the chief anti-money laundering officer for a Canadian chartered bank and provide continuance advice to a financial money exchange business.

I have been able to maintain my knowledge through my current position and over the years by reading various RCMP and Canadian Intelligence Service Canada (CSIS) open reports, other reports received from agencies throughout Canada, the United States, and Interpol, and by reading published works by recognized authors/journalists dealing with organized crime. I have published extensively on organized crime and money laundering and testified before the Cullen Commission in British Columbia; I was consulted by Dr. Peter German in the preparation of the first Cullen report and testified before Justice Cullen. In 2024 I wrote Under Cover: In the Shady World of Organized Crime and the RCMP, published by Optimum Publishing.

As noted previously I was asked to assist my team members with their journalistic investigation into what was believed to be the elite capture of government officials by the People's Republic of China's Belt and Road Initiative, resulting in their alleged corruption and to uncover what facts existed to highlight possible money laundering occurring in PEI. We relied on interviews with well-positioned whistleblowers, concerned citizens, and open sources. However, without an official police lead investigation, our findings fall short of the standards of evidence, since in a journalistic approach there is no ability for corroboration using search warrants, production orders, and/or sworn statements.

As my experience indicates, I was also afforded a depth of education pertaining to triads, (Chinese organized crime groups), including details of their organization, operating methods, and their objective to establish themselves in North America. During my tenure in Hong Kong, volumes of evidence surfaced pertaining to their relocation to Vancouver and Toronto. I was instrumental in getting the Canadian government to include being a member of or associated with an organized crime group as a prohibitive ground for refusing an immigration application, which did not exist is 1991. My support for this resulted in my providing "expert" opinion evidence in a number of immigration challenges before our Federal Court in Vancouver.

Reviewing what was uncovered during our PEI investigation, I will rely on what an expert would explore to demonstrate money laundering. Expert opinions on money laundering cases are often influenced by a range of factors that help to establish whether money laundering activities have occurred, the intent behind certain transactions, and the culpability of the individu-

EVIDENCE OF MONEY LAUNDERING

als or entities involved. Key factors typically considered include patterns of suspicious transactions, suspicious cash-handling activities, questionable real estate transactions, use of complex financial instruments, documentation and recordkeeping, behaviour of individuals or entities, and connection to predicate offenses. Each of these factors is considered in detail in the following pages.

PATTERNS OF SUSPICIOUS TRANSACTIONS

Structuring or smurfing: Transactions deliberately structured below reporting thresholds.

Fact: Interviews with an auditor involved in reviewing the books of Bliss and Wisdom revealed that new "monks" consistently deposited $9,900—just $100 below the $10,000 reporting threshold required by Fintrac. This pattern strongly suggests structuring.

The same auditor also assisted in preparing personal tax returns for the monks and nuns. It was common practice for both to purchase homes in PEI using Guaranteed Investment Certificate (GIC) funds and then rent the properties to themselves. On one occasion, a monk purchased an entire street of homes and later transferred ownership to the Great Enlightenment Buddhist Institute Society (GEBIS). Others acquired homes allegedly for family members, but the auditor questioned the legitimacy of these claims.

Other questionable transactions included the following:

- $60,000 spent on MP3 purchases.
- $280,000 home cash for paying a service provider
- $800,000 in cash allegedly paid to construction workers for building dormitories, of which four were constructed
- $870,000 cash purchase of a property, highlighted here

There are many more transactions and accounts of the amount of cash paid by both the Great Wisdom Buddhist Institute (GWBI) and GEBIS to contractors, homeowners, politicians' homes, building suppliers, and furniture retailers. These are not crimes, but they do demonstrate a disturbing pattern when the bills are sequentially numbered and are paid from briefcases, paper bags, and red envelopes, as witnesses have confirmed.

I have included below an actual email from GWBI Financial which highlights very large financial transactions, the actual genesis of which is unknown but involved a property in Heatherdale purchased for $870,000 according to source documents reviewed for my analysis.

---------- Forwarded message ----------

From: GWBI Finance <gwbi.finance@gmail.com>
Date: 2016-05-21 20:37 GMT-03:00
Subject: Banking Issue
To: ▮

Hi ▮:

Sorry for the tardy response. Please find attached my bank statements for your reference.

1. 2015 March 09 Lent out $580,080 to GFBIS Toronto by wire transfer with promissory note
2. 2015 July 07 GEBIS Toronto returned $581,792.53 (with interest)
3. 2015 July 03, July 17 money transferred from Taiwanese bank account of Yvonne
4. 2015 July 30 Donated $800,000 to GWBI through bank draft
5. 2015 Jan 12 Paid $215,000 by bank draft for purchasing land.
6. 2015 Feb 2 Paid $123,442.54 by bank draft for purchasing land.

Please kindly advise after your review on those bank statements, and let me know if you wish to review the bank statements of other two nuns that own properties too.

Thanks,
Yvonne

Below I have included an email detailing discussions on land purchases and a second email which establishes the fact that the ongoing purchases of property was a noted concern. Additionally, a strategy appears to have been developed to respond to any housing/property issues.

EVIDENCE OF MONEY LAUNDERING

Walter picked option two, for your reference. Please try not to say anything unless Janet brings it up first.

---------- Forwarded message ----------

From: nick tsao <damoutsao@yahoo.com>
Date: 2016-03-17 23:01 GMT-03:00
Subject: FW: Draft Responses - Grain & Splendid
To: <shixewalter@gmail.com>, GWBI Finance <gwbi.finance@gmail.com>

法師吉祥如意,

Richard Collier <richard.collier@keymurraylaw.com> 於 2016/3/17 (週四) 5:28 PM 寫道:

Hello all,

Please find attached draft responses for Grain and Splendid. Please note there are three options for how to respond to question 5, which are explained in further detail as follows:

1) Option one provides the requested information for Ms. Jin and Mr. Lu, the shareholders with land holdings. As payments were made by cash, and the Order requested copies of cheques, copies of confirmed cash payments are not being provided. Furthermore, the wording notes that the taxes were paid, but does not indicate that Mr. Lu or Ms. Jin paid the taxes personally.

(選項一:提供股東金女士與盧先生之土地持有資料,說明由於土地稅以現金支付,所以無支票影本可提供,因此也不會提供現金支付之證明。 在陳述上,只說明有支付土地稅,未說明金女士與盧先生是否自己支付稅金。)

Please note providing this information may still result in the Commission requesting further details, including confirmation of the cash payment, and who made the payment.

(請注意，提供這些資訊後，IRAC 可能要求進一步資料，包括現金支付之證明、及由誰支付。)

2) Option two outlines that we are of the opinion the Lands Protection Act does not provide that the Commission may request property tax payment information, that we are of the opinion the information requested does not factor into aggregate land holding calculations, and furthermore, Splendid/Grain is being asked for the information and Splendid/Grain do not have the authority/ability to provide the personal information of its shareholder's land holdings to the Commission on behalf of its shareholders.

(選項二: 表達我們認為土保法並未規定 IRAC 可以要求支付土地稅之資訊，表達我們認為 IRAC 所要求之資訊與計算併計土地量無關，此外，IRAC 命令要求華/谷提供這個資訊、但華/谷並無權利/能力代表股東提供股東持地之個人資訊。)

This response may still attract a further Order from the Commission seeking the property tax information and providing its justification for requesting same.

(這樣的回覆，還是會讓 IRAC 繼續發出命令，證明其司法權力，然後要求同樣的資訊。)

3) Option three also forms part of option two, but leaves out the argument that the Lands Protection Act doesn't permit the Commission to request the information, and that said information is not relevant in determining aggregate land holdings. Essentially, option three takes the approach that the information is being requested from Splendid/Grain and Splendid/Grain do not have the ability to provide the personal information of its shareholders, beyond the land holdings listed in question 3.

(選項三: 與選項二相似，但是將" 我們認為土保法並未規定 IRAC 可以要求支付土地稅之資訊，表達我們認為 IRAC 所要求之資訊與計算併計土地量無關" 之用句去掉，僅表達 IRAC 命令要求華/谷提供這個資訊、故除提供股東持地資料外，但華 / 谷並無權利 / 能力代表股東提供股東支付土地稅之個人資訊。）

Similar to option two, option three may still attract a further Order from the Commission.

（與選項二相同，這樣的回覆，還是會讓 IRAC 繼續發出命令，要求同樣的資訊。）

Subject to any further comments on the options from Lynn and Ryan, if you have any questions regarding the foregoing options please do not hesitate to ask. After you have had a chance to review and discuss, please advise which option for question 5 you would like us to include.

（若你對於 Lynn Ryan 的回覆建議有任何意見，請不吝指教。若您內部討論完畢，請告知您對問題 5 之回答選項。）

Additionally, in the Moonlight response please note that Yen-Wei Lai, is incorrectly spelled as Yen-Wen Lai. I have corrected this error.

If you have any questions or comments about the responses or the issues discussed above please let me know.

Best Regards,
Richard

Richard A. Collier
Associate
tel +1 (902) 368 7830 | **fax** +1 (902) 368 3762

From: Heart Light <lightinourheart@gmail.com>
Date: Feb 16, 2019, 1:25 AM
To: me

Just want to check with you that you didn't receive my text message sent by cell phone and zoom yesterday, is that correct? Because if so, in the future, I know I will only be able to interact with you through emails. Thanks

The content of my message is at below:

I think the housing issue is quite a big thing before election.

I would like to hear your strategy on how we should advise the individual owners as to how to manage their houses in TRL subdivision. Including rental fee, short-term or long-term rental period, AirBnB advertisement, tenants, etc.

How soon do you think you can provide the answers so we can start making the protocol. Can you help include this topic in your agendas when meeting with Ryan and Lynn?

Source document

Date: Feb 16, 2019, 7:56 AM
To: Heart Light <lightinourheart@gmail.com>

I just got up, have the flu.

The issue I see is the parishioners buying farm land and businesses,

There should be no buying of farm land by parishioners. They are not farmers.

If they buy a business and have a legitimate plan to use it, then ok.

But buying everything without plans has to stop.

It's simple, we need control.

EVIDENCE OF MONEY LAUNDERING

What the parishioners do will hurt everyone and vice versa.

The town of Montague and councillors feel everything is being bought.

This is an internal problem that has to be fixed by the group, not lawyers.

Nuns and monks buying ho.es to live in is not an issue, the people are happy with the monks fixing up and living in heatherdale. I would like to see some nuns living in homes near the monastery in brudenell, especially 117, and 16 red oak.

I just want things to quiet down and stop the parishioners from creating businesses to buy properties, then thr locals seeing chinese nuns ar the properties, like what happened at Mr. Lis farm, and cig in valleyfield where the nuns have been seen many times, even storing vegetables. . . .

From: Heart Light <lightinourheart@gmail.com>
Date: 2018-11-03 11:03 AM
Subject: House update
To: me

1. 778-- don't need winterization, will use it for meetings. Will ask Abbess if we can someone stay every night to watch for security

2. 258-- need winterization. No one will stay in the house during winter.

3. 268-- need winterization. No one will stay in the house during winter.

4. 16-- don't need winterization, will use it for meetings in winter.

5. 117 -- don't need winterization, will use it for meetings in winter. A Buddhist nun will be staying between 11/13-12/3.

6. 44-- need winterization. Tenants will be moving out by the end of November.

7. 88-- need winterization. No one will stay in the house during winter.

8. 102 -- need winterization. No one will stay in the house during winter.

9. 166 --need winterization. Tenants will be staying between 11/13-12/3. Please talk to Jasper about draining the house, thanks!

10. 186 -- need winterization. No one will stay in the house during winter. Mr. Wong's family will only come after they have work permits.

11. 120 --need winterization. Frank will move to Montague at the end of this year, or at the beginning of next year.

12. 96-- don't need winterzation. A couple will be staying in the house in winter time

Thanks so much! Mary also asked me the same question. So please check with her. I believe she will only take care of houses that she gets paid. And she told me she will talk to Jeff through you as well.

Yvonne

Fact: When purchasing homes, monks and nuns privately approached property owners, often offering prices above local market value. Many of these deals included undisclosed cash payments that were not recorded. One such home belonged to former RCMP officer and then-serving PEI MLA Allen Roach. Roach became a strong supporter of GEBIS and GWBI and was a close work associate with Jason Aspin, CEO of Aspin Kemp and Associates (AKA).

EVIDENCE OF MONEY LAUNDERING

According to a source, the tax advisory firm Grant Thornton dropped Bliss and Wisdom as a client after the 2019 review by its Toronto office, citing concerns over the large amounts of incoming cash and the unsatisfactory explanations provided, which were raising money laundering suspicions.

SUSPICIOUS CASH-HANDLING ACTIVITIES

Fact: Russ Compton, who had strong connections with former Premier Ghiz and Jason Aspin, recounted an incident involving an Ontario-licensed vehicle arriving at the Charlottetown offices of Aspin Kemp, where Bliss and Wisdom also maintained an office. Two individuals from the vehicle appeared to notice Compton observing them from a window. At that moment, they were accessing the trunk of their car, but upon realizing they were being watched, they quickly closed it and drove away. They returned approximately 30 minutes later, this time removing large duffle bags from the trunk and taking them into the Bliss and Wisdom office. Compton strongly suspected these bags contained cash. After witnessing these incidents on several occasions, he spoke with Jason, resulting in cameras being installed. Shortly thereafter the Bliss and Wisdom office in the building was closed.

Fact: A former Bank of Nova Scotia teller provided information that between 2017 and 2019, monks and nuns at the Montague branch deposited large amounts of cash through night drop services and ATMs. These cash deposits accumulated to several million dollars in GICs. Bank tellers were instructed by the branch manager not to question the large cash deposits because the monastery was a registered charity. An unusual observation was that many of the deposited $100 bills were sequentially numbered.

On multiple occasions, the head monk personally visited the bank with other monks to deposit cash using a small duffle bag. Similar deposit activity was reported at other Scotia Bank branches. Both organizations had accounts with other large financial institutions including CIBC which eventually dropped them as a client prompting the organizations to transfer their banking activities to other financial institutions including RBC.

Unusual Activity: Transactions inconsistent with the client's typical behaviour or business profile.

Fact: Bliss and Wisdom claims to be a Tibetan monastery associated with the Dalai Lama. However, research has conclusively refuted this claim, revealing that its management has direct ties to businesses in the the People's Republic of China (PRC) and i's monastics to the United Front's Buddhist Association as documented throughout the book. Given these connections, significant red flags are raised regarding the origin of the funds involved in these transactions.

Use of Cash: Our research and interviews revealed the following:

Cash was often a factor in the purchase of homes on the Island and for the payment of contractors. Use of cash does not lend itself to normal business practices, in which you would expect to see wire transfers and/or cheques.

QUESTIONABLE REAL ESTATE TRANSACTIONS

Below are three emails that highlight real estate transactions carried out by the monks which call into question the purpose of the monastery and why they have the hallmarks of what was uncovered in Vancouver.

Fwd: Fox Run — Government × GWBI ×

Forwarded Conversation
Subject: Re: Fox Run

From: 釋宏法師 <chihungwen@gmail.com>   **director of GWBI**
Date: Fri, Aug 5, 2016 at 8:28 AM
To: [redacted]

Good morning, we made the deal yesterday with Betty. $330000 for the house and $110000 for the lots, furniture will be purchased later as you had instructed. There are going to be five buyers to hold title to avoid IRAC application. The deal closes on 9/30. The buyers are pretty happy with the price. Betty wants to keep it confidential so pretend you did not know anything until she tells you herself. By the way, how much would you charge for lawn cutting for the place? Janet

> **When I was first asked by GWBI if they could buy this subdivision and house, they told me GWBI was going to purchase it!!**
>
> **the house is occupied by student nuns from GWBI**

EVIDENCE OF MONEY LAUNDERING

---------- Forwarded message ----------
From: 起宏法師 <chihungven@gmail.com>
Date: Thu, Jun 30, 2016 at 10:02 PM
Subject: Re: Steve ~~~~~~~~~~~~~
To: S ~~~~~~~~~~~~~~~~~~~~

Hi, just to remind you that Steve had given us until 7/4 before he will list the property for sale. You might have to tell him that we do have an interesting buyer and extend the time until we negotiate the price. Also, we have tenants coming tonight to rent for 3 days. Please try to see if we can insure 88 & 44 as soon as possible. Diane will move out completely on 7/3. We will move the people into the main house on Delodder's and rent 44. Do you have people who can rent the house long term for $1500 per month and pay for their own utilities? If you do, let me know. Thank you. Janet

> 44 red oak shows owned by venerable yvonne.
>
> 88 red oak is shows owned by venerable lu.

Re: house purchase   Inbox ×   GWBI ×

Aug 16, 2016, 4:56 PM

起宏法師 <chihungven@gmail.com>
to me ▼

See if this will work. Let's pretend that the lay people are buying first for better negotiation and then transfer to GWBI later before closing. J

Hi, Leslie

Sorry for the late response. Thank you for giving us a quote for your beautiful home. I understand it is not easy for you to come up with such a decision since you have been in the house for so many years and must have so much memory in it. At this time, the IRAC investigation about our land holding is not over yet. However, some of our lay people might be interested in purchasing your house. But due to the investigation, we are advised by our lawyer not to be involved with the lay people's purchasing activities.

The "Vancouver Model" is a term that has been used to describe the way real estate in Vancouver, Canada, has been exploited for money laundering, particularly through foreign investment and the use of complex ownership structures, including shell companies and trusts. Vancouver's real estate market has gained a reputation for being one of the least transparent in the world, creating opportunities for individuals and organizations to launder illicit funds.

KEY FEATURES OF THE VANCOUVER MODEL

1. **Foreign investment**: In the 2010s, Vancouver's real estate market saw an influx of foreign buyers, particularly from China. This demand pushed up property prices, making it difficult for locals to afford homes. Foreign investors, some with ties to criminal organizations or illicit activities, used Vancouver's real estate market to park large amounts of money, often without much scrutiny regarding the sources of these funds.
2. **Shell companies and complex ownership structures**: Money launderers often used shell companies, trusts, and other opaque structures to hide the identities of the true owners of properties. This made it difficult for authorities to trace the real beneficiaries of transactions. The use of intermediaries, such as real estate agents and lawyers, allowed for the movement of money without triggering suspicion.
3. **Overvaluation and "flipping"**: Another tactic used was the overvaluation of properties, allowing for inflated transactions that helped disguise the movement of illicit funds. The practice of "flipping" properties—buying and quickly selling them—was used as a way to launder money while making it appear as though the investments were legitimate.
4. **Use of cash**: Some money launderers preferred to purchase real estate with large sums of cash to avoid scrutiny from financial institutions and to make it more difficult for authorities to trace the funds. This practice contributed to Vancouver's booming real estate market but also raised red flags regarding potential money laundering.
5. **Involvement of organized crime**: While not all foreign investors in Vancouver's real estate were involved in illicit activities, organized crime groups, including Chinese triads, have been implicated in using the Vancouver real estate market to launder money. These

groups used the complex market to integrate their criminal proceeds into the formal economy.

The potential for the Vancouver Model of money laundering through real estate to be employed in Prince Edward Island exists, particularly as real estate markets become increasingly globalized and investment in Canada's more affordable regions rises.

Here are some factors that could influence the likelihood of such a model emerging in PEI:

1. **Growing Interest in Atlantic Canada Real Estate**

    - **Real estate demand:** As Vancouver's market became increasingly more expensive, more foreign investors looked to less-expensive areas of Canada, like Alberta, Quebec, and PEI, for opportunities to park money (exit China) or launder illicit funds. PEI, while traditionally less attractive for high-profile foreign investment, has seen significant growth in its real estate sector in recent years. Factors like the growing popularity of the Island as a tourist destination, more remote working opportunities, and increasing property prices in larger Canadian cities could drive demand for real estate in PEI.
    - **Tourism and retirement:** PEI is known for its tourism industry and as a destination for retirees. These demographic trends may attract wealthy individuals, some of whom might be looking to hide illicit gains through real estate investments.

2. **Lower Scrutiny in Smaller Markets**

    - **Less regulation and oversight**: Smaller markets like PEI may not have the same level of regulatory scrutiny faced by larger markets, such as Vancouver or Toronto. This could make it easier for money-laundering techniques to be employed without raising red flags. Smaller jurisdictions often have less sophisticated systems for detecting complex ownership structures, and enforcement might not be as robust as in larger cities.

- **Fewer resources for AML enforcement**: While Canada has national anti-money laundering (AML) regulations, PEI, as a smaller province, might have fewer resources dedicated to investigating financial crimes. Criminal organizations might perceive this as an opportunity to move illicit funds without immediate detection.

3. **The Impact of Global Capital Flows**

- **International investment**: Although PEI may not currently attract significant foreign investment in the same way Vancouver does, global capital flows are becoming increasingly dynamic. With more foreign buyers looking for real estate options in smaller, more affordable Canadian markets, there's a risk that PEI could become an attractive location for money laundering activity, especially with foreign nationals or organized crime groups seeking more discreet markets.
- **Increased use of shell companies**: Like Vancouver, PEI could see the use of shell companies and trusts to disguise ownership of properties. These structures could facilitate the movement of money without triggering suspicion, especially if investors use intermediaries to complete transactions.

4. **Smaller and Less Competitive Market**

- **Less competitive real estate market**: The relatively smaller and less competitive nature of PEI's real estate market may make it a less obvious target for large-scale laundering schemes, as properties do not generally appreciate at the same rate as those in larger urban centres like Vancouver. However, this could also make it easier to manipulate prices or use real estate to launder smaller sums of money without drawing as much attention as in the larger urban centres.
- **Luxury homes and high-value properties**: Certain luxury real estate in PEI (e.g., waterfront properties, large estates, etc.) present opportunities for individuals looking to use real estate as a way to move illicit funds. If demand

EVIDENCE OF MONEY LAUNDERING

increases for high-end properties, this could attract money laundering schemes.

5. **PEI's Economic and Political Landscape**

   - **Government response**: PEI's government has not been proactive and therefore is not fully prepared for the kind of widespread money laundering that has occurred in Vancouver. However, as the real estate market grows and attracts more external capital, there could be increasing pressure to implement anti-money laundering measures such as improving transparency in real estate transactions and tightening regulations on foreign buyers.
   - **Local financial institutions**: PEI's smaller local financial institutions might not have the same anti-money laundering infrastructure or capacity to detect suspicious transactions as banks in larger cities. This could create an environment where illicit actors feel they can move money through real estate with less risk.

While the likelihood of the Vancouver Model being replicated on a large scale in PEI is currently low, the growing appeal of Atlantic Canada as an alternative real estate investment destination means there appears to be a risk, especially as the market continues to evolve. The province's smaller, less competitive market and relatively lower regulatory scrutiny make it vulnerable to potential money laundering schemes.

It is also worth noting that this same real estate activity is occurring in other parts of the country. Recently a real estate agent briefed me on how approximately 40 condos along the waterfront in Cobourg, Ontario, have been purchased by a Chinese investor, Wajung Jiang-Li Xiaobai, along with part of the old Kraft plan Beneco packaging plant. Like PEI, some of the real estate is vacant and others are short-term leases, which calls into question million-dollar properties being under-utilized. Also, Beneco only employs Mandarin-speaking individuals who are bussed in for all shifts from the Greater Toronto Area.

ORIGIN AND DESTINATION OF FUNDS

Frank Zhou is a Chinese-Canadian businessman who has been described as a "Red Princeling," a term used to denote the descendants of prominent

Chinese Communist Party leaders. He has been noted for his connections to former Canadian Prime Minister Jean Chrétien and former Prince Edward Island Premier Joe Ghiz.

Zhou's relationship with Jean Chrétien dates to the 1990s, when Chrétien was prime minister. Zhou was involved in facilitating business interactions between Canadian and Chinese enterprises, leveraging his political lineage and business acumen. He played a role in organizing trade missions and fostering economic ties between the two nations.

Regarding Joe Ghiz, Zhou's connection is primarily through political and business networks in Canada. While specific details of their interactions are less documented, it is known that Zhou engaged with various Canadian political figures to promote bilateral relations and business opportunities.

These associations have been part of broader discussions about the influence of foreign actors in Canadian politics and the ethical considerations surrounding such relationships. Zhou's activities have been scrutinized in the context of Canada's foreign policy and its approach to international business dealings.

As a Chinese-Canadian entrepreneur, Zhou has played a significant role in Prince Edward Island's (PEI) Provincial Nominee Program (PNP), which aimed to attract immigrant investors to the province. Through his company, Sunrise Immigration and Investment, Zhou has been authorized to facilitate the immigration process for immigrants including Chinese nationals seeking residency in PEI. His firm is among a select group designated by the provincial government to identify and process immigrants through the PNP.

Zhou's influence extends beyond immigration services. He has been instrumental in fostering economic ties between PEI and China, organizing trade missions, and promoting business ventures. Notably, he has accompanied various Canadian political figures, including former PEI premiers Robert Ghiz and Wade MacLauchlan, on trips to China, highlighting his deep involvement in strengthening bilateral relations.[92][93]

In relation to the Great Enlightenment Buddhist Institute Society (GEBIS) and (GWBI), which have a significant presence in PEI, Zhou's connections are evident. Our source confirmed that when both he and his wife Sherry would descend upon the monasteries it was like a whole other level of worship and devotion. His close ties with PEI's political leadership may well have helped to advance GEBIS's and GWBI's interests, including the establishment of monasteries and other facilities. The group was also successful in the removal of the English language criteria from the teaching curriculum in the monastic schools, as well as having a once-a-year organized visits to see how children were being treated in the monasteries. During a recent trip we were informed that the Minister of Education has recently changed the curriculum guidelines, and all private schools must now use the approved PEI curriculum including English. But who is overseeing compliance?

Deborah Parks, a PhD candidate at the University of Ottawa, wrote a 2019 paper for submission to the United Nations Committee on the Rights of the Child. The paper was titled "Canada and the Provinces' Duty to Fully Consider Children's Best Interests in All Matters, Including Education, Immigration and Separation from Parents: The Case of Children Received in Canada to Train as Buddhist Monks."

In a conversation with her at an Ottawa book event, Dean expressed his concern once again that no one was interested in the welfare of anybody on the Island if it meant challenging the good money the monks and nuns were bringing to the Island. She told me she was quite concerned as no one was listening in any government.[94] According to our sources, they are preparing to apply for university licences, and their real plan is to open a Harvard-like University on Prince Edward Island.

Given all of these facts should this be of concern to our national security apparatus and to the 5-Eyes intelligence agencies? Some think so, and in a 2023 short video from Lei,[95] who hosts Lei's Real Talk she highlights many disturbing elements of the PEI, story a lot of which our team has validated. Lei produced a couple of short news docs, including, "Does Immigration Fraud on Canada's PEI Cause U.S. Concerns Over Security? — Lei's Real Talk." Lei's reports suggest that there is a lot more to Frank Zhou than meets the eye as it relates to Beijing. But Sherry Huang on our call last August said they have no association with the Bliss and Wisdom entities or the United Front Work Department.

Zhou's activities have not been without controversy. His central role in PEI's immigration and economic development has drawn scrutiny, particularly concerning potential conflicts of interest and the influence of foreign entities in local affairs. Despite these concerns, Zhou remains a key figure in shaping the province's demographic and economic landscape.

USE OF COMPLEX FINANCIAL INSTRUMENTS

Layering techniques: Use of shell companies, trusts, or other vehicles to obscure the ownership or source of funds. Below is just one example the corporate structure of GEBIS and its multitude of companies. The use of multiple companies is often found in complex money laundering schemes in order to thwart any investigative activity and help conceal the origin of funds. What it does demonstrate to me is that further investigation by the RCMP is warranted.

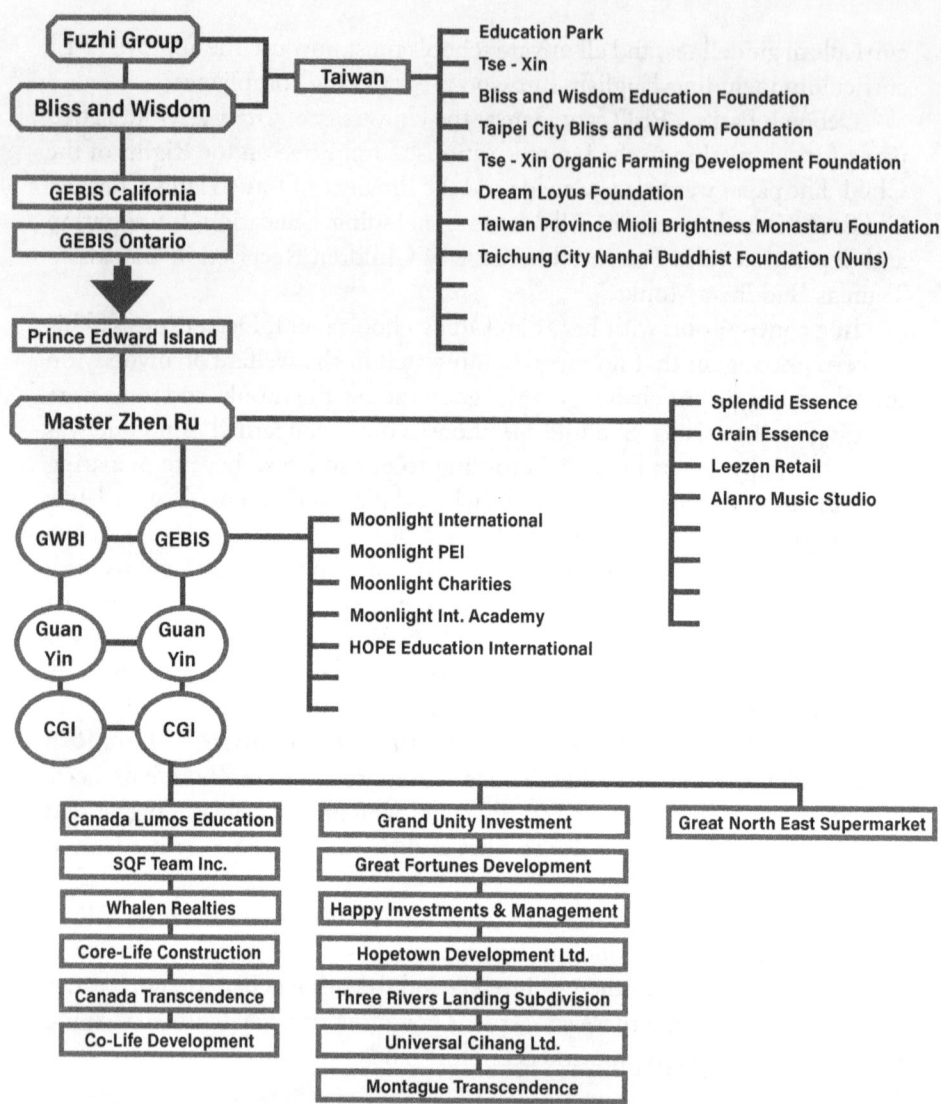

Intermingling funds: Mixing illicit funds with legitimate business income. We know that the monastic group is claiming that all funds are from charitable giving. The fact that the amounts are in the tens of millions of dollars and that the group is constantly dealing with cash raises considerable red flags. Grant Thornton dropping them as a client based on concerns surrounding the genesis of the money is extremely telling. Grant Thorton who was their accounting firm and had to sign off on the records prior to 2019 had concerns with their record keeping and cash being used communicated that concern.

EVIDENCE OF MONEY LAUNDERING

It was confirmed with our team that Grant Thorton dropped them as a client in 2019 due to irregularities stemming out of transactions between the Toronto operation and PEI. This naturally implies that there were concerns with the organization's supporting documentation. I would suggest this is indicative of missing records and/or inconsistencies in the financial documentation and record keeping supporting donations and cash deposits.

DOCUMENTATION AND RECORDKEEPING

Incomplete or false documentation: Use of fabricated invoices or contracts. The fact that Grant Thornton dropped GEBIS as a client would imply that there are concerns with the organization's supporting documentation. I would suggest this is indicative of missing records and/or inconsistencies in the financial documentation.

BEHAVIOUR OF INDIVIDUALS OR ENTITIES

Use of nominees: Transactions conducted through proxies or nominees to obscure true ownership. It is my belief that the real estate transactions involving the monks and nuns are an example of nominee ownership, whereas the true owner is the GEBIS organization.

CONNECTION TO PREDICATE OFFENSES

Illicit activity links: Evidence tying the funds to predicate offenses like fraud, drug trafficking, or corruption.

UNRAVELLING THE ORIGINS: ALLEGATIONS, INTELLIGENCE, AND THE BLISS AND WISDOM MONASTIC GROUP

Without the benefit of a full investigation, any conclusions about the origin of the funds remain speculative. However, discussions with U.S. intelligence officers have raised the possibility that the money may be linked to the international fentanyl trade, similar to patterns previously observed in Vancouver. What is clear is that the monastic group in question has no official affiliation with the Dalai Lama or the Tibetan government-in-exile. However, there appear to be significant ties between the group's development and leadership, particularly during the period from 1999 to 2008. It was during this time that the first monks arrived at the Lobster Shanty, and their leader, Mary Jin, began establishing the group's presence. These connections seem to extend to the Buddhist Association of China (BAC) and the group's original spiritual head, Master Jih-Chang. The BAC, which operates under China's United Front Work Department, plays a key role in religious affairs in the PRC, and the association's influence over the group raises important questions.

The organization Bliss and Wisdom strongly denies any affiliation with the Chinese government or the United Front, instead reiterating their devotion to His Holiness the Dalai Lama. Both narratives could contain elements of truth. However, based on currently available information, there is substantial evidence to support the claim that the group does not maintain any direct or administrative ties to Dharamshala India where His Holiness and the Central Tibetan Administration are headquartered.

We know that precursors for the manufacture of fentanyl flow out of China, and therefore it is possible that rich Chinese are paying the manufacturers of these chemicals in China with renminbi and obtaining property in Canada from the sale of fentanyl. The extent of the fentanyl money laundering was recently the subject of a major report in *The Wall Street Journal*.[96] The report highlighted how Chinese money brokers are controlling the fentanyl profits and investing for Chinese individuals back in China. The money laundering scheme works as follows:

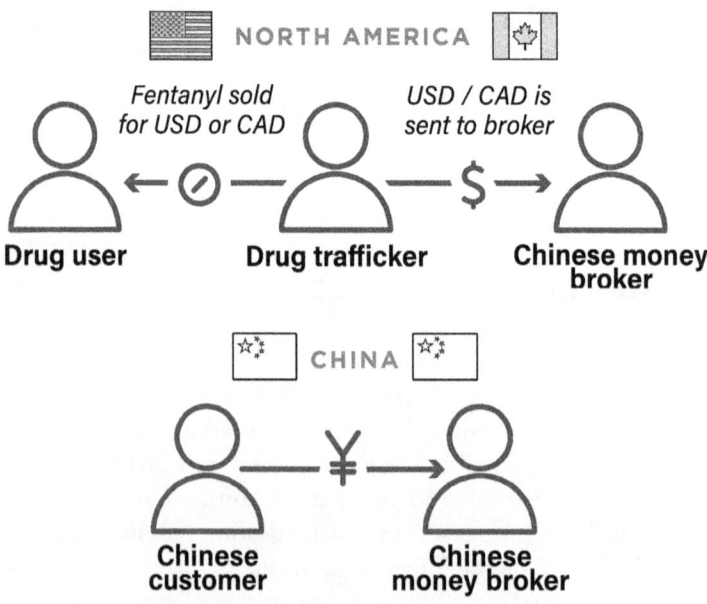

EVIDENCE OF MONEY LAUNDERING

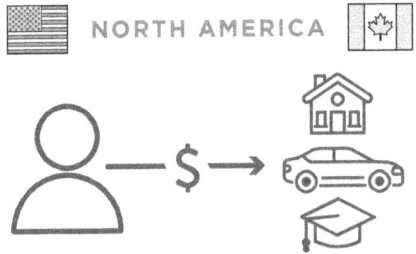

Broker releases USD / CAD to Chinese customer who uses it to purchase real estate, pay tuition, gambling, or to make othher investments.

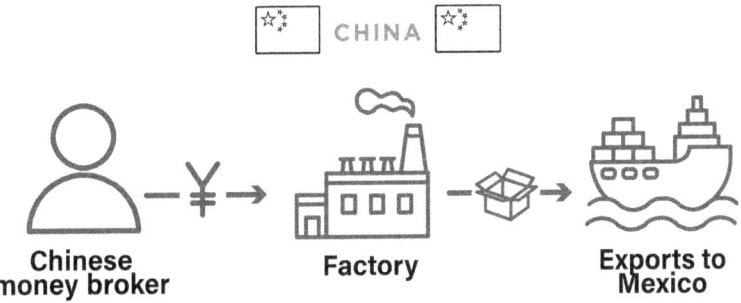

To move CNY to drug traffickers in Mexico the broker exchanges CNY for MXN through a business that is looking to buy Chinese goods for export to Mexico.

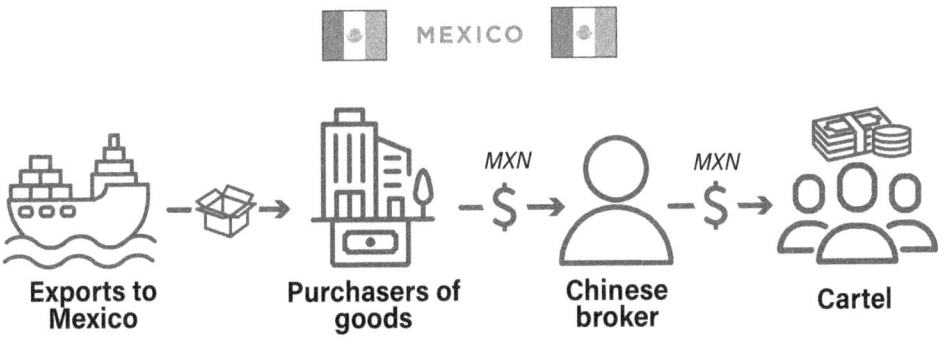

To move CNY to drug traffickers in Mexico the broker exchanges CNY for MXN through a business that is looking to buy Chinese goods for export to Mexico.

Although there is presently no definitive intelligence confirming that the aforementioned framework is actively in operation, current indicators exhibit several hallmarks commonly associated with money laundering, as documented in British Columbia's Vancouver Model. When considered alongside the substantial inflow of capital into Prince Edward Island—particularly in the real estate sector—these indicators warrant a comprehensive and methodical investigation. Such an inquiry would not only help determine the origin and intent of these financial movements but also reinforce transparency, ensure regulatory compliance, and safeguard the province's economic and social integrity.

The following transcript documents the flow of funds from criminal activity:

----- START OF TRANSCRIPT -----

"Regarding the claim related to Fan Yin's bank account and fund transfer, I found it from an interview with the former Abbot and other people hosted by Sanlih E-Television Inc. (三立电视台) on Sep. 14, 2017." [97] [98]

There is a two-part video piece of the interview in its full length:

54新觀點 2017-09-14 福智-接班上師/真如老師/金女士 - 風雨專輯《1》
54新觀點 2017-09-15 金女士*釋梵因 福智接班上師風雨專輯《2》

There is also a shorter version:

54新觀點 (9/14) 違背戒律的通緝犯當「佛母」？ 金夢蓉評價兩極……(上)
54新觀點 (9/14) 違背戒律的通緝犯當「佛母」？ 金夢蓉評價兩極……(下)

In the 3rd video listed above, from 18'59"to 21'37", the host and the former Abbot Ven. Fan Yin had a conversation on the issue.

For reference, I copy the Chinese transcript below:

主持人: 好, 那剛剛談到了錢的問題, 我們聽到如得法師（福智副住持）跟如偉法師說所有的錢都是清清楚楚的, 而且是, 財團法人都是有賬的, 甚至有會計師事務所簽證的, 到底錢有沒有不清楚、有沒有流向不該流向的地方？

梵因法師（福智前住持）：這我這邊可以證明, 就是說他們對於所謂募那個根本道場月稱光明寺的錢, 他跟信徒講是募月稱光明寺, 可是他給的收據裡面竟然增加了所謂的海外道場的支出, 所以這個是明顯的欺騙了信徒。這些錢就是

EVIDENCE OF MONEY LAUNDERING

不曉得,當然一定是拿到國外去的,還有很多信徒他們反映說,當初跟他們講說,如果不要開收據會比較好處理,所以很多信徒都是在這種情況下就沒有開收據,所以這些錢肯定就是被他們挪用。

主持人: 你是前住持,你有沒有曾經瞭解或查過到底有多少錢被挪用?

梵因法師: 這個因為當初我還被蒙在裡面,我完全相信賬務人員的說法,所以我把我所有的印章、所有的戶頭都全部交給他們處理,我從來沒有過問過。所以我是都不知道的。一直到今年我離開的時候,那我要去銀行開戶的時候,結果銀行的人跟我講,說我是洗錢的高危險群,不讓我開戶。所以我就很緊張了。然後我就透過所謂的銀行公會去查,查我的帳。那查出來我的賬戶裡面竟然有一億多元的資金流向。

主持人: 透過你的賬戶流出的?

梵因法師: 對,就是那裡面有一億多元資金流向。那我這是其中一個戶頭。我後面除了這個以外,還有四個戶頭。那就我所知道呢,整個福智僧團體,它這個戶頭,至少有上百個戶頭。

主持人: 那這些戶頭都有一些流向不明的資金在進出?

梵因法師: 對。

主持人: 那你一個戶頭就上億了?

梵因法師: 對。

主持人: 那上百個戶頭很有可能,不排除上百億啊!

梵因法師: 沒錯。

主持人: 那這些錢到哪裡去,你有去查嗎?因為你是有資金流向,那流到哪裡,總有一個銀行總會給個說法。

梵因法師: 現在這個流向呢,已經請政府在調查。

主持人: 哦,你們已經請司法機關調查了。

A literal translation:

HOST: Okay, we just talked about the issue of money. We heard from Ven. Ru De (Deputy Abbot of Fu Zhi) and Ven. Ru Wei that all the money is clear and transparent. The charitable foundation also has accounts and even has certification from an accounting firm. So, have there been any instances of funds being unclear or diverted to unauthorized places?

FAN YIN (FORMER ABBOT OF FU ZHI): I can attest to this. They told the believers that the money was for fundraising for 月稱光明寺 (Yueh Cheng Guang Ming Sih, Guang Ming Temple), but in the receipts they provided, they included expenses for so-called overseas temples. This is clearly deceiving the believers. These funds are unknown, but they must have been transferred abroad. Many believers have also reported that they were told it would be easier to handle if they didn't receive receipts, so many of them didn't request receipts. So, these funds were misappropriated.

HOST: As a former abbot, have you ever investigated or found out how much money was misappropriated?

FAN YIN: Initially, I was kept in the dark. I completely believed what the accounting staff told me, so I handed over all my seals and bank accounts to them for management without ever questioning. So, I had no idea. It wasn't until this year when I tried to open an account at the bank, and they told me that I was in a high-risk group for money laundering and wouldn't allow me to open an account. So, I became very nervous. I then used the Banking Association to investigate my accounts. It turned out that over a hundred million yuan (Taiwan Dollar) had flowed out of my account.[1]

HOST: Through your account?

FAN YIN: Yes, over a hundred million yuan had flowed out of it. That's just one of my accounts. Besides this one, I have four other accounts. As far as I know.

2) I did not find further reports delving into the relationship of the absconding Huang Li-hsiung (黃立雄) or others to Fu Zhi in Taiwan or Canada and to its leaders. However, there has been further news about Huang since the 2018 report by Taipeitimes.com and the *Globe*'s coverage "Taiwan seeks Ottawa's help deporting three fugitives accused of fraud," with the most recent one on Jan. 3, 2024:

---

1 . Note: 100 million New Taiwan Dollar = 3.17M USD

EVIDENCE OF MONEY LAUNDERING

苦主求償有望 檢調急追貴婦奈奈5豪宅
<鏡週刊> 2019年4月5日

Victims' claims hopeful, prosecutors rush to catch up with Lady Nainai's 5 mansions

獨家》 與媳婦貴婦奈奈倒帳10億 台大前名醫是欠稅大戶！ 檢舉獎金出爐 <中時> 2024/01/03

Exclusive: Operating fraudulent accounts with his daughter-in-law Lady Nainai and owing 1 billion, the former top doctor at National Taiwan University is a major tax delinquent! Whistleblower rewards have been announced. China Times.

貴婦奈奈公公 欠稅大戶前台大名醫黃立雄檢舉最高百萬獎金 <CNEWS 匯流新聞網> 2024年1月3日

Lady Nainai's father-in-law, Huang Lihsiung, a major tax delinquent and former top doctor at National Taiwan University: whistleblowers could earn a maximum reward of one million for a report on him.

— CNEWS News Network, January 3, 2024

欠稅大戶「貴婦奈奈」公公黃立雄7130萬未繳 檢舉獎金最高 100 萬 <NOWnews今日新聞> 2024-01-03

Unfortunately, the latest news did not mention anything about Huang's relationship with Fu Zhi in Taiwan or Canada. In 2019, media reports suggested that investigators suspected Huang, Lady Nainai's renowned physician father-in-law, of being a major financial supporter of the Fu Zhi Buddhist group, and that he fled to Prince Edward Island, attended ceremonies in temples, made donations specifically designated for his family and clinics. There were suspicions that someone aided them in hiding, enabling Lady Nainai's entire family to prolong their stay and complete their refugee application.

I hope to find more valuable reports providing in-depth insights into their relationship with Fu Zhi."

Our research further found the following:

One of the posts in the Chinese language blogs that you sent to me contains a mention that Venerable Fan Yin, the former Abbot of the Hanai Temple and right hand man to Master Jih-Chang, said that when he was Abbot, Fuzhi opened a bank account in his name and put several million dollars into it, without him knowing, and at one point he has $8M in the account and became a politically exposed person that was tracked for money laundering, without his knowledge. Can you find the original interview from which this statement came?

It may help to know that Fan Yin was the designated successor to Jih-Chang, who became very angry when Zhen Ru charmed the Master and took over the Fuzhi organization. He went on a massive PR campaign, apologized to the followers in several press articles and videos on YouTube, and also said a lot about what fraudulent practices Zhen Ru brought into the organization (such as using monks' accents to transfer funds to China, Canada and the US).

If you can find other statements that will show the fraudulent practices of Fuzhi, it will help us understand how they operate.

2. *The Taipei Times*[99] carried a report stating that Taipei prosecutors are investigating a prominent cosmetic doctor Paul Huang (黃博健) and his wife, Internet celebrity Su Chen Tuan (蘇陳端), better known as Lady Nai Nai (貴婦奈奈), for alleged financial fraud, after they left Taiwan on a flight to the US, with local media reporting that they might be "hiding" on Canada's Prince Edward Island. They defrauded investors of USD32M.

Paul Huang's father, Huang Li-hsiung (黃立雄), is a leading expert in obstetrics, while his elder brother Huang Po-hao (黃博浩) is a surgeon at National Taiwan University Hospital.

After the case received media attention, Huang Li-hsiung also disappeared, with reports saying that a number of family members had also flown to the United States and that all of them held U.S. or Canadian passports.

A man surnamed Chen (陳), who said he was a fraud victim, told reporters that the couple was on Prince Edward Island, where they own a house. The purchase showed that they had been scheming to illegally transfer assets to Canada, as they had acquired citizenship there, Chen said.

The family members are followers of the Bliss and Wisdom Foundation (福智佛教基金會), a Taiwanese Buddhist organization, and Huang Li-hsiung is a major financial backer of the organization's leader, who is a relative, Chen said.

EVIDENCE OF MONEY LAUNDERING

The foundation has established overseas headquarters on the island and encouraged followers to transfer their assets there, which could qualify them for Canadian citizenship through the Immigrant Investor Program, he added.

I can confirm that people have seen these three fraudsters in PEI, where they made a large donation to Bliss & Wisdom's local church, called GEBIS (Great Enlightenment Buddhist Institute) and GWBI (Great Wisdom Buddhist Institute) and are living in a house the church made available or sold to them.

----- END OF TRANSCRIPT -----

The above story supports my theory that real estate is purchased for wealthy Chinese and that the money flows from criminal activity.

In addition, the aforementioned interviews conducted by Dean in Taiwan revealed a curious and telling pattern: monks travelling to Canada were consistently carrying just under $10,000 Canadian in crisp, new $100 bills. The amount—just shy of the legal threshold that would trigger currency reporting requirements—was small enough to avoid notice on its own. But over time, the steady stream of cash added up to millions.

This wasn't just pocket money. It was flight capital—wealth quietly moving offshore, out of reach of Taiwanese regulators and tax authorities. What stood out even more was the nature of the bills: freshly issued and sequentially numbered. That detail points to something more organized than simple personal savings. Access to large quantities of new, consecutive banknotes typically requires cooperation from a financial institution, suggesting the involvement—witting or not—of a domestic bank.

The method was simple but effective: regular trips, just under the radar, carried out by individuals unlikely to draw suspicion. Taken together, the pattern hints at a sophisticated system designed to move money discreetly and systematically out of Taiwan, raising questions not just about the source of the funds, but about the institutions that may have helped move them along.

BUILDING THE MONASTERY

Having worked extensively in the field of organized crime and having observed the strategic fortification of outlaw motorcycle clubs, I find the fortification of the Bliss and Wisdom Monastery deeply concerning. According to an individual with detailed knowledge of the monastery's construction, the facility is equipped with an extensive network of high-end surveillance cameras, and many of its doors are remotely controlled and monitored from a central control room. Furthermore, the monastery reportedly secured its own dedicated fibre optic line in 2012 at a cost exceeding $2.1 million. The entrance is fully gated, supported by a guard house and electronic access controls.

Based on my professional experience, such a high level of security is highly unusual for a religious institution and is more consistent with the infrastructure found at military installations or sensitive government intelligence facilities. This observation, combined with recently surfaced intelligence, supports concerns regarding the legitimacy of the organization. Specifically, emerging evidence suggests that Bliss and Wisdom may be operating under false pretenses, and that Mary Jin is allegedly an officer of China's Ministry of State Security (MSS). This would align with the strategic objectives of China's Belt and Road Initiative, which has enabled the establishment of organizations on foreign soil through real estate acquisitions and land development—often with a mandate to serve national interests abroad.

The countless examples of all cash transactions and opaque accounting practices by Bliss and Wisdom in Prince Edward Island, when viewed alongside reported Chinese operations elsewhere in Canada, raises serious concerns related to financial crime.

Evidence suggesting that Bliss and Wisdom may be part of a localized laundering operation connected to broader international networks implies that Canada could be a conduit for illicit financial flows. These networks may extend their operations into larger urban centres, where international criminal groups—including those with ties to China—are active.

Of particular concern is the potential nexus between these financial activities and the fentanyl trade. If proven, such a link would significantly elevate the gravity of the threat, given the devastating impact of fentanyl in Canada and the United States. This underscores the urgent need to address both the financial mechanisms and public health implications associated with transnational criminal operations.

The broader implications of this case suggest systemic vulnerabilities in Canada's financial and regulatory systems. The potential infiltration by foreign state-linked actors and criminal organizations underscores the need for a reassessment of current frameworks governing real estate transactions, foreign investment, and non-profit registration. To effectively counter these threats, Canadian authorities must enhance cooperation at all levels—federal, provincial, and international—and prioritize intelligence sharing, joint investigations, and policy reform.

In conclusion, the alleged activities associated with Bliss and Wisdom demand serious scrutiny. Whether these operations are indeed part of a broader geopolitical strategy or a complex network of illicit finance and trafficking, the risks they pose to Canada's security, economy, and public health cannot be dismissed. While it is theoretically possible that the movement of large sums of cash and the cultivation of local influence may be benign or misinterpreted, the confluence of red flags warrants thorough investigation. Canada must remain vigilant in protecting its institutions, communities, and financial systems from exploitation under the guise of sanctuary or cultural outreach.

BOILING IT ALL DOWN

Very much like what I witnessed first-hand during my tenure in Hong Kong, Chinese state-linked interests have successfully ingratiated themselves with segments of Canada's political elite under the guise of foreign investment purportedly made for Canada's benefit. In reality, this is a form of "fool's gold"—a deceptive strategy that has contributed to documented political interference and the large-scale acquisition of Canadian property and natural resources. It is increasingly apparent that these acquisitions serve the strategic interests of the Chinese Communist Party, rather than making any meaningful contribution to Canada's prosperity.

Foreign-generated proceeds of crime are being laundered within Canada at alarming levels, with professional third-party money laundering presenting a serious and persistent threat. According to a 2020 estimate from the Criminal Intelligence Service Canada, between $36 billion and $91 billion in illicit funds are laundered and fully integrated into the Canadian economy each year. More than 175 organized crime groups are currently active in Canada, with approximately half of them maintaining international ties.

To quote The Bureau (Sam Cooper, February 2024):

> In response to Ottawa's pledge to tackle fentanyl-linked money laundering—including the appointment of a "fentanyl czar" and new intelligence-sharing initiatives with the United States—The Bureau is reposting this February 2024 investigation estimating tens of billions, potentially several hundred billion, laundered through Vancouver and Toronto real estate via underground banking networks tied to China and global narcotics trafficking, including fentanyl.

A 2023 analysis by FINTRAC of 48,000 transactions involving members of the Chinese diaspora revealed substantial wire transfers originating from Hong Kong and Mainland China. These funds were funnelled through "money mule" accounts linked to international students, homemakers, and shell businesses—including law firms. Despite the magnitude of these findings, which raised grave concerns about Canada's financial oversight, no prosecutions have resulted. The same laundering patterns appear at the core of the U.S. Justice Department's $3 billion investigation into TD Bank. According to U.S. investigator David Asher, Chinese international students tied to United Front organizations were key actors in laundering operations.

The so-called Vancouver Model—originally centred on laundering drug proceeds through British Columbia casinos—has evolved into a more complex and embedded financial ecosystem, involving Canada's banking and legal systems. These developments align with urban planning research by Andy Yan (Simon Fraser University), who has documented the severe distortions that foreign capital imposes on Canada's housing market, where mortgage approvals and home purchases frequently exceed local income levels.

Central to recent investigations is HSBC Canada whistleblower "D.M.," who identified at least $500 million in questionable Toronto-area mortgages, often supported by fictitious remote-work incomes from China. D.M. alleges that after internal reporting, HSBC Canada implemented only superficial reforms and pressured him to destroy critical records—reinforcing concerns of institutional complacency.

Calvin Chrustie—a former RCMP Senior Intelligence Officer from Vancouver—and I reviewed D.M.'s documentation which emphasized that Canada's systemic regulatory weaknesses continue to enable global underground banking tied to transnational criminal groups, including those in China, Iran, and Mexico. Chrustie also referenced the 2012 U.S. Department of Justice case in which HSBC was fined $1.9 billion for facilitating more than $881 million in cartel-linked transactions.

As Andy Yan rightly notes, governments at all levels must be held accountable for enabling unchecked foreign capital flows into Canada's real estate sector. The lack of transparency surrounding beneficial ownership and the failure to reconcile income-to-home-price disparities have made Canadian markets a soft target for criminal exploitation.

In response, Ottawa appointed a "fentanyl czar" on February 11, 2025, to coordinate intelligence sharing and law enforcement efforts with the United States. The federal government has also pledged to designate major drug cartels as terrorist organizations—an initiative that could expose Canadian financial institutions to increased scrutiny and regulatory consequences under U.S. law.

CONCLUSION

The accumulation of circumstantial evidence and testimonial accounts paints a troubling picture of potential large-scale money laundering activities involving Bliss and Wisdom and its associated entities in Prince Edward Island. The recurring use of structured cash deposits below FINTRAC reporting thresholds, sequentially numbered currency, real estate acquisitions through nominee purchasers, and a lack of verifiable financial documentation strongly resemble laundering typologies observed in British Columbia's Vancouver Model.

The presence of massive surveillance infrastructure at their monasteries, foreign nationals from Taiwan and China, and possible United Front involvement raise legitimate national security concerns. While no single piece of evidence proves criminal activity without the benefit of judicial inquiry, the aggregation of these red flags—unsubstantiated sources of wealth, the use of shell entities, avoidance of financial oversight, and known associations with persons of interest—demands urgent and thorough investigation.

This case must be prioritized by law enforcement and investigated using a coordinated, intelligence-led, multi-agency approach. Recommended tools include production orders, search warrants, beneficial ownership reviews, forensic accounting, and cross-border cooperation with international financial crime enforcement bodies.

Particular attention should be paid to tracing incoming and outgoing funds, mapping connections to the illicit-goods and fentanyl trade, analyzing immigration-linked remittances, and evaluating suspicious real estate holdings.

Ultimately, only a well-resourced, transparent, and uncompromised criminal investigation can uncover the true scale and nature of these activities. While it's possible that some of the hundreds of millions in cash transactions have legitimate explanations, we cannot afford to assume so. As a forty-year police veteran and money laundering expert, the red flags in the documents and interviews I reviewed are undeniable. The signs point to serious vulnerabilities that demand immediate action. The cost of delay is dangerously high: Canada's national security, the integrity of our legal and financial systems, and our international reputation are all on the line. We are at a crossroads—and failure to act decisively now will invite consequences we may not be able to contain.

To quote John F. Kennedy: "Let us not seek the Republican answer or the Democratic answer, but the right answer. Let us not seek to fix the blame for the past—let us accept our own responsibility for the future."[100]

CHAPTER 18
72 HOURS IN TAIPEI

"But then at that time, that was about ten years ago. I don't think they really saw the whole picture . . . They only saw the surface."

SENIOR TAIWAN GOVERNMENT OFFICIAL

With our book shaping up and our possible documentary to chronicle it also looking interesting Chris, the director, said it would be great to get to Taiwan. I remember saying it would be but not sure I can afford to take that trip and what more would it deliver because we already had a lot of the story just from our research in Canada and Washington. Still, I agreed to consider it.

I continued to ponder the prospect of going to Taiwan. The risk. The cost. Whether we really needed to go. Whether it would deliver anything more than what we'd already assembled through months of open-source documents, countless in-person and telephone interviews which all formed part of the HUMINT side of the investigation, as Garry and Michel referred to the process in their respective disciplines. I simply saw it as getting to know the people and getting to the truth.

But as the year turned over and we got to January, I had a conversation with Chris. "I don't know," I said one night over the phone. "Maybe we've got enough."

"But you're not sure," Chris replied. Chris had been making documentaries for a long time, and he felt from his end that we didn't have enough, and he was right. I wasn't sure. And that uncertainty had been growing until eventually I realized that getting to Taiwan would close the loop for our book, and who knew what might turn up once we got there.

So, about a week later there was a persistent itch at the back of my mind as I mulled over what we had and what we didn't. We had a substantial case: evidence of suspicions cash transactions, which indicated some form of financial misconduct inside the Bliss and Wisdom Buddhist monastic order, testimonies about internal manipulation, and unusual activity tied to Canadian financial flows. We had spent countless hours with various whistleblowers who had collected and shared their evidence with us. But we were still missing some of the connective tissue—real-world, face-to-face accounts that could tie the spiritual, financial, and geopolitical elements together.

No one had gone to the island of Taiwan with the insights, documents, and first-hand accounts that our team had collected. But the *Globe and Mail*[101] had published an exposé by Greg Mercer and Jimmy Huang in August 2023 that presented a lot of never-published insights from meeting with a number of sources, and then they conducted their own trip to Taiwan. They also had a source we were familiar with who had provided us with critical research data, and from the same whistleblower we had interviewed for countless hours for our executive report that Garry had delivered to the RCMP Commissioner, Mike Duheme[102] by email. In hindsight, and what persuaded us that the book was a must-do, was his reaction.

The *Globe* article began with all the elements:

> Monks, money and the fierce debate over PEI's scarce land.
>
> Bliss and Wisdom's growing real estate empire has raised alarms on PEI, but the Taiwan-based Buddhist group says it's following the rules.

The direct evidence from our investigation (i.e., emails) indicating that lawyers were helping them cover up their cash sales practices suggested that once again there was more to the operation than meets the eye. Greg Mercer and Jimmy Huang's article painted the following picture, which was consistent with what our research and contacts were telling us.

BLISS AND WISDOM'S EXPANSION INTO PEI: STRATEGIC, NOT SPIRITUAL

The *Globe*'s investigation uncovered that Bliss and Wisdom's land acquisitions in Prince Edward Island (PEI) were not merely the result of religious growth but a strategic and highly coordinated expansion. The group, through a network of affiliated individuals and companies, has amassed up to 17,000 acres—approximately 4% of Kings County. Many of these properties were acquired through means that seemed designed to circumvent PEI's strict land-ownership laws for non-residents. Former residents described the gradual erosion of their communities, driven by persistent purchase offers from monks linked to the group's expanding institutions. The Great Enlightenment Buddhist Institute Society (GEBIS) and the Great Wisdom Buddhist Institute (GWBI) have suggested otherwise.

LEGAL LOOPHOLES, CORPORATE VEILS, AND THE ROLE OF "FOLLOWERS"

Despite claims that all land purchases were made independently by followers, the investigation revealed how many transactions were funnelled through shell companies or laypeople acting under instruction. This is a typical process used by criminal organizations, as highlighted in Chapter 16, Evidence of Money Laundering. Former insiders detailed the use of personal bank accounts (claims made by monks and Fan Yin), cash-filled suitcases, and blurred lines between personal and organizational funds—all pointing to a financial structure that lacked transparency and accountability. The organization's response has largely been to deflect blame onto "former disgruntled members" while maintaining that any irregularities were due to cultural misunderstandings or logistical necessity. Given our meeting with the highly educated middle management at GEBIS, all of them educated in North America, this explanation seems implausible.

POLITICAL QUIET AND THE SHADOW OF A UNITED FRONT STRATEGY

At the heart of the concern is not just real estate—it's influence. Bliss and Wisdom's leadership, particularly Master Zhen-Ru and executive Ke-Zhou Lu, maintain deep roots in China and Taiwan. Their expansion into PEI coincided with an era of heightened Chinese overseas engagement and the use of soft power via religious organizations. While Bliss and Wisdom denies political ties, the pattern aligns with tactics used by the Chinese United Front: influence through religious front organizations, property acquisition, and localized political engagement. The lack of transparency, combined with signs of systemic coordination, has prompted calls for a formal public inquiry.

So, the Islanders who were sharing insights with the *Globe and Mail* wanted action and were hoping that the *Globe* report might lead to further investigation. According to our sources, the paper was going to publish another piece but could not validate some of the claims and backed away from it. But our team had a sense we were on the right track, so between our trip to Taiwan and our collective insights, we had a better handle on the United Front's strategies and their interest in Bliss and Wisdom. In the end, we concluded that no one from the media, nor from any of the so-called watchdog institutions, and certainly no one in the Canadian Security Intelligence Service (CSIS) was doing the deeper and necessary dive. No one had followed the threads to where they began—inside Taiwan, inside the religious network. We had gathered the outlines. What we needed now was the voice inside the walls.

I spoke again with Garry and Michel. Michel, as expected, was enthusiastic. "Yes, someone should go. Let's just do it, I say."

I shook my head, thinking we were not CBC or CNN. "We don't have that kind of funding." But as a publishing and documentary project we had already invested heavily in the investigation and, thank goodness, we had the kindness of people like Jan and Carolyn who put us up in their house on several occasions to defray our costs. I paused. "I'm leaning towards going, but we'll need to be strategic." Problem was I had a lot going on and was heading to the Munich Security Conference in mid-February.

When Chris told me that Shaun, our Director of Photography for the documentary, was going to Japan and available to fly with camera equipment for photo shoots if I committed to going, that tipped it. I made some calls to Washington and Ottawa to try to secure a meeting with a representative of His Holiness in Taipei. I needed support and the proper introduction, and once again, friends and colleagues were about to make it happen. I also needed introductions to top-level officials in the government, and I got that too.

So, I booked a flight for February 3. Chinese New Year had inflated prices, but the Air Canada route worked. Chris flew out of Tokyo and landed a day before me.

By the time I arrived, he'd already been working with Jeff Wang, our local coordinator, a calm, reliable force who'd spent a week lining up contacts. We had a rough schedule. A few appointments. A few possibilities.

But, as always in investigative work, the biggest moments came from the smallest signs.

I landed in Taipei the night of February 4, stepping into the weight of humidity and possibility. Chris had been laying the groundwork from Calgary, coordinating logistics and leads with Jeff. We weren't travelling with a full crew—just me, Chris, a camera, a recorder, and a notebook, armed with questions no one else seemed willing to ask.

When I landed, Jeff and Chris were already on a Zoom Google Meets call with Michael Lee (a pseudonym) so I quickly got on the call to glean what I could from Michael, the Taiwanese journalist who had interviewed a professor who had created a huge controversy in 2017 on Taiwanese television. As part of his preparation for us getting to Taiwan, Chris had unearthed the professor, and Jeff had engaged him on our behalf a few days before. Michael was a seasoned and very senior journalist. He wasn't a stranger to difficult topics.

"This is probably bigger than we thought," he said quietly as I watched and listened intently.

Michael had recently spoken with Professor Zhang Jiang-hui, a respected Taiwanese scholar known for his cross-strait academic work and numerous publications on and in China. The professor had declined a direct interview, citing age, health, and risk—but he had spoken to Michael at length.

What he said reframed the scope of everything.

> "张教授跟我讲说，这个团体 2017 掌门人之争背后的问题很大。"
>
> "Professor Zhang told us that the leadership dispute within the group in 2017 revealed major underlying problems." This wasn't about infighting or theological divisions. It was about money, structure, and influence. Monastic religious (charitable status) were involved in helping the CCP and apparently organized crime move NT$60 billion or 11.5 billion Canadian out of China and Taiwan to various overseas jurisdictions.
>
> "通过台湾的慈善团体把中国的钱，透过台湾转出去海外 … 而不是中国对加拿大。"
>
> "Through Taiwan's charitable organizations, China's money was moved overseas—not directly from China to Canada but routed through Taiwan."

According to Michael, Zhang believed the Bliss and Wisdom group was being used as a financial corridor that masked political and ideological intent under the guise of religious charity.

Then came the demographic target.

"军公教的公务人员小孩往这边送 ... 长大之后,
直接留学加拿大。"
"Children of civil servants in the military and government were sent to monastic schools . . . and later sent to study in Canada."

Zhang, Michel said, saw this as a deliberate strategy: educational insertion leading to international positioning and went on to further state on the call: "In fact, in Canada, both levels are working as agents."
际上在加拿大这边, 两层都是做特务的人员。"

"Wow," I said to myself in the moment, "that is a revelation that intelligence agencies and our government might want to look at." Something I didn't need to share with the local team, who I was just getting to know, as Michel and Garry had coached me always to be careful with what you share and who you share it with. However, this was not a revelation but rather a confirmation of something our team already had on our radar. Michel and I had come to a similar conclusion during our first trip to the Island, given that the province had ceded its right to oversee the curriculum being taught at the monasteries. Nope, some wise politician probably either too naïve or too stupid, or just someone trying to get along at the Ministry of Education, had granted the group an exemption from provincial educational requirements, and now someone in Taiwan, a celebrated scholar and published author, was making this claim. Again, this is an analysis and not a fact until proven. It could all be about higher education for those devoted to monastic training and dedication to Buddhism, no matter what the form.

Zhang wouldn't say it publicly, but he had told Michael, and Michael was now telling us.

"这个团体是台湾三大宗教团体之一 ... 但如果用海外据点推不动的话,那就用买的方式介入。"
"This group is one of the three largest religious groups in Taiwan . . . and if they can't expand overseas by growth, they buy their way in." From our analysis they are probably not number three in size but certainly in the top ten and are well known to citizens and government officials alike."

The infrastructure, the outreach, the targeting of immigrants, the educational pipelines—Zhang believed it was all intentional.

He said the professor warned that Bliss and Wisdom was being used by the CCP to rebrand religious soft power under a Taiwanese face—because overseas, no one would accept Chinese Buddhism post-Cultural Revolution.

> "因为有文革所以人家不会相信你中国的佛教会相信台湾。"
> "Because of the Cultural Revolution, people don't believe in Chinese Buddhism. But they will believe in Taiwanese Buddhism."

This was consistent with the papers the government-in-exile had already published and backed up by various scholarly accounts that we had researched for the past year prior to this trip.

That night, I left that call meeting with a stack of notes and one clear conclusion. Our hypothesis based on the analysis by Garry, Michel, and I was that on all fronts this wasn't just spiritual, it was strategic.

DAY ONE: BELLA'S TESTIMONY

The morning of February 5, we set up the camera in Shaun's room in anticipation of our first formal interview in Taiwan—this one with a woman who had lived inside Bliss and Wisdom for six years. For her safety, we agreed to refer to her by a pseudonym: Bella.

Jeff had arranged the meeting. Bella arrived early, and alone, clutching a folder. She looked exhausted but focused, the kind of weariness that doesn't fade with sleep. As we settled into our chairs, she began talking, quietly, but without hesitation.

> "福祉的大部分的下面的信徒或者学习的人，基本上是很善良的 ... 但是最上面那一层的人的邪恶，他们永远都看不到。"
> "The majority of Bliss and Wisdom's followers are very kind and sincere ... but the most terrible part is the top leadership, whose evil remains invisible to outsiders."

Her voice was calm, but she glanced occasionally at the door.

She told us she joined the group in 2007, looking for spiritual depth. What she found instead, over time, was something else.

> "他们利用意识形态来操控整个福祉组织以及下面的信徒。"

"They use ideology to manipulate and control the entire Bliss and Wisdom organization and the people under them."

She described how the teaching became more about loyalty than enlightenment. Doubt was punished. Internal silence was rewarded.

"对一般人来说，要认清福祉，是一件很困难的事情。"
"It's very difficult for the general public to recognize the true nature of Bliss and Wisdom."

"你必须自己经历，你才能知道。"
"You have to go through it yourself to understand."

I asked what finally made her leave.

"有一个晚上，我突然意识到，我们不是在修行，我们是在服从。"
"One night I suddenly realized—we weren't practising spirituality. We were obeying commands."

She left in 2013. Quietly. Without ceremony. One thing that struck me was the fact that one of her jobs was to transcribe conversations among followers inside the monastery that Bliss and Wisdom would record. They said it was for security reasons, but she felt it was to monitor the dialogue to ensure there was no dissent; if there was, other followers could then be engaged to counter the dissenters' fears or criticisms.

What happened next was about to change our entire time in Taipei. We were scrolling through the computer when she said, "This might interest you." It was an innocent photo, but she had a copy in her folder. Reaching into her folder, Bella pulled out the single photo.

She placed it face down on the table, then slowly flipped it to face us.

It was Fan Yin—clearly visible in full robes—standing beside a local pastor from southern Taipei. Fan Yin, the former monk who had left Bliss and Wisdom when Mary Jin took over as Master Zhen-Rhu.

"He was here," she said. "Recently."

"How long ago?" I asked through Jeff. She said in early January. She said he was at a Presbyterian church in the southern part of Taipei City.

Jeff leaned over, studying the church logo in the background. He looked at me.

"I know this place," he said. "We can be there in 45 minutes." I looked at Shaun, our cameraman, and said "Wow, this is awesome. We can't pass up an opportunity like this." After all he was the one interview that would make the entire trip worthwhile, and I hoped would fill in the gaps in our investigation. "Yep," Shaun replied, "you have to follow the trail and sometimes it leads to a pot of gold.' I was certainly hoping that would be the case. Shaun and I both went to our rooms to grab some things and then met Jeff in the lobby. We ordered an Uber, and on the way, we talked about the luck of finding such a lead and what it might tell us. Shaun recalled a few similar experiences when shooting documentaries, but he sensed how important this one was to me and our investigation for the book and the documentary.

As we travelled along the highway, a great red building emerged to our right. It was a magnificent building. "What's that?" I asked Jeff, "That's the Grand Hotel," he told me. Located in the Zhongshan District of Taipei,[103] the hotel was established in May 1952, and the main building was completed on October 10, 1973.

Jeff explained that the hotel was originally build by Chang Kai Shek's[104] government to host dignitaries who might travel to the new republic. It was as lavish on the inside as it appeared from the outside, as I would discover later in my trip, but not before the hard work was completed and the interview was in the bag.

As we neared the protestant church, I was anticipating something very traditional, but what I saw resembled a political campaign office filled with forms and petitions. Shaun and I had mapped out how we would approach the people in the church but that went out the window once we arrived.

DORCAY CHURCH

As we entered the front door around 1:30 in the afternoon we were thinking that this was the place that we had seen in the picture of Fan Yin with the Dorcay Church pastor. Had Fan Yin been here? Had he really come out of hiding to attend a protestant church? That question would be answered very soon.

The church was wedged between low-rise buildings, at the T of an intersection, and was very modest indeed. The first floor resembled a community centre more than a place of formal worship. There were a few congregants inside—young, mostly—and one woman in her thirties who met our eyes directly.

She introduced herself in English. "I'm Sze."

Sze asked me to use her pseudonym because, like many others in this book and others with whom I have been in contact in the Chinese diaspora community, identities are sacred, and putting a target on your back in Taiwan is not an ideal survival practice. We would learn that she had been an organizer during the Hong Kong democracy movement before relocating to Taiwan. Now, she worked with the Recall Movement,[105] coordinating outreach aimed at unseating Kuomintang (KMT) legislators suspected of having ties with Mainland China.

Over the past few months, she and her church volunteers had mobilized to gather signatures for the recall of the KMT legislators. Despite facing challenges such as public scepticism and opposition from the KMT, her efforts and those of others have gained substantial traction. As of mid-May 2025, thirty groups successfully submitted the required number of signatures to advance to the second phase of the recall process. She told us how the process worked and shared information with us. Of course, we were most anxious to find out about the pastor who was pictured with Fan Yin.

We asked her about the monk in the photo.

"Yes, he came here," she said. "Didn't say much. Quiet. Respectful. He came to volunteer and help our movement. He wanted to help stop the CCP from taking over Taiwan. I thought to myself, if all I have read about Fan Yin was true, then this fit his profile 100%."

She wasn't familiar with Bliss and Wisdom, other than that Fan Yin had shared his story with the pastor extensively. But she understood its aim and lamented how many are fooled by some "Tibetan churches," as she called them. Jeff asked in Mandarin if the pastor was available. "He's out of town," she said. "But I can see that based on what you do and what you are trying to find out this is important; I can help you reach the monk through the pastor."

I then spent the next twenty minutes listening to her and her team tell us about the Recall Movement, which I had read about before coming but knew little about it or its operations. As it turned out, this was ground zero for the resistance. She asked a lot of question and was hoping I could help her promote the movement in other countries and put her in contact with others who have taken on the CCP. Jeff traded numbers with her, and we thanked her.

When we got back into our Uber, Shaun was still hopeful that we were going to get the interview with the monk. Jeff felt confident that it would work out, but we decided to head back to the hotel to debrief and plan for the next day. Jeff looked at Shaun and said, "We'll see."

When we got back, Chris pinged us from Calgary. "How was the day?' I responded "Phenomenal . . . and we may have found Fan Yin."

"Get out!" came his response.

"No," I said. "I'm serious but we won't find out for sure until later this evening."

We got a text from Jeff around 10:00 p. m. on our WhatsApp group, a somewhat secure communications platform in a peer-to-peer setting.

"He said yes. Fan Yin will meet us tomorrow night at his apartment."

Fantastic, I couldn't believe it. I was so excited I couldn't sleep. I sent a note back to Garry and Michel and exclaimed that we had found him. "Who," Michel asked? "*Fan Yin*,' I said. Garry chimed in "Excellent, my friend." And Michel said "Fantastic work." Coming from my two friends and mentors, those words meant a lot to me as I sat all alone in my Taipei hotel room contemplating the next part of my journey. But I had no time to relish one success and quickly jumped to sending them another note through our Signal Group named "Project Anne."

"The story is bigger that we could ever have imagined now that we're here. According to my conversations with various officials, Bliss and Wisdom as an organization had been able to penetrate the Taiwanese government, and many Bliss and Wisdom adherents were influencing government decisions," I wrote. That was a familiar tune for me as a publisher, given that I had published books—*Hidden Hand*, *Wilful Blindness*, and *The Mosaic Effect*—that all address, with examples, how of many of our politicians have been influenced or compromised by or were simply positioned on the side of Beijing. I was told that the former mayor of Taipei was a Fuzhi (Bliss and Wisdom) practitioner.

My assessment went further, as the information and insights I had obtained were pointing to the Tibetan government in exile and the Taiwanese government having known about Bliss and Wisdom and its objectives for a long time. But given its community advocacy, charitable work, and corporate footprint (Leezen Organic), and money (power) it continued to avoid higher levels of scrutiny. I was told by someone who knew very well that the organization, like at least four other even larger Tibetan monastic groups, had been penetrated and were now under the influence of the CCP through its United Front operations that focused on the monastic side of Bliss and Wisdom. Michel, Garry, and I had read countless documents, but they had the added benefit of in-field training. My assessment would later be supported by documents that RCI / CBC Radio Canada would share with us in early May. The documents were scraped from Chinese and Taiwan websites rendered in traditional Chinese and then translated to English. See Exhibits 4 and 5 on p. 217.

These documents in some cases came from the Bliss and Wisdom site itself, so there could be no denying the tone, direction, or complicity with the CCP's Sinicization and influence-and-control objectives regarding Bliss and Wisdom or the countless others operating in Taiwan. Bliss and Wisdom has been and continues to engage with the Buddhist Association of China, and since Mary Jin's takeover this has been considered acceptable within the monastic leadership. It would also secure the corporate ambitions of Master Zhen-Ru and her partners as they expanded their business empire in Asia and North America.

The CCP's Sinicization plan, as we articulated in Chapter 8 on Tibetan Buddhism, seem to support our evaluation that Fuzhi (Bliss and Wisdom practitioners) are instruments of the CCP's statecraft operations re the control of all religions, but especially Buddhism in China and beyond.

Master Hsing Yun of Bliss and Wisdom Sanghu, in December 2014 participated in the so-called "Cross strait Buddhist exchanges," which are part of the CCP's master plan for taking over Taiwan's religious groups and spiritual masters before the main invasion takes place militarily.

The CCP's desired outcome is through the so-called "peaceful reunification" process as promoted throughout Western democracies but here in Canada by the likes of former Canadian Senator and United Front sympathizer Victor Oh.[106] Master Yun said, and emphasized, "The focus of this exchange meeting was to promote exchanges between the Buddhist communities on both sides of the strait." Bliss and Wisdom's own venerable Abbot Ru-Zheng, also known as Ru Jing, proposed the plan, according to the Bliss and Wisdom site "All parties put forward constructive plans for the future development of Buddhism on both sides of the Taiwan Strait." He suggested that the Buddhist Association of China and Fo Gang Shan should serve as windows for a cross-strait association for Buddhist friendship promotion that should be established in the future.

"We are truly one family on both sides of the Taiwan Strait, and we are all disciples of Shakyamuni Buddha."[107]

Bliss and Wisdom's own Facebook page and website published reports of their participation in the goal to synthesize the Buddhist religious orders in Taiwan via the Buddhist Association of China. To some it might suggest that resistance will be futile, and that is part of the CCP's long-term strategy. After all, they think in one-hundred-year cycles, while from a political perspective we work in four-year cycles.

In the end, if the CCP influences and/or controls the long-term leadership of these monastic groups and they are all aligned with China, then practitioners in a time of crisis might take counsel from their monastic leaders. And if the leaders all agree with the unification of the religious orders of Tibetan Buddhism under CCP control, they may well suggest to followers "We should not resist, since the Han dream of a peaceful reunification of the Chinese nation is naturally in our best interests."

It is one thing to apply academic treaties, open-source intelligence, and public statements by the CCP to our investigation, but tomorrow evening's interview would provide us with a face-to-face engagement with the former right-hand person to Master Jih-Chang, who for survival reasons had a close working relationship with Mary Jin. I hoped he would confirm much of our open-source insights and research that had been collected by many on PEI and had been published openly in publications and on their websites. But what I was hoping to get for both our documentary and the book was an opportunity to record this humble, gentle man's experiences inside Bliss and Wisdom.

Tomorrow wouldn't be just another day in Taipei.

DAY TWO, MORNING

On the morning of February 6, we met with Kelsang Gyaltsen, His Holiness the Dalai Lama's official representative, in Taipei. The tone was cordial—serious but not strained. I introduced myself, sharing my background in investigative journalism and publishing and my continued efforts to expose malign influence operations by the CCP. We were late because our last shoot and engagement with one of Bliss and Wisdom's many corporations, Leezen Organic, had taken a little longer than expected. I naturally apologized for our tardiness, and he expressed his understanding. Formalities out of the way, it was time to get down to business.

The setting was modest, befitting the humility of the man we had come to meet. As Jeff interpreted, I described the scope of our work.

"We're doing this book and we're doing this investigation on Prince Edward Island in Canada, where a group of supposedly Tibetan Buddhists, originally based here in Taiwan, has set up a large monastery called Bliss and Wisdom. Our concern is that it may be aligned with the CCP."

He nodded. The name wasn't unfamiliar.

"Of course," he said through Jeff. "Bliss and Wisdom is quite controversial. There have been years of discussion about them—both their internal structure and their spiritual leadership."

When I raised the issue of Mary Jin, also known as Master Zhen-Ru, Gyaltsen leaned forward. His expression sharpened with nuance.

"The role of Mary Jin inside Bliss and Wisdom has been the subject of real division. Some claim she is a legitimate successor to Master Jih-Chang. But others argue her position defies traditional Buddhist norms. She is not a nun. She has not received traditional monastic training."

According to Kelsang, in 2016 and 2017, serious disputes erupted within the sangha, the community of Buddhist believers.

"Many senior monks left the organization during that time. There was a clear fracture. And debates intensified, especially concerning her authority over monastic communities."

This was not a minor internal schism—it was a structural collapse.

He confirmed hearing of Fan Yin, the former monk who later became one of the loudest critics of Mary Jin's leadership.

"Yes, I've read the reports. I have not met him personally, but I am aware of his allegations," he said.

We discussed the Panchen Lama, the child whom Beijing named as their chosen incarnation—one unrecognized by His Holiness. I asked him bluntly whether he believed Bliss and Wisdom was part of Beijing's broader spiritual strategy to control global Tibetan Buddhism.

His answer was equally direct:

"Yes. The Chinese Communist Party absolutely wants to insert itself into the spiritual succession of Tibetan Buddhism. Their plan is clear: discredit the Dalai Lama, elevate their own Panchen Lama, and influence organizations like Bliss and Wisdom to provide legitimacy to their version of Tibetan Buddhism."

He paused. Then added:

"They want to dominate forums of global Buddhism, not because they respect religion, but because they want to weaponize it. Religion is power. The CCP knows this."

I asked whether Taiwan had any concrete evidence of CCP infiltration of Bliss and Wisdom.

"Not directly. But the signs are there. We cannot confirm, but we can observe."

He clarified that Taiwan's government had not declared Bliss and Wisdom a CCP-controlled group, yet he acknowledged that many in civil society and within the Tibetan religious diaspora viewed them as politically compromised.

We moved on to the issue of scripture translation. I told him about our interviews with the nuns in PEI who admitted that no Tibetan scholars were overseeing the translation of ancient scriptures into Traditional Chinese.

He listened intently.

"In principle, such work must be overseen by highly trained monastics. Any alteration—even unintentional—can distort sacred meaning. Without proper oversight, these translations could become tools for soft ideological subversion."

I agreed.

"That's my fear as well. Especially when I hear that some of these groups are translating without external validation."

He added with calm clarity:

"In Tibet, religious leaders undergo decades of training. Authority is earned through discipline, not proclaimed through charisma or business success. Mary Jin does not fit this mould."

I asked him if he saw this pattern elsewhere—groups claiming Tibetan legitimacy but tethered to Beijing's agenda.

"Yes, of course. There are hundreds of Buddhist centres globally. Many are legitimate. But others have political backers and function more like cultural consulates than places of worship."

We returned to Bliss and Wisdom in PEI. I asked whether he believed their global footprint—spanning agriculture, education, even real estate—reflected genuine religious growth or a hidden political architecture.

His answer was sobering:

"They are wealthy. I've heard of their landholdings in Canada. I've also heard that they have access to large financial flows. And while I do not claim to know their internal accounts, any monastic group with over $500 million in assets should be treated not only as a religious body—but as an economic and political entity."

As we closed our discussion, I asked the final question, one that had lingered since my arrival in Taiwan:

"Do you believe Mary Jin is acting in good faith?"

Kelsang Gyaltsen did not answer immediately. He folded his hands. Then he spoke, not with outrage, but with gravity.

"I cannot say what is in her heart. But I can say this: if she sits atop a monastic hierarchy without having received proper training, without having earned that position by our traditional standards, and if she operates without transparency or oversight—then it is only right that the global Tibetan community ask serious questions."

INVESTIGATIVE SUMMARY: INTERPRETATION OF KELSANG GYALTSEN INTERVIEW

Our interview with Kelsang Gyaltsen, the representative of His Holiness the Dalai Lama, confirmed what many within Tibetan and Taiwanese religious circles have long suspected: Bliss and Wisdom, under the leadership of Mary Jin (Zhen-Ru), represents a divergence from traditional Tibetan Buddhist practice—not just in theology, but in political proximity.

Gyaltsen articulated clear concerns over Jin's unorthodox rise to authority—absent formal monastic training and operating from a model that is more corporate than clerical. He described how traditional lines of religious succession and discipline have been circumvented, echoing criticisms from defectors like Fan Yin. His most pointed concern, however, related to China's strategic ambition to co-opt Tibetan Buddhism through figures like the state-sanctioned Panchen Lama, and organizations like Bliss and Wisdom, which may serve as ideological conduits.

From an investigative standpoint, this interview validated our broader thesis: that Bliss and Wisdom's expansion in Canada is not merely a religious phenomenon, but a complex intersection of soft power, wealth, and potential influence operations. With no Tibetan scholars overseeing scripture translation and a layperson-turned-spiritual leader exercising sweeping authority, the organization bears the hallmarks of an engineered religious front—potentially useful to actors aligned with Beijing's United Front strategy.

In short, Gyaltsen's testimony underscores the risk: what appears as faith may function as political theatre—and Canada, like Taiwan, must decide how to respond.

DAY TWO, AFTERNOON: GOVERNMENT EYES OPEN

Later that same day, we met discreetly with a senior official from Taiwan's Ministry of Foreign Affairs (MOFA). He had previously served in Canada and had first-hand knowledge of the political engagements involving Bliss and Wisdom. The meeting was private, off-record in format but on-the-record in substance, with direct permission to quote him, so long as his name and current title were withheld.

He carried himself with the calm gravitas of someone who'd been observing quietly for years.

We spoke in a secure location. Jeff translated where needed, but the official's English was fluent. He began not with briefing notes, but with a memory.

"When I was in Canada, I was so surprised to see that in your small island, there's a big monastery, at least four hundred people or more, living there. . . . When we approached your premier of island province and also those elected officials, they were very proud of this monastery. . . . Not only bringing a good virtue and good immigrants, but also good money, good business."

He paused briefly, measuring the next sentence.

"But then at that time, that was about ten years ago. I don't think they really saw the whole picture. . . . They only saw the surface. And they didn't know that behind it, there's a very complicated relation between the monastery and the Chinese CCP and all those United Front Work Department efforts."

That assessment stuck with me; it wasn't just a concern. It was confirmation.

This was not a vague suspicion from activists or dissidents—it was a formal recognition from within the Taiwanese diplomatic and intelligence establishment that Bliss and Wisdom's outward spiritual mission was entangled with state-backed ideological operations. But I was struck by the fact that so many innocent followers had bought into the organization's mission to create a 1,000–year monastery on PEI and continue to donate to these goals.

I pressed him for further details.

He confirmed that the Taiwanese government had observed multiple indicators of alignment between Bliss and Wisdom and Beijing's soft-power strategies, including deepened interactions with the Buddhist Association of China, and organizational mimicry of the outreach patterns of the United Front Work Department.

"Do you believe the Canadian government understands this?" I asked.

He smiled faintly. "You're writing the book," he said. "I think they will." I thought to myself it is a bit crazy that as a publishing enterprise that we now were responsible for informing the public and government, but it certainly fit our fifty-year-long DNA. He then suggested I needed to work on publishing *Wilful Blindness* in Taiwan. I said I had, and you have the Taiwan book. No, the same story is here; you should ask Michael Cole to write it. He is the expert here and has studied this and written about it extensively. Political influence, corruption and organized crime all playing a role in trying to undermine democracy. The CCP's playbook is global and yet back at home our political, bureaucratic and business class don't seem to want to know.

A project for another time but for now on with the rest of the investigation.

DAY TWO, EVENING

We arrived at the apartment building a few minutes before 7:30. Jeff had spoken with Fan Yin earlier that day, and he had agreed to meet. No conditions, just caution. He understood who we were, and more importantly, why we were there.

When the elevator doors opened in the lobby, he was already waiting. Dressed in his monastic robes, simple and brown, his presence was calm, quiet. He bowed slightly, and we returned the gesture.

Without speaking, he turned and led us to the elevator. The ride to the eighth floor was silent.

Inside the apartment, the air was warm. Dim light. A small two-bedroom unit modestly furnished. His mother, whom we did not meet, stayed in the second bedroom. The living room was arranged around a low coffee table with a couch and two straight-back chairs. On the table was dinner: a homemade vegetarian meal, traditional in Chinese Buddhist households—braised tofu, stir-fried greens, rice, and a light mushroom broth.

We sat around the coffee table. Fan Yin smiled faintly. No words yet. There was a hospitality to him—measured, respectful, but sincere.

Shaun moved quietly around the edge of the room, setting up the camera. He adjusted angles, tested audio, kept the setup as discreet as possible. Fan Yin never flinched.

As we began eating, Jeff handled the early exchanges. No rush. No pressure. Fan Yin spoke softly, answering our early contextual questions as we ate.

I knew what was happening. This wasn't just a meal. This was a man—once silenced, once expelled, once anonymous—deciding whether we were worthy of the truth.

He had not spoken openly in nearly eight years.

And now, here he was.

After dinner, Fan Yin cleared the bowls and quietly set them in the kitchen sink. He returned and took his place cross-legged on a cushion, facing us squarely. He folded his hands.

There was no declaration. No speech. He simply said:

> "那时候，我们每一个人都要带钱去，每个人都带一万、两万加币。"
> "At that time, each of us was required to carry money—we each carried $10,000 or $20,000 in Canadian dollars."

I asked him how these trips were framed within the organization.

> "每年每年都有这样的活动 … 都是以修行名义组织的，但实际上是带现金。"
> "These trips happened every year, organized as 'spiritual retreats,' but in reality, it was about transporting cash."

I noted the precision of his phrasing. Not "gifts." Not "donations." Transporting.

> "很多很多人。不是一次，是连续几年。"
> "A lot of people. Not just once—this continued for years."

He spoke clearly, without emotion, but never with detachment. There was gravity in every word.

I asked whether Bliss and Wisdom had help moving the funds. Did the banks ever raise issues?

> "台湾这边的银行经理人 … 他们很多都是佛教徒，他们帮忙兑换，加拿大那边就不用申报。"
> "Many of the bank managers in Taiwan were Buddhists. They helped convert the currency. In Canada, there was no need to declare anything."

There was no bitterness in his voice—just observation. I asked what became of the money. Where did it end up?

> "PEI 的那个地方 … 表面上是修行中心，其实是他们的金钱和影响力中心。"
> "That place in PEI … it looks like a spiritual centre, but in reality, it's the core of their financial and influence network."

He then described the monastery's size, and how it became more than just a place of worship.

> "他们在那里建了大庙，还试图影响当地的政治人物。"
> "They built a large monastery there and attempted to influence local politicians."

The message was clear: Prince Edward Island wasn't chosen by accident. It was chosen for its remoteness, its openness, and its silence.

When we brought up Zhen-Ru, Fan Yin didn't flinch. He spoke plainly:

> "现在的这个组织，已经不是我们当初的那个修行团体了 … 是一个以她为核心的思想体系。"
> "This organization is no longer the spiritual group we once knew … it's a structure built entirely around her ideology."

He told us that she became a spiritual authority beyond question, elevated through repetition and enforced belief.

> "他们把忠诚当成修行的标准。"
> "They treated loyalty as the standard of spiritual cultivation."

Then we asked about support from China.

> "我认为福智他们之所以会变得这么强大，是因为他们背后有中国佛教协会支持。"
> "Bliss and Wisdom became so powerful because they had the backing of the Buddhist Association of China."

So this backs other open source intelligence on the infiltration of Buddhist monastic groups in Taiwan and other nations. We asked if he believed this was a spiritual alliance, or something more strategic.

He answered without hesitation.

> "他们利用宗教外衣，进行的是政治和经济渗透。"
> "They use religion as a cover for political and financial infiltration."

I asked why he had stayed silent for so long.

> "后来我提出问题，他们说我是精神有问题，就把我赶走了。"

> "When I started asking questions, they said I had mental problems. They forced me out."

And why speak now?

> "我觉得不能再沉默了."
> "I feel I can no longer remain silent."

There was no anger. Only resolve.

Near the end, I asked: "What would you say to Canadians? To the people on Prince Edward Island who may not know any of this?"

He looked directly into the camera.

> "First of all, I am ok. I want to tell Canadians—wake up. This is not a normal Buddhist group."
> "如果没有人说出真相，他们还会继续骗下去."
> "If no one tells the truth, they'll keep deceiving people."

I was thinking to myself, he must know the risks in telling his story and yet he had allowed us to film him on camera.

As I stood up to thank him Fan Yin spoke in Mandarin and Jeff was interpreting his final off the record comments to me. Jeff said "Dean, he wants to let you know that he is praying for you and that he is here for you. He is committed to helping you get the truth to the people."

I couldn't believe what I was hearing and as I spoke, I was filled with emotion and started to cry. I was astonished to have a person who had endured so much at the hands of what appeared objectively to me as a victim of systemic abuse, isolation, torment and one can even say evil. Now he was telling me (us), he was committed to me and here to serve me and our collective mission.

I thanked him and told him. "I am here for him, for His Holiness and for the preservation of Tibetan Buddhism as taught by qualified masters." I thanked him profusely and presented him with a copy of the Taiwan edition of *Wilful Blindness*, translated by 1841 Press and released in 2024 in Taiwan as my gift to him. It was a small token of my appreciation for his sacrifice.

As Jeff, Shaun, and I left his small apartment and reached the elevator having bowed to him on our exit, I now realized the enormity of our mission.

As a journalist, publisher, and now a documentary film producer in the moment I understood what was at stake. By this point in time our team had interviewed and consulted with over one hundred people and read over a thousand documents, but nothing mattered more to me than ensuring that those who had put faith and trust in our team to tell their story would finally be given a voice through the book you are reading and the documentary you can watch.

The responsibility was ours.

DAY 3

As I woke up the next morning, I realized I had to continue to absorb the incredible engagement over past two days with a Bliss and Wisdom follower, government officials, a journalist, and a key whistleblower who had risked his life to come forward to tell the truth. It was also evening back in Ontario and Quebec, so I sent my report to Garry and Michel on what yesterday had delivered.

I had a few conversations with Garry and Michel as well as Chris because we had gotten some phenomenal interviews that validated our research, and interviews with the countless people our team had been engaged with for more than fifteen months now.

So, we agreed we would convene for a more extensive meeting in Ottawa when I got back to Canada.

But for today I still had another meeting with Member of Parliament Fan Yun and Paster Chen, who had helped to make our trip such an overwhelming success through the Fan Yin interview.

MEETING MP FAN YUN: DEMOCRACY, DELAYS, AND DIRECT TALK

Before I left for Taiwan I was speaking with my colleague and Canadian Member of Parliament, Kevin Vuong. He had been a target of a nasty campaign by CCP operatives in the Liberal Party to smear his reputation, and it had worked: Justin Trudeau had dropped him from the caucus just after he became an MP for Spadina-Fort York in downtown Toronto. I told him I was on my way to Taiwan to finalize our investigation for the book and to try to get some key interviews in Taipei for our documentary.

He said he knew Fan Yun, who was a member of the Inter-Parliamentary Alliance on China (IPAC), an organization Optimum and I had worked with to highlight the CCP's egregious behaviour in Hong Kong, Tibet, Taiwan, and East Turkestan since 2021. He made the introduction and, of course, when I landed the meeting was arranged.

My meeting with Fan Yun, a sitting member of Taiwan's Legislative Yuan and the country's representative to IPAC, didn't unfold quite as planned. Originally, we had arranged to meet for lunch at a nearby restaurant. But like many things in the world of politics, schedules shifted. When she wasn't able to leave her office, one of her assistants—fluent in English and incredibly gracious—found me and took me directly to the Legislative Yuan.

Fan Yun and I ended up sharing a lunch of Taiwanese chicken and shrimp noodle bowls in the comfort of her office—simple fare, but perfectly fitting for a serious conversation.

Our discussion ranged from Taiwan's place within IPAC to the broader democratic struggle against the CCP's influence. Fan Yun spoke with quiet conviction about the importance of democratic alliances, insisting that IPAC isn't just a symbolic entity, but a strategic bulwark in the growing contest between open societies and authoritarian regimes.

When the subject of the Recall Movement surfaced, she nodded knowingly. She was clearly aware of the grassroots effort under way in Taoyuan and other districts. But as a legislator, she understood her limitations. She expressed admiration for the passion and civic engagement behind the movement, while noting—with appropriate restraint—that it wouldn't be suitable for her to publicly endorse it. Her respect for democratic processes was matched by a strong sense of institutional responsibility.

I naturally brought up Fuzhi (Bliss and Wisdom). She had little awareness of the group but did say that all of the Buddhist groups in Taipei were deeply infiltrated by the CCP. So, our story did not surprise her, but I felt it was better not to continue exploring this subject with her other than to make her aware, and she said she wanted to know when the documentary and the book would be released. I presented her with a copy of *Wilful Blindness* to thank her for taking the time to meet with me. It is something I just naturally do. A little knowledge in exchange for a little knowledge.

What struck me most was her balance—between principle and protocol, between political awareness and civic restraint. Fan Yun remains one of the clearest voices in Taiwan's democratic chorus, working across borders while remaining grounded in the legislative heart of her country.

LAST LIGHT IN TAIPEI: THE PASTOR, THE RECALL, AND A QUIET VISITOR

It was late afternoon in Taoyuan when I finally met Pastor Chen from the Dorcay Church, established in 2012. The unassuming Presbyterian Church set in a bustling neighbourhood stood at the heart of a movement that could shape Taiwan's democratic future. The clouds had hung heavy with an off-chance of rain the whole day and now the temperature was dropping. But the mood inside was unmistakably charged.

This was my last day on the ground in Taiwan, as Shaun our Director of Photography, had left to go back to Calgary earlier that morning—to a country that had just weathered an intense election and was now confronting the aftermath. I had come to speak with Pastor Chen, not just as a clergyman, but as one of the unlikely architects of Taiwan's Recall Movement. This was a civic uprising forged not in parliament or party offices, but in pews, classrooms, and street corners.

Before we began, I took a moment to thank him. The night before, I had interviewed Fan Yin—known publicly now as Zhen Ding—whose insights into spiritual resistance and authoritarian pressure were critical to my investigation. It was Pastor Chen and Sze, my interpreter for this interview, who had made that connection possible. As you now know, we had come to this church searching for someone who might know him. And Pastor Chen did.

But this time, I was alone and had not just come to talk about Fan Yin. First, I needed to understand the storm gathering in Taiwan and in his precinct, Taoyuan.

THE BIRTH OF THE RECALL

Sitting at a table in the small upstairs prayer room with a small, pedestrian-looking altar, Pastor Chen laid out the facts with a clarity that cut through the usual fog of politics. He and his congregation had watched with growing concern as Taiwan's legislature, now controlled by the Kuomintang (KMT) and the Taiwan People's Party (TPP), were pushing through three amendments that, taken together, represented a frontal assault on Taiwan's democratic institutions.

The first amendment made deep cuts to national security and social welfare funding. The second raised the bar for citizen-led recall initiatives, requiring personal ID photocopies and a significantly higher signature threshold, all measures that would chill civic engagement and open the door to data abuse. The third restructured legislative power itself, raising the voting threshold for passing laws from a simple majority to two-thirds. In effect, it handed permanent veto power to the ruling coalition.

"This is about more than law," Pastor Chen said calmly. "This is about control."

The result? A movement that began in one district and is now sweeping across six. Originally, the plan had been to target one or two KMT lawmakers in Taoyuan. But after the amendments were forced through in December, citizens across the political spectrum began showing up—blue voters, green voters, and those who never voted at all. Their message was simple: this was no longer a partisan issue. This was about survival.

A CHURCH TRANSFORMED

What's extraordinary about Pastor Chen is not just what he's doing—but where he's doing it. The church has become more than a place of worship. It is now a coordination hub, a classroom, a safe haven. During the week, children from working-class families gather here for tutoring. Some are the children of blue-collar workers. Others are the children of migrant labourers. All are treated with dignity.

"We tell them that if they work hard, they will have a future," Pastor Chen said. "But what kind of future are we offering them if we let authoritarianism creep into our laws?"

The church is part of the Presbyterian Church of Taiwan, a denomination with a long history of opposing KMT authoritarianism. The spiritual meets the political here—not as campaign slogans, but as moral obligation. "The Bible tells us to stand with those who cannot stand for themselves," he said. "And that is what this is."

A MOVEMENT WITHOUT PERMISSION

The Recall Movement is coordinated across six districts in Taoyuan. But it's not centralized. There's no official structure, no party funding. Just messaging apps, neighbourhood meetings, and people willing to give their time. It's a "team battle," Pastor Chen said, one being fought in living rooms, in schoolyards, and now, in front of television cameras. What started with a single local target now involves the potential recall of all six federal KMT legislators in the district.

"When we started," he said, "we thought maybe we could take back one or two. Now the people are demanding all six be held accountable."

I asked if this expansion risked spreading the movement too thin. "No," he replied. "It has made us stronger. The people are awake."

FIGHTING DISINFORMATION

As we spoke, I asked how the movement had been treated by local media and whether the CCP had attempted to interfere. Pastor Chen was direct.

"At first, only one station would report on us. Now, almost all of them are covering the story. The CCP doesn't want this movement to succeed. And we know they're watching."

He had just returned from one such interview—his third that week. The change was visible. What began in obscurity was now a national story. And the world, slowly, was beginning to pay attention.

When I asked if I could record a short message from him for Canadian viewers, he didn't hesitate. "Let the world see what is happening here," he said. "Taiwan is not asleep."

A QUIET VISITOR

Only after we had completed the formal part of the interview did we circle back to Fan Yin.

"I'm grateful that you introduced us," I told him, "his voice is a vital part of this puzzle."

Pastor Chen nodded. "He came quietly," he said. "Not to lead. Not to speak. Just to help."

Fan Yin—now Zhen Ding—had come to the church not as a known activist, but as a volunteer. His presence wasn't symbolic. It was personal. He wasn't seeking the spotlight. But he understood the stakes.

A religious figure who had told his entire story to Pastor Chen about his experience within Fuzhi, or Bliss and Wisdom. He had dropped out of sight and whether by luck or not we had found the church and him. Fan Yin, or Zhen Ding, had no formal organization behind him. No network. No staff. Just conviction. He had lived through what it means to resist authoritarian control having survived a near-death experience with tuberculosis in the monastery in PEI

It told me a lot about him, and the fact he was engaging publicly once again and working to defend democracy said it all. In one of their communications to our team, the nuns were busy trying to convince our team he was a CCP disinformation agent and a liar.

His presence, "it meant something to us," Pastor Chen said. "To have him here."

For me, it was the final piece of the puzzle.

This church in Taoyuan wasn't just a campaign headquarters. It was a sanctuary of faith, resistance, and quiet courage. A place where democracy wasn't being defended by elites, but by pastors, students, and monks. And that last image, of Pastor Chen and Zhen Ding, standing side-by-side, told the real story of Taiwan's fight and that of Fan Yin.

The Recall Movement sprang from citizens' fear for their democratic freedoms and the need to fight the CCP's attempt to take them over politically, quietly like the Buddhist Association of China taking over Tibetan Buddhism in China, Taiwan, and the rest of the world. Fan Yin was back battling against the tyranny he saw in Bliss and Wisdom's quiet takeover by Zhen-Ru who, as Michel's analysis suggests, has been working in concert with the CCP for decades.

It was a fitting end to three intense days of high-stakes interviews, B-roll footage, and an unfiltered look at Taiwan's precarious frontline with authoritarian pressure. What had begun as a journey of cautious prospects quickly transformed into a critical chapter in our broader investigation.

With Fan Yin—His Holiness's representative—and others who generously agreed to speak on background, we now had what we needed to complete both the book and the documentary. The voices, insights, and quiet defiance we had gathered would form the backbone of our story.

But this new clarity came with a renewed sense of urgency.

With these revelations in hand, we three investigators would now need to head to Prince Edward Island one more time. What has been unfolding there, in its own quiet way, demanded the same scrutiny. Taiwan had confirmed our witnesses and research and had opened our eyes; now we could share some of our findings and get the final interviews on camera and for the book.

With one night to chill I headed out to the Grand Palace for a bite to eat and then a long journey back to Canada.

CHAPTER 19
THE RECKONING
FINAL TESTIMONIES FROM THE FRONT LINES

It had started with a chapter from a book, an improbable lead on an improbable island. In December of 2023, a group of Islanders approached Optimum to talk about doing a book launch with a couple of our books. What some of them had seen going all the way back to 2015 were the first signs involving a new organization on the Island that for many were easy to dismiss: a strangely funded construction project here, a vacant property sold three times in six months there, and out-of-place continuous cash payments for work done and properties purchased. But the organization seemed very legitimate to the many politicians who extolled its virtues, its money, and its numbers.

It presented itself as a religious nonprofit with a clear mandate and a 1000-year plan. But for those trained to see patterns, to look at the mosaic, what had once been scattered anomalies began to form a map and resemble a strategy built around the Game-of-Go,[108] or Wei Chi in Chinese, one that pointed not just to Prince Edward Island, but to the United Front Work Department with ties all the way back to Communist China in late 1999 when Master Jhen-Ru made her presence known to Master Jih-Chang and Venerable Abbot Vanyin (Fan Yin). Something none of the Islanders or intelligence agencies in Canada understood or knew how to act on.

Over the course of eighteen months, the investigation led by our team would spiral outward from its humble Maritime origins and uncover a latticework of CCP-linked influence operations on Canadian, American, Taiwanese, and Mainland China's soil. What they exposed was not merely elite capture—it was the quiet colonization of provincial economics, real estate, immigration, and politics. PEI, once cherished as the "Birthplace of Confederation," had become, in the words of one federal official, "a prototype for foreign-directed community engineering."

Now, in March 2025, the final stage of the investigation was under way. We were there to document the interviews on camera as well so that there was a record, one that would provide us with an accurate reflection of the Islanders who witnessed many pieces of the puzzle over the past decade and a half. Seven interviews, each a thread woven into a single, harrowing tapestry. Each conducted with a specific focus and a specific witness—people who had lived, worked, and suffered within systems warped by foreign leverage.

The interviewers were not academics or journalists detached from the consequences—they were former intelligence officers, law enforcement commanders, and public watchdogs. Michel Juneau-Katsuya, with his decades inside CSIS and intimate knowledge of the CCP's overseas strategies, brought gravitas and precision to each exchange. Garry Clement, a seasoned RCMP veteran and financial crimes expert, had the language and instincts to pursue what most overlook—the flow of money. And Dean Baxendale, publisher and investigator, offered both public credibility and a relentless commitment to truth in an era dominated by curated silence.

Each man carried the burden of knowing that what they unearthed could very well define Canada's national security posture for the next decade. What follows in this chapter is not speculation—it is testimony. These are the voices of those who saw what others refused to see: a former Solicitor General of Canada, a provincial whistleblower who lost everything, a tradesman who found himself in the middle of something far darker than a renovation contract, a shipbuilder who began noticing late-night deliveries that weren't fish, a bank teller trained in anti-money laundering who watched as rules were rewritten, and a real estate agent who saw her community erode from the inside out.

Each account stands alone in its witness yet, together, they form a chilling ledger of infiltration. As Garry Clement would say, "It's not always about the espionage—we must follow the economic compromise." And as Michel Juneau-Katsuya reminded us throughout, "Influence isn't always illegal. But left unchecked, it becomes occupation by another name."

What began on PEI did not stay there. This is the reckoning. This is what the Island saw when the masks came off.

THE CONTRACTOR — "SOMETHING BEHIND THAT DOOR"

(Interviewed by Michel Juneau-Katsuya)

When I sat down with this contractor, I expected a straightforward account of a renovation job. What I got instead was the anatomy of what seems to be a shadow operation.

He was a tradesman—no-nonsense, plain-spoken, the kind of man who measured truth in square footage and torque. He'd worked for the monks before, but this job, out in Heatherdale, was different.

"I was building for the 'Master,'" he said, referring to the spiritual head of the Buddhist organization. "I was renovating a bedroom and master bathroom. The Master's suite was palatial: custom stonework, radiant floors, imported woods, hidden ducts."

He described the great interactions with the monks who were eager to come for a few hours to help and get trained on different aspects of what he was constructing. They were always pleasant, respectful, and always willing to do whatever was needed for Master Jhen-Ru.

However, one thing stuck out in my mind. The level of surveillance in a teaching or training centre, with special quarters for the Master. The contractor told me there were cameras everywhere—inside, outside, in every corridor.

"You couldn't move without being watched. And there were rooms we weren't allowed into. Not just locked. Off-limits."

I raised my eyebrows. "Did that strike you as odd for a residence?"

He nodded. "Everything about it did. We have to get into all the rooms and at first there was one door that felt locked, and I said, 'Okay, well we can't get in there. I'll have to figure out something else.' And [the plumber] was like, 'Oh, just try it again.' So, I jarred the door open and something pushed me back. It wasn't an air balancing issue in the house or anything like that. It was quite a bit of force. It *pushed* me back. Somebody was behind that door."

"You and the plumber were both there?" I asked.

"Yes, he witnessed it happen. He was like, 'you had that door open.' I could see the clasp. I could see the cameras in that hallway."

"So, they saw you?"

"Yeah. There are cameras everywhere."

SUSAN HOLMES — "YOU DON'T GET TO REWRITE INTEGRITY"

(Interviewed by Dean Baxendale)

Dean had seen whistleblowers before. Most wore the quiet fatigue of people who had learned too late that doing the right thing rarely comes with protection. But Susan Holmes carried herself with the calm defiance of someone who had nothing left to lose—and no intention of fading quietly.

When she sat across from Dean, the look in her eyes was not bitterness. It was clarity. For more than a decade, Susan Holmes had been at the centre of the Island's immigration bureaucracy as the manager of the Population Secretariat. A seasoned educator, policy expert, and federal liaison, she was the kind of public servant the system was supposed to rely on. Until it turned on her.

"What happened with that ESL (English as a Second Language) contract?" Dean asked.

She took a moment. "It was supposed to be merit-based. We did everything by the book. Holland College submitted a stronger proposal. The adjudicators—none of them political—agreed. It was unanimous."

Dean nodded, letting her speak.

"But when I brought the results to my director, she said something I'll never forget: 'This is not the outcome we were looking for.'" Holmes stared ahead. "Then she asked me to change the scores. Make it look like Study Abroad Canada matched Holland College."

Susan refused. "I told them I wouldn't do it. That if they wanted to change it, they'd have to find someone else. I knew what that meant. But I wasn't going to sell my name."

From that point forward, Holmes's career was dismantled. Overnight, her duties tripled. Her team was stripped away. She was locked out of meetings, isolated, and harassed. "They wanted me to quit," she said. "Instead, I fought."

Holmes described the key figures: Frank Zhou and Sherry Huang, owners of Study Abroad Canada, individuals later linked to the United Front Work Department through international intelligence channels. "They were always in the building. Not just visitors—fixtures. Smiling, offering help, asking how your kids were. Like they belonged more than we did."

Dean asked, "Do you believe the contract was about more than language training?"

Holmes's reply was immediate. "Yes. It was access. Influence. Control. They weren't just trying to win a bid—they were embedding themselves. Into policy. Into the system."

Dean leaned forward. "Were there consequences when you went public?"

She laughed, without humour. "They watched my house. They followed me. My settlement came after CSIS intervened, after the Privacy Commissioner confirmed my rights were violated. But even then—I lost everything. My job. My name. Years of my life."

Her voice, unwavering, carried the weight of institutional betrayal. "You don't get to rewrite integrity. They did what they could to erase me. But I'm still here."

Dean asked what gave her the strength.

Holmes answered simply: "This Island. I wasn't going to let it be sold off—one contract at a time."

RUSSELL COMPTON — "FOLLOW THE BAGS"

(Interviewed by Garry Clement)

Garry Clement was used to talking to hard men—logistical minds in a dirty world. So, when he sat down with Russ Compton, the shipbuilder turned reluctant witness, he recognized the controlled unease. Compton wasn't used to cameras, but he knew the docks, the roads, and more importantly—the whispers.

"I saw the bags," Compton said. "More than once. Dropped off at odd hours, no logos, no tags. Sometimes three or four at a time. Always delivered to the same place—those Buddhist monastery offices near Montague."

"Cash?" Garry asked.

"I think so. Can't prove it. But I know what heavy looks like. And I know what's in an envelope when it sags like that."

Russ had been in the marine industry his whole life. Built NorCan Marine from nothing. But what started as a modest shipbuilding operation had slowly become surrounded—physically and economically—by an influx of foreign-owned shell groups and "religious" enterprises that didn't act like either.

"They bought up lobster quotas in Nova Scotia. Now they're coming here. It's not just buying—it's boxing us out. Local fishermen can't sell their catch anymore unless they go through their channels."

Garry nodded. "So, you're seeing economic control first?"

"That's the surface," Russ replied. "But it goes deeper. Land being bought at triple value. Homes left empty. It's not development. It's laundering, and it's saturation."

Garry asked about the monasteries.

"They started active. Real farming. Now they let land go fallow. That's not agriculture—it's a front."

Russ grew quiet. "If forty thousand people moved here overnight from anywhere, it'd change the place. But this isn't people—it's structure. Silent, foreign structure. The kind you don't vote out."

He finished with a shrug that said too much.

"You follow the bags, you follow the story. That's all I've done."

THE RECKONING

THE REAL ESTATE AGENT — "A THOUSAND-YEAR PLAN"

(*Interviewed by Michel Juneau-Katsuya*)

I had dealt with foreign agents before. What made this interview different was the civilian nature of the subject—a local realtor, not a spy or politician. But the story she told was no less damning.

"They came to me in 2016," she said. "Said they needed someone local, someone who understood the community. At first, I thought it was just another new investor group."

That illusion didn't last long.

"They gave me a list. Houses they wanted. Not houses for sale—houses with owners. Some weren't even on the market. I called people, and they were confused, sometimes angry. They'd already been approached—directly—by monks or reps. Offering cash."

"Was this organized?"

She nodded. "Absolutely. No inspections. No mortgages. Hundreds of thousands over market value. It wasn't buying—it was removing."

The realtor noticed a pattern. "Once a property was bought, it stayed empty. Ninety percent of one neighbourhood—just gone. People left. The community died in silence."

I asked if she raised concerns.

"I did. And I stopped getting calls. They started buying directly. My name was erased."

One monk had left her with a phrase she never forgot: "This isn't a ten-year plan. *It's a thousand-year plan.*"

She didn't know what it meant at the time. Now, she said, "I do."

THE BANK TELLER — "YOU DON'T QUESTION RELIGION"

(*Interviewed by Garry Clement*)

Of all the interviews, the teller's may have been the quietest—yet the most haunting.

"I was trained in money laundering," she told me. "I knew what placement, layering, and integration looked like. And this matched everything."

For eight years, the teller worked at Scotiabank in Charlottetown. What she saw was not just large cash deposits—it was institutional permission.

"They'd come on weekends. ATM drops. Sometimes $100,000 or more. Always $100 bills. Sequential."

"And you flagged it?" I asked.

"We did everything we were supposed to. Notes. Reports. Internal alerts."

"Did the bank escalate?"

She shook her head. "They told us it was religious. That we don't question religion."

She'd later hear from friends at CIBC that the same deposits were happening there too.

"It wasn't just our branch. It was the system. The silence. Management didn't want attention. And it wasn't just about the cash."

"What else?"

"There were contractors who became millionaires."

"But you never got any sense that the bank was worried?"

"No, no. I didn't sense that there was any worry because banks operate in goals, right? So, we were meeting management's goals."

"So, it's all about bonuses going up?"

"Yeah."

WAYNE EASTER — "THE LAND IS BORROWED"

(Interviewed by Dean Baxendale)

Dean Baxendale had met with many politicians during his career in media and intelligence work, but few exuded the mixture of rural sensibility and institutional command that Wayne Easter did. A former Member of Parliament for Prince Edward Island for twenty-eight years, former Solicitor General of Canada, and longtime Chair of the House Finance Committee, Easter was, by most measures, an unimpeachable source on matters of sovereignty, agriculture, and governance. His legacy was carved deep into the fabric of PEI—not just through federal funding programs and political reform, but through the very land itself, which he farmed and defended for decades.

Their meeting was quiet, intentionally so, and held in a farmhouse with windows overlooking red-soil fields outside of Hunter River. Easter preferred face-to-face conversations, away from the din of Ottawa. He had been watching the investigation unfold from a distance—closely enough to know it was serious, and grave enough to finally speak publicly.

Dean opened simply. "What do you see happening to the Island, Wayne?"

Easter didn't hesitate. "The land is borrowed from our children. What's happening now . . . it's theft by complexity."

He leaned forward, both hands resting atop a notepad he hadn't touched. He spoke like a man used to giving testimony—not in sound bites, but in substance.

Easter recounted the history of land protection laws in PEI with reverence and clarity. "After Confederation, the first major political battle on this Island was about land. It was owned by absentee landlords in England. Islanders fought for the right to own the land they worked. What's happening now is a betrayal of that fight."

He referenced the Belize Bliss and Wisdom Group, a foreign-backed enterprise linked to a series of shadowy land acquisitions. "There are people coming in, buying up farms, entire sections—using shell companies, offshore accounts. It violates not just the letter, but the spirit of the law."

Dean nodded. "Why hasn't it been stopped?"

"Because we don't know what we're up against," Easter replied. "And when we do, we call it 'investment.' That word has become a shield. But it's not investment when the land is empty, the buildings are vacant, and the moneys untraceable. That's laundering."

He didn't mince words. "I was part of the committee that created NSICOP (National Security and Intelligence Committee of Parliamentarians) to investigate national security threats. I can tell you with confidence—Canada is behind. The other Five Eyes partners have raised the alarm. We're not just losing land—we're losing credibility."

Easter reflected on the influx of CCP-related assets not as a theoretical risk, but as a proven pattern. "You don't need soldiers when you can buy the land under someone's feet and silence them with a foundation grant or political donation."

Dean pressed him gently. "Do you believe this goes beyond economic distortion?"

Easter looked at him and said plainly, "I think it's about control. Quiet, persistent, legal-looking control. If you don't know the origin of the money or the goal of the buyer, how can you pretend it's just business?"

Then, softer: "I've seen families forced to sell. Not because they wanted to—but because they couldn't match offers inflated beyond market logic. Then the buyers leave the land untouched. It becomes ghost territory."

Dean paused. "So, what should Canada do now?"

Easter's answer was sharp. "Public inquiry. No more task forces with soft findings. If we can't protect PEI, the Birthplace of Confederation, from foreign capture, what hope does Vancouver or Toronto have?"

The interview ended with a silence that spoke louder than the transcript. Wayne Easter's testimony was not the beginning of the investigation—it was its indictment.

JACK AND BRAD — "ALL IN CASH"

(Interview Conducted by Dean Baxendale)

I wasn't sure what to expect when I met with Brad, who owned a successful equipment sales and service centre, but I had some high expectations. Jan Matajcek had set up the meeting and told me this guy has known the monk group (GEBIS) for a long time. I reached out to Brad and told him I was flying back to Toronto in the afternoon and was hoping he could fit me into to his schedule. He readily agreed.

I had just finished an interview with Jack, a supporter of the nuns and monks who had been on the Island for more than forty years. He was an old-timer and had been advocating for GWBI for years. Jack had also sold his properties to them and was clearly sold on the virtues of GWBI and all the good they could bring to the Island. Good virtue and good money, I suppose. He was at the Three Rivers town council meeting the night before where the mayor and council had approved the permit to expand the GWBI's incredible facility by another 80,000 square feet (7,432 sq. metres) to house more nuns wishing to study Tibetan Buddhism on PEI.

I asked him what he thought of the meeting. "It was great for those approving of the nuns and the establishment and all that, and not for the dissidents."

For me that was a telling description. Dissidents. That is what the CCP tells the world when describing journalists, academics. Intel analysts, Tibetans, Uyghurs, Falun Gong and pro-Democracy Hong Kongers, and Taiwanese individuals and groups when they try to paint them as being enemies of the CCP.

Our interview was interrupted by a patron of the local Tim Hortons (where we met) because I was wearing my "Canada is Not for Sale" hat. The patron wanted to express her gratitude for Doug Ford and his stand against the Trump administration regarding his threat to impose a 25% reciprocal tariff[109] on electricity being exported to New York State and others. She said she had a friend that would kill to get that hat. How much is it? We had a pleasant chat and finally I told her the hat was not for sale. She laughed and we ended our conversation.

Next, after Jack asked about my interest in this story and how he understood I was a journalist, I talked of Ben Roger's book The China Nexus and the fact that His Holiness was interviewed for the book. Ben and had I travelled to Dharamshala to present a copy of the book to his Holiness in 2023. Jack was impressed by my dedication to Tibetan Buddhism. I was also hoping it would help him to trust me.

He then said about the nuns, "I am not 100% sure but I am 90% sure they are Tibetan Buddhists under the Dalai Lama."

And there it was, the illusion that His Holiness was directing this group or overseeing it in some way! They are not, as the Tibetan Central Administration has stated to us through our various in-person and telephone interviews. The nuns and monks represent Buddhism of some form, but one that's influenced by the Sinicization and influence operations of the CCP as outlined by Michel in Chapter 12, "The Poor Guru Who Wears Prada."

He then told me he was taking Master Zhen-Ru's teachings online from a monk who works for Bliss and Wisdom in the United States. Those texts are filled with good virtues to be sure, but she is the "TEACHER" so her philosophy, her take, her brand—the CCP's brand of Tibetan Buddhist philosophy—is being taught to unsuspecting people. Some are drawn to Bliss and Wisdom by the virtues of releasing lobsters back into the ocean, picking up garbage from side of the road, or offering muffins to the poor.

We were 45 minutes into the interview, and Jack said I could quote him but not to use his proper name in the book. I thanked him and said I had to go because I had to meet a couple more people before I left.

On my way I stopped by the Aspin Kemp parking lot, where Russ gave me another hat I had left behind during Garry's interview with him for the documentary. I thanked him for all of his help and honesty and for agreeing to be part of the story and tell the world about what he saw.

I told him that Jason Aspin had declined an interview on camera after we had got to the Island. I suggested that Jason had been all in on China like every other Islander who had access through Frank Zhou to China.

We must emphasize that there is nothing illegal or wrong about that strategy, as it has been a focal point of the federal Global Affairs Department since the '90s, as you learned earlier.

What I did not tell him was that during my conversation with Jason he had confirmed that he was introduced to a wealthy Bliss and Wisdom investor and patron in China. His son even came to live with Jason.

Yet on numerous occasions Bliss and Wisdom told us they have no operations in China, which seemed once again to confirm our investigation and flew in the face of the middle management here on the Island who probably do not understand the bigger picture. That investor is now in business with Jason Aspin and his former wife in hotel investments on the Island. Like many Chinese nationals, they are loyal to their party, but they are also loyal to diversifying their risk and moving capital into place in the West.

Bliss and Wisdom seems to be a conduit for that opportunity, given their three-week investment and Buddhist sanctuary retreats held on the Island every six months or so. Who says money and religion don't mix, something Michel and Garry had been hammering home to me for the past eighteen months.

Follow the money, they said and so I did while driving like a bat out of hell to get to Brad. I am glad I did because the interview with Brad was the cherry on top of the cake.

I arrived knowing I only had thirty minutes or could press my luck by getting to the airport thirty minutes before departure.

Brad offered me a coffee and then we got straight to the conversation. He has dealt with the monks for more than a decade. He slipped me a piece of paper with dates and transaction amounts hand-written on both sides.

"All cash," he said. I was a bit startled because there was one transaction that stood out amongst the others. Dated July 25, 2015 for $102,600 (see Exhibit 6 on p. 219).

"That payment came in cash?" I asked again, knowing the answer.

"Yes, always cash."

"How did they explain it to you?"

"Well, Eli who represents GEBIS said whenever they make a payment, we are just waiting for the donation to come."

A donation of $102,600 handed over in a paper bag.

"How did the bills come?"

"They were crisp, clean fifties and hundreds."

"As if they were taken from one bank and then given to you," I said. "It looked that way to me." I then said, "No cheques, no e-deposits?"

"No, all cash, except for one."

It had me thinking, had the cash come in with monks travelling to PEI or in a black bag out of Ontario or from one of the retreats that brought wealthy Buddhist followers from Taiwan and China to PEI?

Before I left I thanked him on behalf of our team who, I had explained to him earlier, had the collective experience and knowledge of more than ninety years in law enforcement and intelligence gathering. I told Brad I would send him an invitation to the book launch in the spring. For me it was verification of the patterns that said this needs to be thoroughly investigated by the RCMP and a full-on inquiry, as Wayne Easter recommends. As I got into my car, I called Garry first and then Michel and said, "You will never guess what I found out today."

They could, and it just confirmed everything they already knew. No one on the Island, not the businesses, not the banks, and certainly not the politicians gave a rat's ass about the flood of money and where it came from. It was good for an impoverished province and that is all that matters.

But in a game of shadows, nothing is as it seems!

CHAPTER 20
THE FORWARD OPERATING BASE YOU DIDN'T SEE COMING
PRINCE EDWARD ISLAND

Throughout the book we have attempted to present a story consistent with a bigger strategy. Whether strategically planned or simply an outcome of China's Belt and Road Strategy, Prince Edward Island and Eastern Canada in our opinion are part of a larger strategy to envelop Canada from coast to coast.

But for readers to better understand the bigger context of how the concept of and what constitutes an FOB (forward operating base) fits into the CCP's larger 2049 strategy[110] today, we need to take you on a short journey from past to present.

Forward operating bases, by other names, have been with us for more than two millennia. The Romans had their castra[111]—fortified outposts strung across frontiers, enabling projection of power deep into contested regions. Genghis Khan[112] used mobile yurt cities[113] to control the conquered steppes. The British seeded the seas with coaling stations,[114] ready to refuel their empire. These weren't merely military encampments, they were instruments of influence. And in today's age of grey zone warfare—where adversaries prefer subversion to confrontation—forward operating bases don't need airstrips or armories. Some come disguised as language schools. Others as ports, farms, or religious centres. But their function remains the same: to influence, to surveil, and ultimately, to control.

During the Cold War, the Soviets deployed sleeper cells, trade delegates, and cultural attachés across the West. The Chinese Communist Party (CCP) has refined this playbook for the twenty-first century. I remember attending a Montreal roundtable hosted by the U.S. Consul General. There, a senior State Department official said in conversation with Michel and me "It's not just Havana or Caracas. We're watching Barbados, given China's influence

THE FORWARD OPERATING BASE YOU DIDN'T SEE COMING

on the government and its transition from being a former colony to a republic. Accounts were that PRC representatives simply showed up with more cash to buy the now president's support. China had entrenched itself in the Caribbean, using economic aid, infrastructure investment, and diplomatic charm to establish leverage. When Barbados distanced itself from the Crown and declared itself a republic, many assumed a natural evolution of sovereignty. But for those of us who were watching and follow grey zone activity, it bore the fingerprints of soft power encroachment.

That brings us back to our story on Prince Edward Island (PEI)—a province previously rarely associated with international intrigue. And yet, we couldn't ignore what we were seeing. PEI had become a proving ground of quiet influence operations, supported by economic engagement, political relationships, and spiritual outreach. We weren't speculating. We were tracking a pattern, eerily familiar to those of us who'd watched the Caribbean shift towards Beijing, and having control and influence on the northeastern flank of the United States was something few could now ignore.

Back in 2016, PEI Premier Wade MacLauchlan was pursuing a bold vision: quadruple the province's trade with China to $160 million. At the time, PEI exported approximately $40 million worth of goods to China—primarily lobster, mussels, naval technology, and frozen vegetables.

That strategy, cloaked in economic logic, bore an uncomfortable resemblance to CCP tactics used in other jurisdictions. By 2023, a change in government had brought China's trade rank down to fourth place, with exports totalling roughly $41.5 million. It was a reversal of the earlier trajectory. But the infrastructure of influence remained—relationships, agreements, and the echo of a previous path. Trade had not expanded, but neither had the CCP's foothold been dismantled.

Let us be clear: this is not about a trade figure. PEI's total exports hit $2.6 billion in 2023. China accounts for just over 1.6% of that. The concern isn't numerical dependency—it's strategic vulnerability. When a foreign power has successfully built soft power bridges through local elites, educational exemptions, and economic incentives, it gains something more valuable than GDP share: access and influence. As a good student of Sun Tsu, Michel taught us that "influence is a far easier strategy to execute than control or siege."

PEI's strategic location makes it far more than a sleepy fishing province. It is within reach of Halifax, home to Canada's East coast naval operations. It lies along NATO shipping routes, and important undersea communications cables are just a few miles off its coast. It is part of North America's maritime perimeter. It is also where our fleet will leave to patrol and defend the Canadian Arctic. The Chinese Communist Party's People's Liberation

Army doesn't need a naval base here to matter. A forward-operating influence centre, concealed within dual-use infrastructure or civilian cultural initiatives, would suffice. Just ask Sri Lanka or Djibouti or the Solomon Islands outlined earlier in the book.

In our research, we noted several markers consistent with China's forward operating base model in Eastern Canada. These include:

- **Civilian infrastructure with strategic utility:** Seafood processing facilities, agricultural logistics, strategic industries, and academic partnerships. Any of these could be co-opted for surveillance, data gathering, or cyber intrusions.
- **United Front Work Department outreach:** CCP-affiliated groups working with diaspora populations to monitor, influence, or suppress dissident voices. These aren't theoretical. Canada's security agencies have already acknowledged the presence of such operations.
- **Curriculum-exempt educational institutions:** Schools linked to the Taiwanese-originated but mainland-complicit Bliss and Wisdom organization have reportedly received exemptions from curriculum oversight on PEI where English is not even taught. Annual checks prearranged with school officials? That's not oversight—that's optics. When we spoke with PEI government employees responsible for the education program and asked how many children were kept at the Bliss and Wisdom monastery, they did not know.
- **Political softening via economic carrots:** Investment in export-based industries that align provincial fortunes with foreign buyers. While Premier Dennis King has since pivoted toward stronger U.S. trade relations, the previous government's open door to Beijing remains a cautionary legacy.

China's doctrine of Unrestricted Warfare,[115] authored by PLA colonels Qiao Liang and Wang Xiangsui, outlines a chilling strategy: win without fighting. Cyber warfare, economic coercion, legal warfare, and information manipulation are the tools. You don't need tanks to dominate a region. You need leverage over its economy, its networks, and its political and business elite. Perhaps the most telling reference comes from Chapter 5, when the authors state: "Most of these attacks are not military actions, and yet they can be completely viewed as or equal to warfare actions which force other nations to satisfy their own interests and demands."

Could PEI be militarily useful in a conflict? Unlikely in the traditional sense. But in a grey zone scenario—where signals intelligence, economic instability, and political division matter more than missiles—the Island becomes a vulnerable node. A CCP-aligned infrastructure project here could serve as a quiet sensor. A data centre, port, or telecom hub with hidden capabilities? All feasible, all deniable.

This brings us to the quietest—and perhaps most dangerous—front: spiritual soft power. The Bliss and Wisdom Buddhist group has long-standing plans for a massive thousand-year monastery on PEI. On the surface, it seems to be a cultural and religious initiative. But if leadership of this organization is either dependent on, or actively serving, CCP interests, the implications are profound. A spiritual FOB is far harder to challenge. It cloaks influence in benevolence. It preys on our multicultural tolerance. It survives scrutiny because few dare to question its intent.

This is why we raise the alarm. PEI may not be under direct siege. But it has been scouted, softened, and, in some ways, compromised. The right kind of infrastructure. The wrong kind of oversight. The continued willingness of officials to invite foreign partnership without due diligence. All of this signals one goal: vulnerability, manipulation, and, ultimately, influence. All that facilitated tacitly by greed and wilful blindness.

As we've seen from the Caribbean to East Africa, and from the South Pacific[116] to the Port of Hamburg,[117] once a forward operating base is established, it rarely stays dormant. It expands. It evolves. And when the next global crisis erupts, it activates.

If you really want to get into the strategic mind of the CCP, learn the game of "Go." A thousand-year-old game that is still today the most strategic game learned by all political and military Chinese. In that game, you come to understand the role and influence of an FOB.

Eventually, when it comes to CCP soft power initiatives, always remember to follow the money.

EXHIBIT I

Reference Letter: Susan Holmes [11/10/2010 1:02 AM]

Dear Dr. Mayne,

As a co-chair of the FPT Settlement Working group, I would like to take this opportunity to express my appreciation and acknowledgement of the contribution of Prince Edward Island's representative, Susan Holmes, to the work of this committee over the last year. As you know, over the past several months all jurisdictions have been collaborating to define national settlement and integration outcomes. This work has brought together many different perspectives across the country on how to define Canada's success as a nation in settling and integrating the many immigrants we welcome to our country.

    Susan has brought valuable insight and analysis to our discussions, both at the full committee and as a member of the subcommittees. She has conveyed the particular challenges and perspective of Prince Edward Island, and her contribution has helped our work reflect the complexity of newcomer settlement and integration across the country. In addition, Susan has helped us break through deadlocks and turn the corner on difficult issues. She brings a particular dynamic to the team that has greatly enhanced our effectiveness and the positive interaction of the working group. I look forward to continuing to work with Susan as we finalize our reports for Ministers in the year ahead.

I would also like to thank you for your role in supporting this work. I have found this to be a very collaborative working group.

Sincerely,
Angela Arnet Connidis,
Co-chair, FPT Settlement Working Group, (Canada)

EXHIBITS

Angela Connidis
Director, Horizontal Policy Development and Coordination | Directrice, Elaboration et coordination de politique horizontale

NHQ - Integration | AC - Intégration

Citizenship and Immigration Canada | Citoyenneté et Immigration Canada
180 Kent Street Ottawa ON K1A 1L1 | 180 rue Kent Ottawa ON K1A 1L1 Office | Bureau KENT 8-76

Angela.Connidis@cic.gc.ca
Telephone | Téléphone 613-946-0572
Facsimile | Télécopieur 613-954-9144
Government of Canada | Gouvernement du Canada

EXHIBIT 2

Phone call with Serge Serviant transcribed by Susan Holmes in 2010 following her dismissal.

- Literal Chiz objective extortion of the PEI economy to create a even larger elite class
- They need to increase this elite to stay in power —
- to stay in power means to create an even bigger elite & a greater number of poor or impoverished citizens.
- the objective of the perversion of the PNP was to maintain the establishment & keep people poor.
- Only 7% of the Investor's group in PEI (through the Immigrant Program) met the criteria

EXHIBITS

Official Languages  Les langues officielles

www.peifc-cfipe.gc.ca

without meeting the criteria we open ourselves as a country or a province to national security issues.

This government is in need of investigation

RE: embezzlement, Money laundering & income tax evasion

95% of businesses in PNP are solely owned by the Manager (director) or the family

2007 = 11 ministers got PNP Money

EXHIBIT 3

Date: May 25, 2025 at 17:44:40 EDT

To: Dean Baxendale <deanb@optimumpublishinginternational.com>
Cc: Garry Clement <gclement@clementadvisorygroup.ca>, "mjk@tngcorp.com" <mjk@tngcorp.com>

Dean—

Thank you for reaching out to us and trying to provide a balanced perspective to the book.

We appreciate you wanting to do your part as a global citizen and shed light on a critical global issue. However, we would like to point out that much of your "evidence" in trying to show Bliss and Wisdom ("B&W") to be a CCP agent is actually oversimplified assumptions. In addition, we will not provide any personal information that is unrelated to the public.

Our responses are below in bold

Thank you for waiting for our response.

Heather, Sabrina, Joanna and Jingli

On Mon, May 12, 2025 at 3:20 PM Dean Baxendale <deanb@optimumpublishinginternational.com> wrote:

Good Afternoon Heather, Sabrina, Joanna, and Jingli.

As you know we asked if you would participate to tell your side of the story on GWBI and GEBIS which run under Bliss and Wisdom, (known as Fuzhi in Taiwan and China) and the development of the monastic organization in China via Mary Jin.

B&W is a community of people who follow Late Master Jih-Chang and Teacher Zhen-Ru, studying and practicing Buddhism. Under the guiding principles of Buddhist values, there are a few core NPOs or social enterprises, but there is no legal entity that oversees the community. B&W does not run GEBIS and GWBI.

CASH TRANSACTIONS:

You are known to have purchased homes and farms using several methods. We have several witnesses that have confirmed that land or real estate was purchased using cash and through bank transfers but with no mortgages.

Please explain if you wish to have an opportunity to express your position regarding your land purchases, heavy use of cash, and cash being deposited into Canadian banks that were presented as donations.

In the event of receipt of cash donations from lay followers during annual retreats, GWBI would deposit the cash into banks. GWBI has not used cash to pay for land purchases. Any individual using cash to pay for land does not represent GWBI.

BLISS AND WISDOM AND MARY JIN:

According to your website, Mary Jin met Master Jih-Chang in the late 90's during one of Master Jih-Chang met in the late '90s. The venerable Abbott Fan Yin also came to China and worked with the Master and Mary Jin.

https://www.blisswisdom.org/topic/announcements/h/1905-1008

Ven Fan Yin was abbot only from Jan 1995 to Dec 1998, before Teacher Zhen-Ru was appointed. While Ven Fan Yin received teachings from Teacher Zhen-Ru, he was not involved in the work of Master Jih-Chang and Teacher Zhen-Ru.

Was one of her sister's a former broadcaster in China. Is one of her sisters or sister-in-law with Bliss and Wisdom in Singapore? They all own land in and around the monastery or more generally on Prince Edward Island. Is that correct?

China has complete dominion over media and religion, with all media outlets run by the state. Anyone who concludes from China's highly regulated media industry to suggest a media employee is a CCP agent clearly oversimplifies the situation. Stating this incorrect assumption in the media, allowing it and other disinformation to be widely quoted by the greater public who may not be as aware of the situation in China, creates fake news and harms the parties involved.

Teacher Zhen-Ru's family members are not affiliated with any Leezen outlets. Any land holdings by Teacher Zhen-Ru's family are listed publicly on Geolinc (PEI government website).

What was Mary Jin's association with the Buddhist Association of China and the United Front formalized? You have claimed there are no links to China or the Fuzhi temples inside China to Bliss and Wisdom

Teacher Zhen-Ru is neither associated with the Buddhist Association of China ("BAC") nor the United Front.

Regarding links to China, please see answer to "When did Bliss and Wisdom register with the Buddhist Association of China (which year?)". There are Buddhist monks and nuns in China who want to study Buddhist teachings from Teacher Zhen-Ru.

EXHIBITS

Compassion and Grace institute are nuns from the Chinese monasteries of Bliss and Wisdom. Which temples are the nuns coming from in China?

To protect these nuns and their family members, we are unable to disclose the names of these monasteries in China.

BAC President, Xuecheng (2015-2018): Xuecheng. He was a key figure during the 1999 through 2007 period prior to Mary Jin arriving on PEI via mainland China. What was there relationship.

Prior to 2004 (Late Master Jih-Chang's passing), Lamrim teachings were given to Ven Xuecheng. Teacher Zhen-Ru does not have a relationship with Ven Xuecheng.

When did Bliss and Wisdom register with the Buddhist Association of China (which year?)

Bliss and Wisdom monasteries cannot possibly be registered with BAC. B&W monasteries have roots in Taiwan and study Tibetan Buddhism. The Chinese government will not allow B&W to set up monasteries in China due to these two factors.

Also did Mary Jin come through the PNP program? Who processed her? Did she arrive in 2007 0r 2008?

Given Mary Jin's importance to Bliss and Wisdonm and within Tibetan Buddhism has His Holiness ever met or received Mary Jin formally?

Due to political sensitivities (China-Taiwan, China-Tibet), we are unable to disclose any information regarding His Holiness and Teacher Zhen-Ru. Below is His Holiness the Dalai Lama's answer:

> "HHDL: We have to consider the possibility that because they want to spread the

teachings in Mainland China, it may really be inconvenient for her to see me. I hope you have considered this point. This can be due to general political reasons. In Tibet many people have faith in me, but do not dare to come and see me. This year when I gave the Kalachakra initiation in Bodh Gaya, many people wanted to come and receive the initiation, but they were afraid their friends and relatives could come to harm, so they were hesitant to come. I advised them that, "If coming to the Kalachakra initiation could bring harm to your family, then it is better to go back! I hope you will pray sincerely during the Kalachakra initiation, I will also pray sincerely for you!"

BLISS AND WISDOM PARTICIPATES IN CROSS-STRAIT BUDDHIST EXCHANGES

According to your website Master Hsing Yun participated in the exchange with the Buddhist Association of China in 2014. It is clear you were working with the BAC to promote Tibetan Buddhism on both sides of the strait. Please confirm that you are still working for the same objective which is to unify Buddhism on both sides of the strait?

This is another example where a prevailing oversimplification has led to erroneous theories. As mentioned above, China highly regulates everything, including religion e.g. Catholicism, Christianity, Buddhism. All legal religious groups have to be registered with the authorities. For Buddhism, the relevant authority is BAC. In addition, there are no religious exchange programs that are not overseen by the BAC (CCP). Anyone who concludes from China's highly regulated religious landscape to suggest that all Chinese religious organizations or anyone

participating in China's religious exchange programs are CCP agents clearly over-simplifies the situation.

Bliss and Wisdom is non-partisan and does not identify with any political ideology to maintain its independence so it can carry out its preservation work of Tibetan Buddhism.

Bliss and Wisdom has numerous corporations in China. These businesses have to be registered in China and are known to the government. If you are allowed to operate and prosper in China, does that mean you have the official approval and acknowledgement of the government?

It is incorrect to state that B&W has numerous corporations in China. The main NPOs and social enterprises within the B&W community have not set up any corporations in China. Any business in China is a personal business set up by lay followers. In addition, China does not allow private Buddhist study groups.

The assumption behind your question neglects to consider the reality that no organization is able to operate unless they register with the government.

FLOYD SANDERSON AND DAVID WEALE

Why did you feel it necessary to generate this campaign? https://www.youtube.com/watch?v=ck2TU414ukg

GWBI did not generate, support or participate in this campaign.

Below you suggest that Fan Yin is an unriable source and in fact was and may still be part of the CCP's disinformation operations to discredit Fuzhi, GEBIS and GWBI. There is no question that, along with Master Jih-Chang, they worked with Mary Jin and the Buddhist Association of China.

Do you believe he is a CCP agent who is spreading disinformation about your organization?

Ven Fan Yin is publicly spreading massive disinformation about Bliss and Wisdom and Teacher Zhen-Ru.

Thank you and we look forward to your responses. We would naturally include any statment or your answers in the book as is customery in an journalisitc investigation.

We thank you for taking the time previously to meet with us and will be sure to represent that meeing and interview objectively.

If you have any formal statement on behlaf of the nuns and monks we would certainlty entertain publishing it in the book.

On behalf of our team thank you for your time. Please send your responses back no later than 2:00 p.m. Thursday May 15, 2025.

Thank you,
Dean Baxendale

EXHIBITS

EXHIBIT 4

This document clearly shows that Bliss and Wisdom's Master Monk Ru Zheng (Master Rujing on next document). It comes from their own Chinese language Facebook page.

09/05/2025 08:16   Bliss and Wisdom participates in cross-strait Buddhist exchanges

 福智之聲 (/publications/bwvoice)

Fan Page(https://www.facebook.com/bwvoice1991)   Featured Articles (/publications/bwvoice/topics)

Each issue of Fu Sheng (/publications/bwvoice/number/1005-246)

Bliss and Wisdom participates in cross-strait Buddhist exchanges

Issue 219 (/publications/bwvoice/number/954-219) 2015/01/30

♦Compiled by the Voice of Bliss and Wisdom editorial office

From November 30 to December 2, 2014, at the invitation of Master Hsing Yun of Fo Guang Shan, 32 Buddhist masters from Taiwan participated in the first cross-strait Buddhist friendship and exchange meeting for young and middle-aged Buddhists. The abbot of Fengshan Temple, Venerable Ru Zheng, and three other Buddhist masters were also invited to attend. This exchange activity was hosted by the State Administration for Religious Affairs of China and was held at the Lingshan Giant Buddha in Wuxi and the Dajue Temple in Yixing.

The Friendship and Exchange Meeting for Young and Middle-aged Buddhists from Both Sides of the Taiwan Straits has opened up opportunities for cross-strait Buddhist exchanges. The person in the picture is Director Wang Zuoan, and the third from the right is Master Hsing Yun.

Director Wang Zuo'an of the State Administration of Religious Affairs of China expressed his pleasure at the interaction in this exchange, which provided a platform for Buddhists on both sides of the Taiwan Strait to communicate. He also thanked Master Hsing Yun and other religious elders for their efforts in promoting the development of Buddhism and creating a situation where "before the two sides of the Taiwan Strait are connected, religions are connected first; before religions are connected, Buddhism is connected first."

Faced with the current problems in mainland China such as the lack of Buddhist teaching staff, cultivation of monks, and a sound system, Director Wang hopes to learn from the fruitful results of Master Hsing Yun's Dharma propagation in Taiwan as a guideline for future development. He encouraged the public to always be willing to communicate, and that promoting traditional Chinese culture is the common responsibility of both sides of the Taiwan Strait, and requires Chinese people around the world to inherit and promote it together.

During the meeting, Master Hsing Yun emphasized that the focus of this exchange meeting was to promote exchanges between the Buddhist communities on both sides of the Taiwan Straits. He praised Director Wang for initiating the first religious dialogue between young and middle-aged people on both sides of the Taiwan Straits, which showed his far-sightedness and macro perspective.

Monk Ru Zheng (pictured) participated in a cross-strait Buddhist exchange meeting.

All parties also put forward constructive plans for the future development of Buddhism on both sides of the Taiwan Strait. Monk Ru Zheng suggested that the Buddhist Association of China and Fo Guang Shan should serve as windows for cross-strait Buddhist exchanges; Master Ji Shen of Yuanguang Buddhist College suggested that a long-term cross-strait Buddhist friendship promotion association should be established in the future; Master Guo Jing of Dharma Drum Mountain proposed that Buddhist forums could adopt in-depth dialogues to effectively promote mutual understanding and generate substantive interactions.

Taiwan has a relatively complete Buddhist system, which can benefit the future development of Buddhism on both sides of the Taiwan Strait. Master Hsing Yun encourages the Buddhist community in Taiwan to interact with each other, because we are all inheritors of the Buddha's teachings and are all Buddhist disciples, and there should be no distinction between you and me. With the earnest expectation of representatives of Taiwan's Buddhist community, it is hoped that Fo Guang Shan will take the initiative to integrate and establish the "Chinese Humanistic Buddhism Association" to represent Taiwan's Buddhist community and become a window corresponding to the Chinese Buddhist Association, promoting future cross-strait Buddhist exchanges, jointly promoting Buddhist culture, and contributing to the Buddhist community.

EXHIBIT 5

Master Rujing is an Abbot based in Tiawan from the Blessing and Wisdom Sangha. He is a leader at Bliss and Wisdom (Fuzhi) and has actively participated in working with mainland Chinese groups under the control of the Chinese Buddhist Association. It is hard for BW to refute its associations, engagements and ties to the CCP's United Front Work Department through the Chinese Buddhist Association.

Tibetan Buddhism has seen significant growth in Taiwan over the past few decades. As of 2018, there were 473 Tibetan Buddhist centers across the island, a notable increase from 82 in 1996. This expansion reflects a growing interest in Tibetan Buddhist practices among the Taiwanese population.

Additionally, the Tibet Religious Foundation of His Holiness the Dalai Lama, founded in 1997, serves as the de facto representative office of the Central Tibetan Administration in Taiwan, further indicating the institutional presence of Tibetan Buddhism on the island. This is where we met his Holiness' representative.

EXHIBITS

EXHIBIT 6

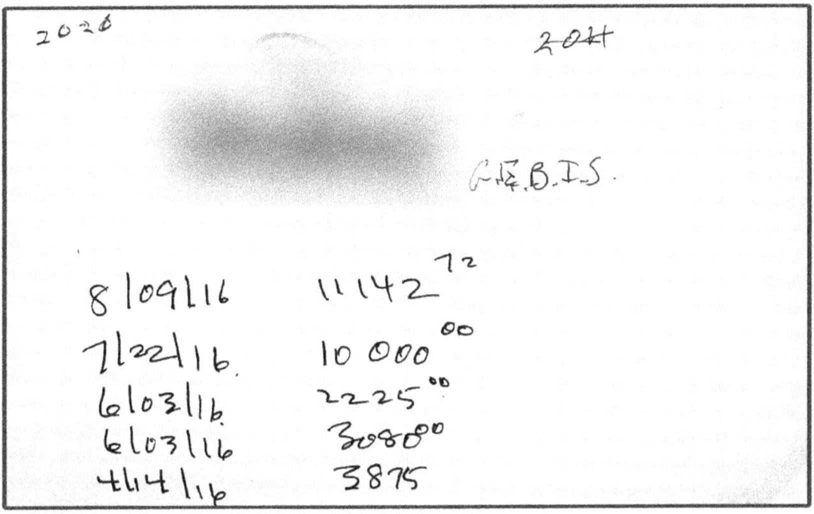

2020   2011

G.E.B.I.S.

8/09/16   11142 72
7/22/16   10 000 00
6/03/16   2225 00
6/03/16   3080 00
4/14/16   3875

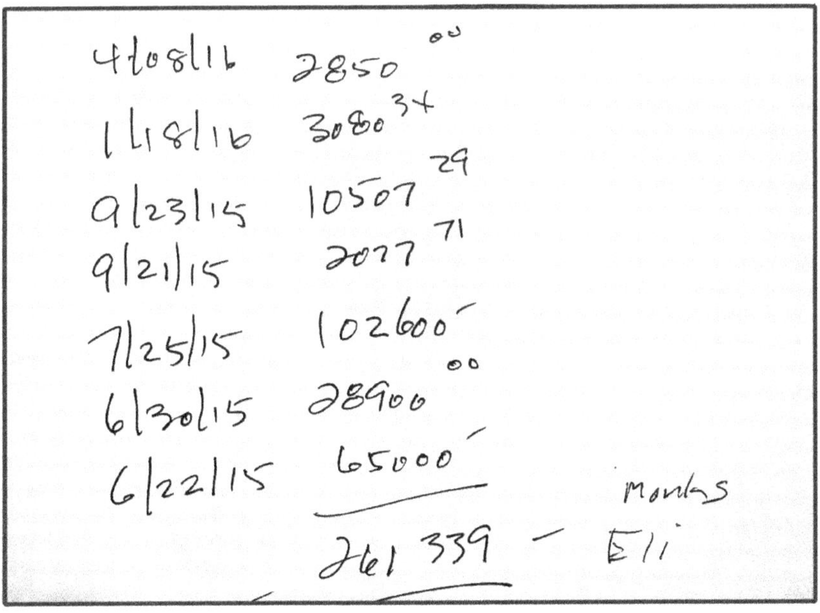

4/08/16   2850 00
1/18/16   3080 34
9/23/15   10507 29
9/21/15   2077 71
7/25/15   102600
6/30/15   28900 00
6/22/15   65000
           ───────   Montas
           261 339   —   Eli

PHOTOS

The Beautiful GWBI (The Nuns) Monastery, Montague, PE.

Nuns on clean up duty around the new monastery in Brudenell.

On our first trip to PEI, Juneau-Katsuya reviews our check list of possible issues on the island. This based on the interviews and documents were given to inspect. December 2023.

Duncan MacIntosh, with partner and former Premier Wade MacLauchlan with Sherry Huang and Frank Zhou. Frank Zhou Partners in Anne in China Inc. with Wade and Duncan (2011). The book was a great success in China according to reports and Laureen Harper wrote a forward for it.

Three River town council meeting, March 10. Councilors agreed to issue a building permit for an 88,000 Square foot expansion of the GWBI facility in Brudenell. Some residents of the area are trying to appeal that decision based on their having not been a public consultation of the original master plan.

"North America Under Siege" event, March 17th, 2024. Eventually the right side wall was opened to accommodate the close to 600 who showed up for the book launch and panel discussion.

Image to advertise the March 17th at the Delta Hotel in Charlottetown.

Premier Robert Ghiz receives a honorary certificate from Ke-Zhou Lu known as "General" Lu on the island. CEO of its non-charitable corporate divisions. The United Front also presents friendship and appreciation awards to many political and business elite in Canada.

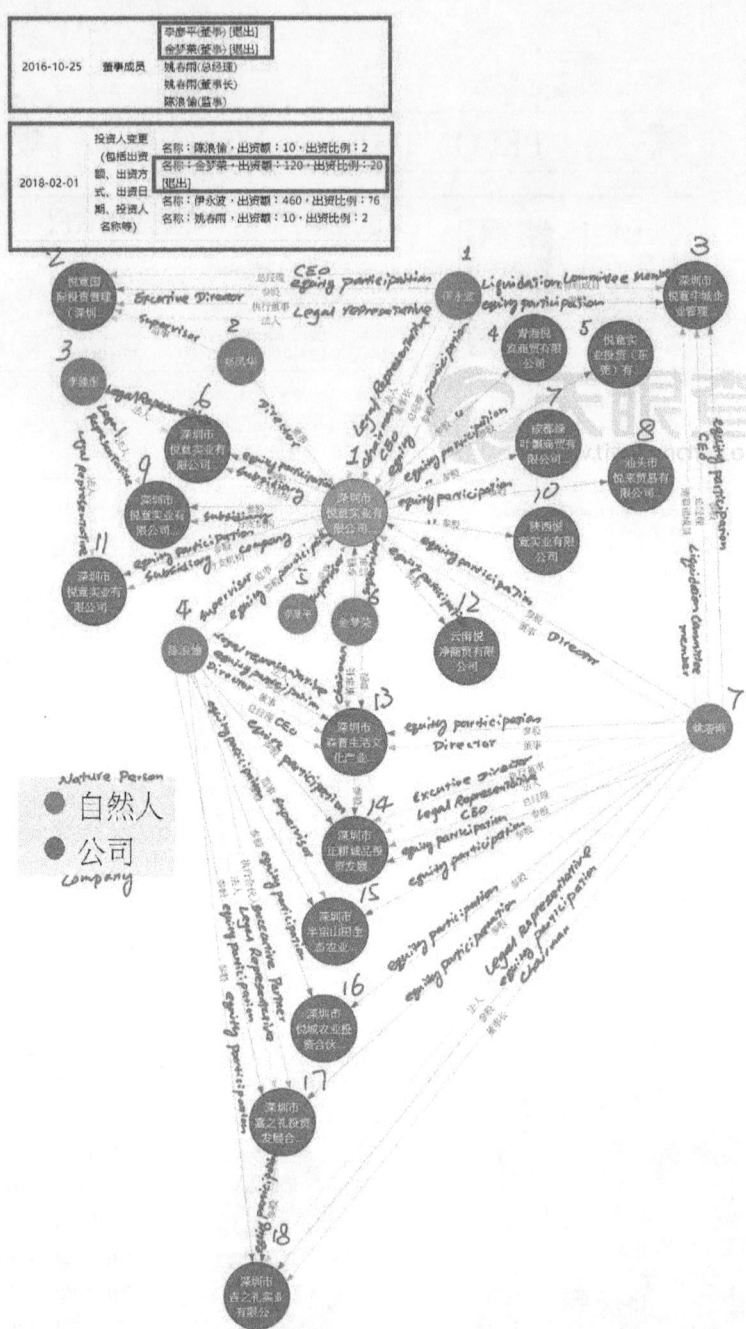

Complicated flow chart of various Directors of Bliss and Wisdom and their ownership or directorships in various mainland Chinese companies. Number 6 is Master Zhen-Ru. This chart is from 2018. She no longer has ownership in the company she was CEO of at that time. Reviewed by and translated by an expert sinologist.

SEan Casey MP

Tabs: Sean Casey MP Family | Spencer Campbell | brooke MacMillan | Sheet6 | Billy Dow | Dennis King

D. SPENCER CAMPBELL PROFESSIONAL CORPORATION

55 Queen Elizabeth Drive
Charlottetown, PE

CIA 3A8 (MAP)

Shareholders, Directors and Officers

D. Spencer Campbell
55 Queen Elizabeth Drive Charlottetown, Prince Edward Island C1A 3A8 (MAP)
someone with this name is also a shareholder or officer of:

101239 P.E.I. INC. PROVINCIAL
6331688 CANADA INC. FEDERAL
6937942 CANADA INC. FEDERAL
D. SPENCER CAMPBELL PROFESSIONAL CORPORATION PROVINCIAL
DSC PROFESSIONAL SERVICES CORP. PROVINCIAL
GLOBAL PEI PRODUCTS INC. PROVINCIAL
GRAFTON STREET PROPERTIES INC. FEDERAL
LEGAL MANAGEMENT INC. PROVINCIAL
SOUTH SHORE VILLA INC. PROVINCIAL
YORK RIVER PROPERTIES INC. FEDERAL

Owns Interest In

DSC PROFESSIONAL SERVICES CORP.

Related Links

PEI Corporations Registry Official Record
Royal Gazette search for: D. SPENCER CAMPBELL PROFESSIONAL CORPORATION.
Generate DOT file

Entities with the name 'SPENCER CAMPBELL'

are listed as shareholders or officers of D. Spencer Campbell

101239 P.E.I. INC. PROVINCIAL
6331688 CANADA INC. FEDERAL
6937942 CANADA INC. FEDERAL
D. SPENCER CAMPBELL PROFESSIONAL CORPORATION PROVINCIAL
DSC PROFESSIONAL SERVICES CORP. PROVINCIAL
GLOBAL PEI PRODUCTS INC. PROVINCIAL
LEGAL MANAGEMENT INC. PROVINCIAL
SOUTH SHORE VILLA INC. PROVINCIAL
YORK RIVER PROPERTIES INC. FEDERAL

DE ZHI YANG
JIAN XUN WANG
JING HONG JIN

KIRK DEBOER
someone with this name is also a shareholder or officer of:
100960 P.E.I. INC. PROVINCIAL
6937942 CANADA INC. FEDERAL
REORED HOLDINGS INC. PROVINCIAL
SOUTH SHORE VILLA INC. PROVINCIAL

SEAN J. CASEY
someone with this name is also a shareholder or officer of:
101217 P.E.I. INC. PROVINCIAL
4145311 CANADA INC. FEDERAL
6937942 CANADA INC. FEDERAL
GRAFTON STREET PROPERTIES INC. FEDERAL
LEGAL MANAGEMENT INC. PROVINCIAL
Padinox Inc. FEDERAL
SEAN J. CASEY PROFESSIONAL CORPORATION PROVINCIAL
SN PROFESSIONAL SERVICES CORP. PROVINCIAL
SOUTH SHORE VILLA INC. PROVINCIAL

STEPHEN DUNNE
someone with this name is also a shareholder or officer of:
100451 P.E.I. INC. PROVINCIAL
100745 P.E.I. INC. PROVINCIAL
100970 P.E.I. INC. PROVINCIAL
100819 P.E.I. INC. PROVINCIAL
100877 P.E.I. INC. PROVINCIAL
101010 P.E.I. INC. PROVINCIAL
2BDM STRATEGIES INC. PROVINCIAL
060903 CANADA INC. FEDERAL
6618034 CANADA INC. FEDERAL
6937942 CANADA INC. FEDERAL
CANADIAN INTERNATIONAL OPPORTUNITIES INC. PROVINCIAL
DUNNE CONSULTING INC. PROVINCIAL
HERITAGE DEVELOPMENT INC. PROVINCIAL
IMAGEWORKS P.E.I. INC. PROVINCIAL
MAKE-A-RESERVATION INC. PROVINCIAL
R.O. ENTERPRISES INC. PROVINCIAL
S. DUNNE PROPERTIES INC. FEDERAL
SOUTH SHORE VILLA INC. PROVINCIAL
ntrepreneurs.ca Incorporated PROVINCIAL

WENDY SUE DEBOER
someone with this name is also a shareholder or officer of:
6937942 CANADA INC. FEDERAL
8110613 HOLDINGS INC. FEDERAL

Related Links

Federal Corporations Registry Official Record

6937942 CANADA INC.

65 Grafton Street P.O. Box 2140
Charlottetown
Prince Edward Island
C1A8B9
Canada

Shareholders, Directors and Officers

CHAN QIN JANG

D. SPENCER CAMPBELL
someone with this name is also a shareholder or officer of:

101239 P.E.I. INC. PROVINCIAL
6331688 CANADA INC. FEDERAL
6937942 CANADA INC. FEDERAL
D. SPENCER CAMPBELL PROFESSIONAL CORPORATION PROVINCIAL
DSC PROFESSIONAL SERVICES CORP. PROVINCIAL
GLOBAL PEI PRODUCTS INC. PROVINCIAL
GRAFTON STREET PROPERTIES INC. FEDERAL
LEGAL MANAGEMENT INC. PROVINCIAL
SOUTH SHORE VILLA INC. PROVINCIAL
YORK RIVER PROPERTIES INC. FEDERAL

FOUR SEAS INC. Janet Campbell

Traveler cottages at Cavendish - Lakeview Lodge and Cott

Lakeview Lodge & Cottages
RR 1 Hunter River, PE
C0A 1N0 (MAP)

Shareholders, Directors and Officers

Kathleen Casey
Vice President
c/o 65 Grafton Street Charlottetown, Prince Edward I
C1A8B9 (MAP)
someone with this name is also a shareholder or officer of:

FOUR SEAS INC. PROVINCIAL
K.C. HOLDINGS LTD. PROVINCIAL

Horace Reinder
Secretary/Treasurer
c/o 65 Grafton Street Charlottetown, Prince Edward I
C1A8B9 (MAP)
someone with this name is also a shareholder or officer of:

100124 P.E.I. INC. PROVINCIAL
FOUR SEAS INC. PROVINCIAL
LAKEVIEW EXECUTIVE COTTAGES INC. PROV

Janet Campbell
President
55 Queen Elizabeth Drive Charlottetown, Prince Edw
C1A 3A8 (MAP)
someone with this name is also a shareholder or officer of:

101239 P.E.I. INC. PROVINCIAL
DSC PROFESSIONAL SERVICES CORP. PROVIN
FOUR SEAS INC. PROVINCIAL
LAKEVIEW EXECUTIVE COTTAGES INC. PROV
SOUTH SHORE VILLA INC. PROVINCIAL

Tracey Clements
c/o 65 Grafton Street Charlottetown, Prince Edward I
C1A8B9 (MAP)
someone with this name is also a shareholder or officer of:

101214 P.E.I. INC. PROVINCIAL
FOUR SEAS INC. PROVINCIAL
LEGAL MANAGEMENT INC. PROVINCIAL
TLC PROFESSIONAL SERVICES CORP. PROVIN
TRACEY L. CLEMENTS PROFESSIONAL CORPORATION PROVINCIAL

HUNDI Shabirar
c/o CICL Suite 1014 Cogswell Tower 2000 Barringto
Halifax, Prince Edward Island B3J3K1 (MAP)

SHENG Xinn
c/o CICL Suite 1014 Cogswell Tower 2000 Barringto
Halifax, Prince Edward Island B3J3K1 (MAP)

Registered Trade Names

LAKEVIEW LODGE AND COTTAGES

Related Links

PEI Corporations Registry Official Record
Royal Gazette search for: FOUR SEAS INC.
Generate DOT file

Key players on the island who accepted or were part of orchestrating multiple units in multiple numbered companies formed just to get the cash from PNP. Billy Dow, Liberal MP Sean Casey and other have not responded to our request for comment.

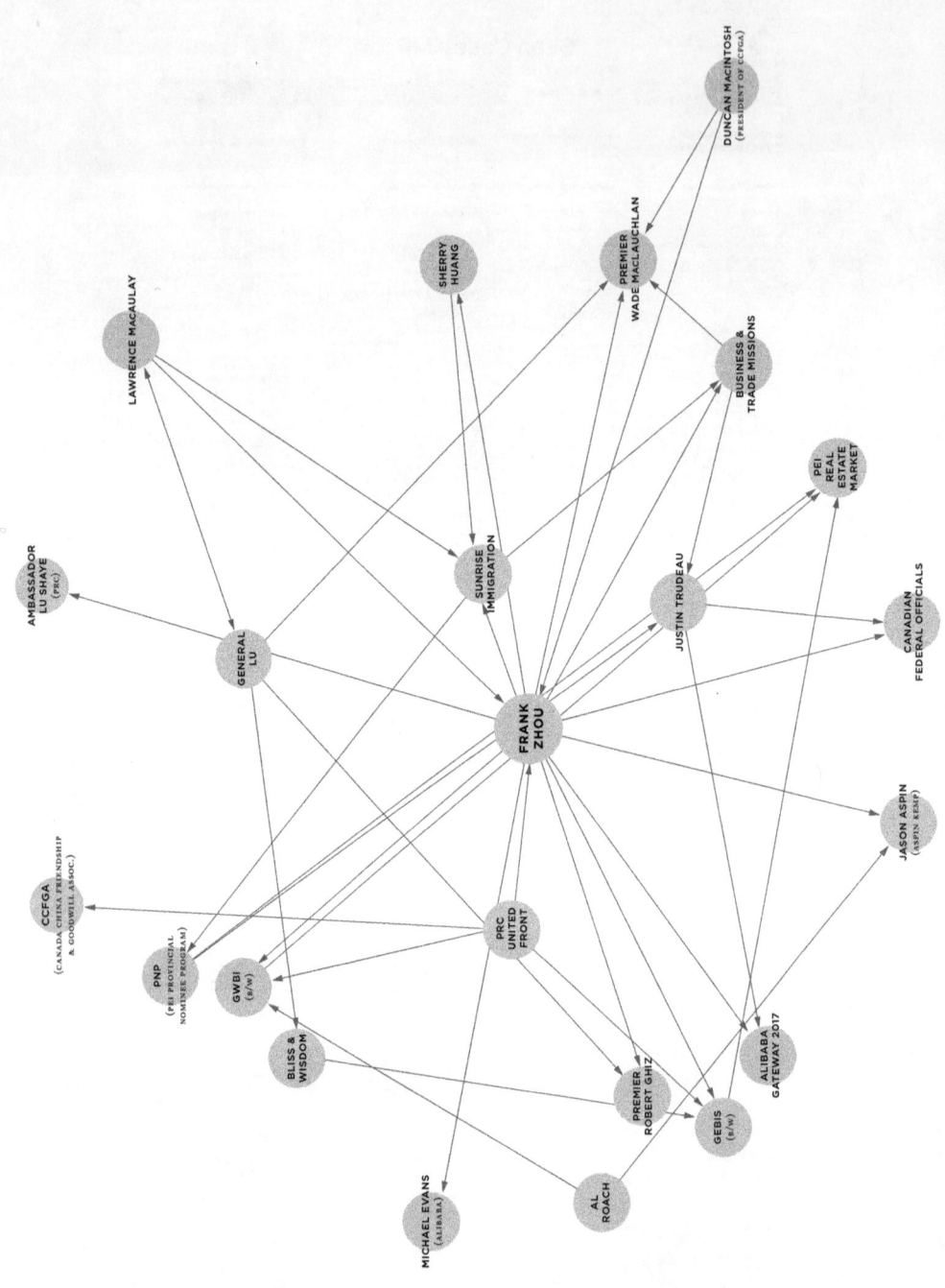

Chart of Frank Zhou's connections (as of 2017) to prominent politicians and business people.

Justice Hogue delivering her report in Ottawa. January 25, 2025.

Former Prime Minister Justin Trudeau testifies at the Hogue Commission on foreign Interference. Michel and Dean attended several testimonies in 2024.

Dorcay Church, Taiwan. It was our meeting here with the Recall movement that helped us to locate the Venerable Fan Yin. February 2025.

Taiwan Buddhist Street temple. February 2025

Little Monk Pretzel Shop in Summerside, PEI. It is closed most of the time and few islanders have eaten one. These business were set up to meet government requirements for active business investment for Permanent Residence status. Another example of poor transparency and oversight by Government.

Three investigators meet at the Charlottetown International Airport on their final trip to the island before ending their investigation. Key witnesses would come forth to be interviewed on camera for the documentary *Game of Shadows* and for the book. March 2025.

Rural PEI countryside. August 2024.

This book represents the outcome of a close to two-year journalistic investigation, undertaken with the participation of two former senior officials from the RCMP and CSIS. Drawing on extensive research, high-level witness testimony, and expert academic analysis, it offers one of the most detailed examinations available into foreign interference, elite capture, and the troubling culture of wilful blindness among those entrusted with protecting Prince Edward Island and Canada.

The authors urge leaders in business, politics, intelligence, and law enforcement to seriously consider the book's findings and to support a full public inquiry—an action already advocated by both Wayne Easter and the authors themselves.

AKNOWLEDGEMENTS

This book and the investigation that powered it could not have been done without the help, the courage, and the commitment of many people. We cannot name everyone because we want to protect your identity and privacy, but we want you to know that we are acknowledging your contribution and support. Thank you to the more than fifty people who came forward and agreed to talk to us and share your stories. We, and the Islanders, owe you a great debt of gratitude for caring. In our line of work, we need people who are seeking justice and want to do the right thing for the simple reason that it is the right thing to do. Your commitment is one of the main reasons why we undertook this project, and we want this book to honour your contribution.

We also want to give a special thank you to Jan and Carolyn. You have been generous, not only with your time and testimonies, but also by hosting us each time we were on the Island. Your knowledge of PEI, the local culture, and history gave us some extremely valuable insights. To say thank you is only a pale expression of our profound gratitude.

To our families also, we are deeply grateful. You accepted many weeks of absence and even disappearance so we could accomplish this task. As you did many times over and over in our lifetimes and careers, you supported us and even patiently listened to our stories, giving us objective and sound advice. Thank you.

A special thanks also to David Weale. We came to know David in the course of many meetings but, more importantly, we understood his commitment going back to the early 1970s to protect the land of this beautiful province. We know your reputation and motives have been virulently attacked, but we can stand today, as your defenders, to testify to your commitment to protect the Island. On behalf of the team and the Islanders, thank you for your service and commitment. We hope one day people will come to realize what you have diligently accomplished over six decades of relentless work and engagement.

Thank you also to our key whistleblowers. We will not name you, as agreed and for obvious reasons, but your insights and knowledge of the situation were of great importance in guiding us in the right direction.

Finally, thank you to the many Islanders who came in great numbers to our events. We would not have been able to truly tell your story and the story of those who follow His Holiness and the traditions, culture, and philosophy of Tibetan Buddhism without guidance and direction from many people and groups. They include numerous Sinologists, those linked to Tibetan Buddhism and those near the intelligence community, the U. S. Congress, the Parliament of Canada, and the various NGOs and non-profits that have been fighting for the rights of the Chinese diaspora communities since the 1960s and 1970s in the aftermath of Mao's Cultural Revolution, the Great Leap Forward, and the Tiananmen Square massacre under Deng Zhou Ping. The Chinese Communist Party has been trying to eviscerate Tibetan culture both inside Tibet and around the world. Your dedication to justice, human rights, and the truth despite the CCP's relentless propaganda operations to discredit you and your advocacy has inspired us all.

Collectively, from Prince Edward Island to Dharamshala and from Washington to Ottawa, your presence and voice carried us through the months of research conducted in Taiwan, Germany, Washington, Vancouver, Ottawa, Toronto, Montreal, and of course, PEI. Your desire for justice and fairness was the energy needed to make this project a reality. YOU are the reason why we wrote this book, why we did all of this. Like you, we love this country and our own connection to the land and the peoples who make up Canada. We are all the descendants of immigrants, and no matter if you are of European, Asian, or Indigenous descent, you became our drive to take on this quest. We hope we met your expectations and those of the brave Islanders who gave us the insight and tools to fix the wrong that has been prevailing for too long. We heard you, guardians of the land, of the culture and history of the Island. Your roar was loud and clear.

Now it is time to demand the changes that you deserve, to demand that our leaders begin to act for all of us Canadians.

GLOSSARY

Buddhist Association of China (BAC): Also known as the China Buddhist Association, it is the official government supervisory organ of Buddhism in the People's Republic of China, serving to enforce the will of the Chinese Communist Party (CCP) on Buddhist communities both within Chinese territory and abroad. Founded in 1953, the BAC is tasked with communicating government regulations to Buddhists and ensuring compliance with national laws, unifying spiritual practice with official state control, using its control to slander the Tibetan government-in-exile, and propagating the Chinese-selected Panchem Lama as the figurehead of Tibetan Buddhism. The BAC is estimated to exert influence over around 47 million Buddhists.

Central Tibetan Administration (CTA): The official name for the Tibetan government-in-exile, headquartered in Dharamshala, India. It is a democratic governing body that represents the Tibetan diaspora and maintains Tibetan cultural and political advocacy globally.

Dharma: The spiritual teachings of the Buddha, representing the foundation of Buddhist ethics, philosophy, and practice. In Tibetan Buddhism, Dharma encompasses both monastic discipline and esoteric Vajrayana rituals.

Dharamshala: The Indian town that houses the Central Tibetan Administration (government-in-exile) and the home of the current Dalai Lama, Tenzin Gyatso. Located in the Indian state of Himachal Pradesh and often referred to as "Little Tibet," Dharamshala serves as an asylum to preserve Tibetan religious and cultural history amid Chinese state incursions and usurpation of the Buddhist hierarchy. It has become the heart of the Tibetan exile community and a symbol of spiritual and political resistance.

Ganden Phodrang: The former Tibetan government established in 1642 under the 5th Dalai Lama. Though dissolved after the 1959 Chinese occupation, its legacy is carried on by the Central Tibetan Administration.

Great Leap Forward and Cultural Revolution: Chinese political movements (1958–1976) under Mao Zedong that led to mass destruction of Tibetan religious sites, forced labor, famine, and the widespread persecution of monks and spiritual leaders.

His Holiness the 14th Dalai Lama: The title "His Holiness" refers to the Dalai Lama, the highest spiritual leader and head of Tibetan Buddhism. **Tenzin Gyatso** is the personal name of the 14th Dalai Lama The term is just part of the full title, "Holiness Knowing Everything Vajrayana Dalai Lama," which is bestowed upon those believed to be a reincarnation of the Buddha of Compassion. According to Tibetan Buddhist doctrine, the Dalai Lama chooses his reincarnation. The Dalai Lama serves not only as a religious leader but also as a temporal head of state for the Tibetan people, governing under the historic concept of *mchod yon*, which through the patronage of secular rulers Tibet maintains a degree of autonomy in religious and cultural matters while ensuring political stability and protection.

Throughout the history of its line, the Dalai Lama has negotiated autonomous freedoms for Tibet with Mongol, Manchu, and Chinese authorities, in turn providing spiritual legitimacy and guidance as the acknowledged head of the Buddhist community. From 1642 and the 5th Dalai Lama until 1951 and the 14th Dalai Lama, the lineage was enjoined with the secular role of governing Tibet. The 14th Dalai Lama, Tenzin Gyatso, was forced into exile from Lhasa in 1959 amid the Tibetan Diaspora, currently living in exile in Dharamshala but maintaining his role as spiritual and temporal leader of Tibetan Buddhism.

Mao Zedong – Founding father of the People's Republic of China, under whose rule Tibet was invaded in 1950. His ideological campaigns drastically disrupted Tibetan culture, religion, and autonomy.

Monastic Re-education: A Chinese government policy in which Tibetan monks and nuns are forced to attend political indoctrination sessions, swear loyalty to the Communist Party, and renounce the Dalai Lama.

Panchen Lama: The Panchen Lama is the reincarnation of Amitabha, the Buddha of Boundless Light, who traditionally, each acts as a spiritual companion to the Dalai Lama and plays a key role in identifying his reincarnation. In 1995, the Dalai Lama recognized six-year-old Gedhun Choekyi Nyima as the incumbent Panchen Lama; three days later, Nyima was kidnapped and forcibly disappeared by the Chinese government, installing a puppet by the name of Gyaincain Norbu.

The Panchen Lama has since detached himself from the Tibetan inner circle of Buddhist practice, declaring himself the sole leader of Tibetan Buddhism with the backing of the People Republic of China in an attempt to give control of the religion over to official state doctrine. The CCP has continued to try to control reincarnation of the Dalai Lama since the leader in exile left Tibet in 1959.

Potala Palace: The historic winter residence of the Dalai Lamas in Lhasa, Tibet. Now a UNESCO site controlled by China, it remains a powerful symbol of Tibet's past sovereignty.

Reincarnation (Tulku System): A core belief of Tibetan Buddhism where enlightened teachers, such as the Dalai Lama or Panchen Lama, are reborn in new bodies to continue their spiritual missions. The Chinese state has controversially claimed control over this process.

Rinpoche: A Tibetan honorific meaning "precious one," used for revered lamas, particularly those believed to be reincarnations of former spiritual masters.

Self-Immolation: A form of political protest by Tibetans—often monks or nuns—who set themselves on fire to oppose Chinese rule and advocate for freedom or the return of the Dalai Lama. This tragic act reflects the deep desperation of the Tibetan people.

Sinicization: Also known as Sinofication or Sinification, the process of non-Chinese societies or groups being acculturated or assimilated into Chinese culture, particularly the language, societal norms, cultural practices, and ethnic identity of the Han Chinese. When it comes to the example of Tibetan Buddhism, tactics include rewriting scriptures, controlling monastic education, and promoting Mandarin over Tibetan.

Sikyong: The Sikyong is the political leader of the Central Tibetan Administration, a Tibetan exile organization in India also known as the Tibetan government-in-exile based on the 2011 Charter of Tibetans-in-exile. The title was created in 2012 after the 14th Dalai Lama decided not to assume any political and administrative authority as the head of the Tibetan Administration for Tibetans-in-exile. The title is currently held by Penpa Tsering.

Tibetan Buddhism: A major Buddhist tradition combining Mahayana and Vajrayana teachings and is characterized by its rich rituals, visual imagery, and emphasis on meditation.. It emphasizes compassion, ritual, meditation, and a unique reincarnate lama system, central to the spiritual life of Tibet. Tibetan Buddhism inherited many traditions from late Indian Buddhism, including a strong emphasis on monasticism and scholastic philosophy. The religion is practiced predominantly in the Tibet peninsula, along with Bhutan, Mongolia, and parts of China, India, and Russia, as well as in the surrounding Himalayan regions and increasingly in the West.

Tibetan Diaspora: The global community of Tibetan refugees and exiles, primarily located in India, Nepal, North America, and Europe, advocating for cultural preservation and Tibetan freedom.

Tibetan Uprising Day (March 10): The annual commemoration of the 1959 Tibetan revolt against Chinese occupation. It marks the day the Dalai Lama fled into exile and is observed with protests and remembrance worldwide.

United Front Work Department (UFWD): A division of the Chinese Communist Party responsible for controlling ethnic and religious groups, including overseeing the manipulation of Tibetan Buddhist institutions to serve party interests. They are tasked with international espionage, focusing on targeting high level personnel outside of mainland China. The UFWD gathers intelligence on, manages relations with, and attempts to gain influence over elite individuals and organizations inside and outside Chinese spheres of influence, often targeting human rights advocates, Taiwanese government officials and international critics of the CCP, especially those who hold political, commercial, or academic influence, or who represent interest groups. Through its efforts, the UFWD seeks to ensure that these individuals and groups are supportive of or useful to CCP interests and that potential critics remain divided.

The United Front Works Department friendship associations number close to 900 in the United States and close to 100 in Canada. This includes One on Prince Edward Island the CCFGA Canada-China Friendship and Goodwill Association (2015); previously Frank Zhou was the Director of the PEI Association for Newcomers to Canada (PEIANC) from 2000-2010.

INTELLIGENCE TERMS

INTELLIGENCE GATHERING AND NATIONAL SECURITY TERMS

All-Source Intelligence: Information derived from the integration of intelligence collected via multiple disciplines (HUMINT, SIGINT, GEOINT, etc.), offering a comprehensive analytical perspective.

GLOSSARY

Assets: Individuals who are recruited to collect information on behalf of an intelligence agency, often inside foreign governments, organizations, or networks.

Backdoor Access: Unauthorized or covert entry points into software or hardware systems that allow surveillance or data exfiltration without detection.

Black Site: A secret detention facility operated by intelligence or military organizations, often used for interrogation of high-value detainees outside standard legal oversight.

Central Intelligence Agency (CIA): The U.S. civilian foreign intelligence service responsible for collecting, analyzing, and conducting covert operations internationally to protect national security interests.

Counterintelligence (CI): Activities aimed at protecting against espionage, sabotage, or other intelligence threats posed by foreign entities or insider threats.

Canadian Security Intelligence Service (CSIS): Xanada's principal national intelligence agency, tasked with collecting, analyzing, and reporting information on threats to the country's security. Established in 1984, CSIS operates under the authority of the CSIS Act and is responsible for counter-terrorism, counter-intelligence, cyber security, and protecting Canada from foreign espionage and domestic threats. It conducts both domestic and international operations, often in collaboration with allied intelligence agencies, including those within the Five Eyes alliance. CSIS plays a crucial role in advising the Canadian government and law enforcement agencies to prevent security breaches and safeguard national interests through strategic intelligence operations.

Cyber Intelligence (CYBINT): Intelligence derived from cyberspace, including computer network operations, malware tracking, and digital forensics for state or corporate security.

Defense Intelligence Agency (DIA): A U.S. Department of Defense agency responsible for military-related intelligence gathering and analysis globally.

Electronic Surveillance: The use of technology (like wiretaps, cameras, GPS) to monitor individuals, often under the authority of national security agencies.

Five Eyes (FVEY): An intelligence-sharing alliance between the United States, Canada, the United Kingdom, Australia, and New Zealand, formed after the Second World War to enable global SIGINT collaboration.

Geospatial Intelligence (GEOINT): Intelligence derived from the analysis of imagery, maps, and geographic data, often used for military planning or threat assessments.

Human Intelligence (HUMINT): Intelligence collected from human sources, including spies, informants, or defectors. It often involves clandestine operations and field agents.

Intelligence Cycle: The process of planning, collecting, processing, analyzing, and disseminating intelligence information to policymakers or commanders.

National Security Agency (NSA): The U.S. government agency responsible for global monitoring, collection, and processing of communications and electronic intelligence (SIGINT).

Open Source Intelligence (OSINT): Intelligence collected from publicly available sources such as newspapers, websites, academic journals, social media, and broadcasts.

Signals Intelligence (SIGINT): Intelligence derived from intercepted communications and electronic signals. Includes monitoring of phone calls, internet activity, and radio transmissions.

Surveillance: The monitoring of behavior, communications, or activities of individuals or groups for the purpose of intelligence gathering or law enforcement.

Tasking: The formal assignment of intelligence collection responsibilities to a specific agency or field unit based on operational needs or national security priorities.

Terrorist Screening Center (TSC): A U.S. agency responsible for maintaining the consolidated watchlist of known and suspected terrorists used across government departments.

GLOSSARY

Undercover Operations: Covert missions where agents infiltrate target groups or organizations using false identities to gather intelligence without revealing their affiliation.

CHINA'S MILITARY INTELLIGENCE, UNITED FRONT, HONG KONG SECURITY LAW, AND TAIWAN CONFLICT

Anti-Access/Area Denial (A2/AD): A military strategy aimed at preventing adversaries from entering or operating within a contested region. China employs A2/AD to deter foreign intervention, particularly in the Taiwan Strait and South China Sea.

Article 23 (Hong Kong): A provision in Hong Kong's Basic Law requiring the region to enact laws prohibiting acts like treason, secession, and subversion. Its implementation has raised concerns over potential infringements on civil liberties.

Central Military Commission (CMC): China's highest military authority, overseeing the People's Liberation Army (PLA) and responsible for formulating military policies and strategies. The CMC commands all branches of the armed forces and plays a pivotal role in national defence.

China Coast Guard (CCG): A maritime law enforcement agency under China's armed police, playing a significant role in asserting China's territorial claims, especially in the South and East China Seas. The CCG has been involved in various maritime disputes with neighbouring countries.

Cyber Espionage: The act of penetrating digital networks to gather intelligence, often targeting governmental, military, or corporate data. China has been implicated in various cyber espionage activities globally, raising concerns about cybersecurity.

Eastern Theater Command: One of the PLA's five theater commands, responsible for operations in the East China Sea and the Taiwan Strait. It plays a pivotal role in any potential Taiwan-related military actions.

Five Eyes Alliance (FVEY): An intelligence-sharing alliance comprising the United States, United Kingdom, Canada, Australia, and New Zealand. While not a Chinese entity, it's often referenced in discussions about countering Chinese intelligence activities.

Grey Zone Warfare: Strategies employed to achieve geopolitical objectives without open warfare, including cyber attacks, disinformation campaigns, and economic coercion. China utilizes grey zone tactics to assert its interests while avoiding direct military conflict.

Hong Kong National Security Law (NSL): Enacted in 2020, this law criminalizes acts deemed as secession, subversion, terrorism, and collusion with foreign forces, leading to significant political and social changes in Hong Kong. The NSL has been criticized for undermining the region's autonomy.

Integrated Network Electronic Warfare (INEW): A PLA strategy combining cyber warfare, electronic warfare, and kinetic operations to disrupt adversary information systems. INEW reflects China's emphasis on information dominance in modern warfare.

Joint Operations Command Center (JOCC): A facility coordinating multi-branch military operations, enhancing the PLA's ability to conduct integrated warfare. The JOCC serves as the nerve center for China's military command and control.

Military-Civil Fusion (MCF): A national strategy aiming to integrate civilian and military sectors, facilitating the transfer of technology and resources to bolster China's defence capabilities. MCF underscores China's approach to leveraging all aspects of society for national security.

People's Armed Police (PAP): A paramilitary force responsible for internal security, border defence, and maritime rights protection, operating under the CMC's command. The PAP plays a crucial role in maintaining domestic stability.

People's Liberation Army (PLA): China's unified military organization encompassing land, sea, air, rocket, and strategic support forces, central to China's defence and power projection. The PLA is one of the world's largest military forces.

People's Liberation Army Rocket Force (PLARF): The strategic missile force of the PLA, managing China's nuclear and conventional missile arsenals. PLARF is a key component of China's deterrence strategy.

Political Warfare: The use of propaganda, psychological operations, and other non-kinetic means to influence, coerce, or undermine adversaries. China employs political warfare to shape perceptions and advance its strategic objectives.

Porcupine Strategy: Taiwan's defence approach focusing on asymmetric warfare to deter or delay a potential Chinese invasion by making it costly and protracted. The strategy emphasizes resilience and deterrence.

South China Sea Arbitration: A 2016 international tribunal ruling that invalidated China's expansive claims in the South China Sea, which China has rejected. The ruling has significant implications for regional maritime disputes.

Strategic Support Force (SSF): A branch of the PLA responsible for space, cyber, and electronic warfare operations, highlighting the modernization of China's military capabilities. The SSF reflects China's focus on information dominance.

Taiwan Relations Act (TRA): A U.S. law enacted in 1979 that governs unofficial relations with Taiwan, providing a legal basis for arms sales and support. The TRA underscores the U.S. commitment to Taiwan's security.

Three Warfares: A PLA doctrine encompassing psychological warfare, media warfare, and legal warfare to shape public opinion and international perceptions. The doctrine is integral to China's information operations.

United Front Work Department (UFWD): A Chinese Communist Party agency tasked with influencing domestic and foreign entities, including diaspora communities, to align with party objectives. The UFWD plays a key role in China's soft power strategy.

Unrestricted Warfare: A concept introduced by two PLA colonels advocating for the use of all means, including non-military tactics, to achieve strategic goals. The concept reflects China's holistic approach to warfare.

Zhongnanhai: The central headquarters of the Chinese Communist Party and State Council, symbolizing the epicenter of China's political power. Zhongnanhai is the seat of China's top leadership.

APPENDIX A

CHINA'S BELT AND ROAD INITIATIVE (BRI)

OVERVIEW

Launched in 2013 by President Xi Jinping, the Belt and Road Initiative (BRI) is China's ambitious global infrastructure and economic development strategy. It aims to enhance regional connectivity and embrace a brighter economic future by building trade routes reminiscent of the ancient Silk Road. The BRI comprises two main components:

- **Silk Road Economic Belt**: An overland network connecting China to Central Asia, the Middle East, and Europe through railways, highways, and pipelines.
- **21st Century Maritime Silk Road**: A sea route linking China's coastal regions to Southeast Asia, Africa, and Europe via major ports.

OBJECTIVES

The BRI seeks to:

- Facilitate trade and investment flows between China and participating countries.
- Promote economic integration and cooperation on a transcontinental scale.
- Enhance China's global influence and soft power.

APPENDIX

GLOBAL REACH

As of recent reports, over 150 countries and international organizations have signed agreements with China under the BRI framework, encompassing projects worth trillions of dollars. These projects span various sectors, including transportation, energy, telecommunications, and industrial parks.

CRITICISMS AND CHALLENGES

Despite its scale and scope, the BRI has faced several criticisms:

- **Debt Sustainability**: Some recipient countries have accumulated significant debts, leading to concerns about "debt-trap diplomacy."
- **Transparency Issues**: Lack of transparency in project financing and execution has raised questions about governance and accountability.
- **Environmental and Social Impacts**: Large-scale infrastructure projects have sometimes led to environmental degradation and displacement of local communities.AP News

ALLEGATIONS OF BRIBERY BY THE CHINESE COMMUNIST PARTY (CCP) IN THE CARIBBEAN
Context
China's growing presence in the Caribbean has been marked by increased investments and diplomatic engagements. While these initiatives aim to foster development and cooperation, there have been allegations concerning unethical practices, including bribery of local officials.

ALLEGED PRACTICES

Bribery and Kickbacks: Reports suggest that Chinese firms have been involved in bribery and kickback schemes to secure contracts and favorable treatment in various Caribbean nations. These practices undermine fair competition and can erode public trust in institutions.

Influence through Investment: Wealthy Chinese individuals obtaining citizenship through investment programs in Caribbean countries have allegedly used their economic clout to influence local politics and policies, potentially aligning them with Chinese interests.

IMPLICATIONS

Such activities, if substantiated, could have several implications:

- **Erosion of Democratic Institutions**: Bribery and undue influence can weaken democratic processes and institutions, leading to governance challenges.
- **Strategic Leverage**: By securing key positions and contracts through unethical means, China could gain strategic leverage in the region, affecting geopolitical dynamics.
- **Reputational Risks**: Both for China and the affected Caribbean nations, these allegations can lead to reputational damage and strained international relations.

APPENDIX B

SINICIZATION OF TIBET AND CONTROL OF TIBETAN BUDDHISM

Michael van Walt van Praag[118] has been a vocal advocate for the Tibetan cause, emphasizing the legal and international dimensions of the Tibet issue. In a presentation for the Lithuanian Parliamentary Tibet Group, he asserted that Tibet is an occupied country and that Tibetans are not an ethnic minority within China but rather an occupied people. He stressed that the international community has largely remained silent on Tibet, often self-censoring to accommodate Beijing's sensitivities, which has shifted the narrative towards human rights violations rather than addressing the Sino-Tibetan conflict as an international issue. Von Praag's arguments are based on the international legal status of Tibet, asserting that the People's Republic of China does not have sovereignty over Tibet and that Tibetans have the right to self-determination. He urged the international community to recognize the true nature of the Sino-Tibetan conflict and to act in accordance with international obligations and the rule of law.[119]

The process of Sinicization of Tibet by the Chinese Communist Party (CCP) involves a comprehensive strategy aimed at assimilating Tibet into the dominant Han Chinese culture. This strategy includes the promotion of Mandarin Chinese over the Tibetan language in educational and official discourses, encouraging the migration of Han Chinese into Tibet, closely monitoring religious institutions and suppressing religious leaders, and enforcing strict controls on Tibetan Buddhists and other religious practices. These policies have led to demographic changes, tensions, and a dilution of Tibetan cultural identity. The CCP's justification for these measures often cites stability, economic development, and progress, despite international criticism of human rights violations and the undermining of Tibetan culture and religious freedoms.[120]

Additionally, economic policies such as the Western Development policy have aimed at exploiting Tibet's resources, further integrating the region into China's economy. This has included attempts to relocate Han Chinese farmers into Tibet, which, despite protests and the withdrawal of a World Bank loan, has continued with Beijing's financing. These moves, alongside suppression of Tibetan Buddhism, banning images of the Dalai Lama, and interfering in the reincarnation of Tibetan Lamas, exemplify the CCP's efforts to control and Sinicize Tibet. The international community's response to these actions and the broader implications of Sinicization strategies in Tibet and beyond raise important questions about cultural preservation, human rights, and geopolitical stability.[121]

Any notion or academic defence of the notion that the CCP's Buddhist Association of China under the United Front Work Department is not engaged in infiltration, influence, and control of any Tibetan monastic group in China, Taiwan and the rest of the world would have a near 0 probability of defence in any recognized academic institution outside of Mainland China.

INDEX

A comprehensive index for this book is available on the page for *Canada Under Siege* at:

www.optimumpublishinginternational.com

ENDNOTES

1. PEI Coat of Arms

2. https://www.theglobeandmail.com/news/national/conflicts-of-interest-strangle-pei-politics/article1372364/

3. https://www.theglobeandmail.com/canada/article-peis-immigration-record-in-spotlight-after-family-caught-in-crackdown/

4. https://www.saltwire.com/prince-edward-island/pnp-whistleblower-says-she-has-lost-everything-98138

5. Also known as ESL. All provinces had versions within their various education ministries for new immigrants to Canada.

6. chrome-extension://efaidnbmnnnibpcajpcglclefindmkaj/https://www.assembly.pe.ca/sites/test.assembly.pe.ca/files/2009-AG-ar.pdf

7. https://www.saltwire.com/prince-edward-island/peis-pnp-a-serious-failure-says-kenney-95214

8. https://www.cbc.ca/news/canada/prince-edward-island/pei-egaming-deleted-emails-1.3871135

9. https://www.theglobeandmail.com/news/national/conflicts-of-interest-strangle-pei-politics/article1372364/2. 2 2

10. https://www.ctvnews.ca/atlantic/article/how-investigators-cracked-an-alleged-business-immigration-scam-on-pei/

11. https://www.saltwire.com/prince-edward-island/migration-from-china-to-canada-subject-of-pei-multi-media-project-343934

12. https://www.ned.org/wp-content/uploads/2017/12/Sharp-Power-Rising-Authoritarian-Influence-Full-Report.pdf

13. https://tinyurl.com/PEI-Population-growth

14. https://kevinjarsenault.com/wp-content/uploads/2025/03/Wade-and-Zhou.mp4
15. https://tinyurl.com/Mosaic-Effect-Book
16. https://en.wikipedia.org/wiki/Project_Sidewinder
17. https://jamestown.org/wp-content/uploads/2019/09/Read-the-09-26-2019-CB-Issue-in-PDF-1.pdf
18. https://www.ourcommons.ca/documentviewer/en/44-1/CACN/report-3
19. Sunrise and it's various entities. https://en.sunriseltd.ca/author/sunrise/

    From Anne in China Inc. to Two Cows Ice Cream:

    If you are looking for a bridge to the CCP and Mainland China, Frank and Sherry are that bridge. Their connections to Beijing are exemplary, as one would expect. They also created significant two-way business opportunities for PEI businesses at a time when Canada was still all in on the CCP and China as both a hedge to U.S. hegemony and a belief that China would continue to liberalize and adhere to the rule of law. Being invited to the 70th annual CCP's celebration in Beijing and the Peoples Consultative congress suggests they are highly regarded in Beijing.

20. https://www.wilsoncenter.org/article/magic-weapons-chinas-political-influence-activities-under-xi-jinping
21. https://www.saltwire.com/prince-edward-island/letter-no-government-for-the-people-404779
22. https://gebis.org/
23. https://www.gwbi.org/
24. https://en.wikipedia.org/wiki/PT_109_(film)
25. https://sundayguardianlive.com/investigation/paradise-lost-is-sogavare-beijings-straw-man
26. https://www.cnn.com/2004/US/12/29/bush.quake/
27. https://www.wilsoncenter.org/blog-post/debt-distress-road-belt-and-road
28. https://indepthsolomons.com.sb/suidani-scores-legal-victory-against-former-sogavare-govt/

29. https://en.wikipedia.org/wiki/Second_United_Front

30. https://www.thechinastory.org/yearbooks/yearbook-2015/forum-ascent/the-expansion-of-the-united-front-under-xi-jinping/

31. https://harrisburg.psu.edu/faculty-and-staff/nicholas-eftimiades
https://www.thetimes.com/uk/royal-family/article/prince-andrew-china-uk-beijing-hw69z93rp?utm_source=chatgpt.com&region=global

32. https://www.cfr.org/backgrounder/chinas-huawei-threat-us-national-security

33. https://www.cfr.org/backgrounder/chinas-huawei-threat-us-national-security

34. https://www.wsj.com/politics/national-security/was-there-a-chinese-agent-working-in-the-new-york-governors-office-0f972d86

35. https://america.cgtn.com/2019/03/02/chinas-two-sessions-2019

36. https://www.canada.ca/en/public-safety-canada/news/2024/06/legislation-to-counter-foreign-interference-receives-royal-assent.html

37. https://www.bbc.co.uk/news/articles/cgm1lg3gj7vo

38. https://www.cbc.ca/player/play/video/9.6707041

39. https://www.thebureau.news/p/liberal-candidate-peter-yuen-reportedly

40. https://www.hrw.org/news/2024/12/02/volkswagens-china-joint-venture-exit-xinjiang

41. https://en.sunriseltd.ca/anne-in-china-inc/

42. https://www.axios.com/2024/08/22/palantir-hires-gallagher-defense

43. https://www.thecanadianencyclopedia.ca/en/article/meng-wanzhou-affair

44. https://thebreaker.news/news/trudeau-mainland-chinese-fundraising

    Bob Mackin first reported this story, and it was later picked up by major media outlets.

45. https://www.cbc.ca/news/canada/prince-edward-island/p-e-i-population-secretariat-shut-down-1.1214015

46. The colloquial term for Robert Ghiz's office.

47. https://stewartmckelvey.com/announcements/charlottetown-partner-spencer-campbell-k-c-appointed-president-of-the-law-society-of-prince-edward-island/

48. https://www.cbc.ca/news/canada/prince-edward-island/pei-pnp-whistleblowers-privacy-breach-liberal-government-1.4516572

49. https://www.cbc.ca/news/canada/prince-edward-island/3-former-civil-servants-file-1-8m-suit-against-former-p-e-i-premier-government-agency-over-privacy-breach-1.5010386

50. https://www.youtube.com/watch?v=jwjbiS-QAss

51. https://www.legnb.ca/en/members/current/15/cardy-dominic

52. Us Congressional Report on Religious Freedoms. https://www.uscirf.gov/sites/default/files/2024-09/2024%20China%20Factsheet%20Sinicization.pdf

53. https://tibetpress.com/2023/07/31/decoding-the-ccps-sinicization-strategy-for-tibet/

    The Sinicization of Tibetan Buddhism by the CCP is well known to anyone who is interested in preserving the philosophy, principles, and religious doctrine.

54. Barbara Demick, *Eat the Buddha: Life and Death in a Tibetan Town* (New York: Random House, 2020).

55. Tibet Policy Institute

56. https://link.springer.com/book/10.1057/9780230601192

57. https://savetibet.org/buddhist-association-of-china-takes-a-leading-role-in-chinas-attempts-to-control-and-forcibly-reshape-tibetan-buddhism/

58. https://tinyurl.com/Buddhist-Association-of-China

    The Chairman of the Buddhist Association of China (BAC) holds a pivotal role in aligning Buddhist institutions with the Chinese Communist Party's (CCP) objectives, both domestically and internationally. This position involves overseeing religious practices, guiding the Sinicization of Buddhism, and engaging in diplomatic efforts to extend China's soft power through religious channels.

    A comprehensive analysis of the BAC's role is presented in André Laliberté's chapter titled "The Buddhist Association of China and Constitutional Law in Buddhist Majority Nations," published in Buddhism and Comparative Constitutional Law by Cambridge University Press. Laliberté examines how the BAC functions as an instrument of the CCP's United Front Work Department, facilitating the integration of Buddhism into the state's political framework and promoting China's influence in Buddhist-majority countries

59. https://tibet.net/representative-dr-namgyal-choedup-speaks-on-voice-for-the-voiceless-at-jifeng-bookstore/

60. https://lop.parl.ca/sites/ParlInfo/default/en_CA/People/Profile?personId=9754

61. https://www.parl.ca/diplomacy/en/friendship-groups

62. https://tibet.net/wp-content/uploads/2014/10/MIDWAY-ENGLISH.pdf

63. https://www.harpercollins.ca/9780063391390/voice-for-the-voiceless/

64. *Damden chos skyong* in Tibetan, "oath-bound Dharma protectors," connected with the Dalai Lamas include especially Palden Lhamo and Dorje Drakden (also known as Nechung).

65. Excerpt from Chapter 15 of the Dalai Lama's book, *Voice for the Voiceless: Seven Decades of Struggle with China for My Land and My People* (New York: HarperCollins, 2025).

66. https://www.thecanadianencyclopedia.ca/en/article/meng-wanzhou-affair

67. https://www.cbc.ca/news/canada/prince-edward-island/pnp-returns-to-haunt-liberal-campaign-1.1124600

68. https://www.chinalawtranslate.com/en/criminal-law-amm-9/

69. https://bitterwinter.org/Vocabulary/xie-jiao/

70. https://www.academia.edu/77846863/Issue_1_The_Journal_of_CESNUR_

71. Craig S. Smith, "Asylum Plea by Chinese Sect's Leader Perplexes the U.S.," *The New York Times*, 31 July 2000.

72. Kevin J. O'Brien, *Popular Protest in China* (Cambridge, MA: Harvard University Press). p. 195.

73. https://www.state.gov/reports/2023-report-on-international-religious-

freedom/china/

74. Alex Joske, "The United Front Work Department," JSTOR, June 2020, https://www.jstor.org/stable/resrep25132.8?seq=1

75. https://www.facebook.com/tsanteng.chiang/

76. Greg Mercer, "How a group of Buddhist monks bought up a chunk of PEI," *The Globe and Mail*, Oct. 3, 2023, https://www.youtube.com/watch?v=_IVSJexRbEs

77. Jichang Lulu and Lin Li, "The party in monk's robe — The cultivation of global Buddhism within CCP influence operations," *Synopsis*, 18 July 2022. https://sinopsis.cz/wp-content/uploads/2022/07/buddhism0.pdf

78. Laliberté, André, "The Buddhist Association of China and Constitutional Law - The International Channels of Influence," Chapter 14 in *Buddhism and Comparative Constitutional Law*, pp. 285-304. Cambridge University Press, 2022. https://www.cambridge.org/core/books/buddhism-and-comparative-constitutional-law/buddhist-association-of-china-and-constitutional-law-in-buddhist-majority-nations/6FD0CF999F6956C2F90B7B39F3597D47#

79. "The Voice of a Propagator of Zhong Gong," bbs.gelupa.org, March 21, 2012. This reference is behind the censorship wall.

80. Alex Joske, "The Party speaks for you: Foreign interference and the Chinese Communist Party's united front system", ASPI Policy Brief 32 (2020). https://web.archive.org/web/20200612072714/https://s3-ap-southeast-2.amazonaws.com/ad-aspi/2020-06/The%20party%20speaks%20for%20you_0.pdf

81. See Joske (2020) and Laliberté (2022) above.

82. Gerry Groot, "Managing transitions: the Chinese Communist Party's united front work, minor parties and groups, hegemony and corporatism", PhD thesis, University of Adelaide, 1997. https://web.archive.org/web/20191119233403/https://digital.library.adelaide.edu.au/dspace/handle/2440/19225

83. Land Use Task Force, *Report of the Task Force Report on the Land Use Policy*, PEI government, January 2014, page 2.

84. https://www.princeedwardisland.ca/sites/default/files/legislation/l-05-lands_protection_act_p.e.i.pdf

85. https://www.islandparty.ca/lands-protection-act.

86. https://www.saltwire.com/prince-edward-island/letter-on-p-e-i-land-holdings-and-irac

87. https://www.theglobeandmail.com/canada/article-pei-land-bliss-and-wisdom-monks/

88. https://www.saltwire.com/prince-edward-island/pei-greens-question-kings-county-land-sale-465565

89. https://irac.pe.ca/about/about-the-commission/

90. IRAC website, « About IRAC » https://irac.pe.ca/about/about-the-commission/

91. http://canada.ca/en/democratic-institutions/news/2025/01/statement-from-minister-sahota-and-minister-mcguinty-on-the-final-report-from-the-commissioner-for-the-public-inquiry-into-foreign-interference-in-.html

92. From China to PEI, The Big Picture. https://www.cbc.ca/news/canada/prince-edward-island/from-china-to-p-e-i-the-big-picture-1.2557795

93. Frank Zhou Building Businesses in PEI.and China https://www.saltwire.com/prince-edward-island/entrepreneur-frank-zhou-building-business-in-pei-and-china-97838

94. https://tinyurl.com/PEI-Buddhist-teachings

95. Lei's Real Talk on Immigration in PEI. https://www.youtube.com/watch?v=MmxnyRFWtTg

96. https://www.wsj.com/world/china/china-fentanyl-trade-network-9685fde2?st=XUYTxk

97. https://vimeo.com/233927958 Interview Part 1 Sahlih E-Television

98. https://vimeo.com/233927958 Interview Part 2 Sahlih E-Television

99. https://www.taipeitimes.com/News/taiwan/archives/2018/12/10/2003705841

100. Speech at Loyola College Alumni Banquet, Baltimore, Maryland, 18 February 1958. Papers of John F. Kennedy. Pre-Presidential Papers. Senate Files, Box 899, "Loyola College annual alumni banquet, Baltimore, Maryland, 18 February 1958." JFK Library.

101. https://www.theglobeandmail.com/canada/article-pei-land-bliss-and-wisdom-monks/

102. https://www.pm.gc.ca/en/news/backgrounders/2024/04/29/mike-duheme

103. https://en.wikipedia.org/wiki/Grand_Hotel_(Taipei)

104. https://sites.asiasociety.org/chinawealthpower/chapters/chiang-kai-shek/

105. https://focustaiwan.tw/politics/202504190015?utm_source=chatgpt.com

106. https://thebreaker.news/news/senator-oh-united-front/

107. https://www.khanacademy.org/humanities/art-asia/beginners-guide-asian-culture/buddhist-art-culture/a/the-buddha-shakyamuni

108. https://uschinatoday.org/features/2016/06/06/the-game-of-go-ancient-applications-and-contemporary-connotations/

109. https://www.cbc.ca/news/canada/toronto/trump-ford-ontario-electricity-tariffs-trade-war-1.7480234

110. https://2017-2021.state.gov/military-civil-fusion/

111. https://study.com/academy/lesson/roman-castra-history-camps-layout-forts.html

112. https://www.britannica.com/biography/Genghis-Khan

113. https://www.thevintagenews.com/2017/11/25/yurts-dwellings-used-by-hun-warriors/

114. https://www.sciencedirect.com/science/article/abs/pii/S0305748817301275

115. https://www.amazon.com/Unrestricted-Warfare-Chinas-Destroy-America/dp/1626543054

116. https://indepthsolomons.com.sb/suidani-scores-legal-victory-against-former-sogavare-govt/

117. https://www.politico.eu/article/germany-to-revisit-chinas-hamburg-port-deal-over-inconsistencies-on-critical-infrastructure-classification/

118. https://www.ias.edu/hs/van_walt

119. https://tibet.net/tibet-is-an-occupied-country-betans-not-an-ethnic-minority-michael-van-walts-tibet-brief-20-20/

120. https://tibetpress.com/2023/07/31/decoding-the-ccps-sinicization-strategy-for-tibet/

121. https://tibetpolicy.net/ccp-and-sinicization-of-tibet/

ABOUT THE AUTHORS

Garry Clement, CFE, CFCS, CAMS, FIS, CCI, CCIA, is an internationally recognized expert in organized crime investigations, money laundering, and financial intelligence. With a storied career spanning over four decades, Garry has been qualified repeatedly in Canadian courts as an expert on drug trafficking syndicates, triads, and transnational financial crime. His tenure includes extensive undercover operations, international liaison roles—most notably in Hong Kong—and expert testimony in landmark cases across Canada. From shaping courtroom narratives with expert affidavits to advising on legislative compliance, Garry's insights have been instrumental in transforming the financial crime landscape. Now turning his penetrating investigative lens to the written word, Garry brings the same precision and insight to his authorship, delivering gripping, authentic narratives rooted in real-world criminal complexities.

He is currently Senior Vice President and Chief Anit-Money Laundering Officer at Versa Bank.

Michel Juneau-Katsuya is a former criminal investigator with the RCMP and Senior Intelligence Officer and Chief, Asia/Pacific with the Canadian Security Intelligence Service (CSIS). With more than 40 years of experience, he is internationally recognized as one of the most consulted Canadian experts on national and international security regarding issues of police operations, terrorism, Chinese espionage, appearing in more than 20 international documentaries and on national and international media regularly. He has been called as expert witness by several Canadian Parliamentary and Senate committees on intelligence, national security and foreign interference issues and helped shaping national policy on the matter. Michel led operations that penetrated foreign espionage networks and exposed critical security vulnerabilities on all continents. His strategic acumen has informed major investigations into terrorism, organized crime, and foreign interference, making him a sought-after expert for governments and media alike. Fluent in the high-stakes language of global intelligence, Michel translates his profound experience into compelling literature that pulls readers deep into the shadows of real-world espionage. As an author, he merges factual depth with gripping storytelling, offering an unfiltered look into the clandestine corridors of international intelligence and the forces shaping our world from behind the scenes. He has been also teaching Criminology at several Canadian Universities for many years.

Dean Baxendale is the Publisher and CEO of Optimum Publishing International, a legacy Canadian publishing house renowned for its fearless and groundbreaking titles on politics, intelligence, crime, and global affairs. With a passion for championing free expression and investigative truth, Dean has positioned Optimum as a leading platform for bold voices exposing corruption, authoritarianism, and geopolitical disinformation. Under his leadership, the company has published numerous Canadian and international bestsellers that challenge state narratives, uncover transnational threats, and give voice to suppressed stories from around the world. Dean's work has attracted international recognition, particularly for Optimum's role in advancing democratic values and press freedom against foreign influence operations. As a columnist, publisher and thought leader, Dean is a tireless advocate for intellectual courage, transparency, and the indispensable role of publishing in upholding democratic discourse. He serves on a number of boards and also heads the China Democracy Fund to defend those targeted by the CCP's lawfare operations globally.

INDEX

A
Abegweit, 2
Acadians, 3
Anne of China Inc., 9, 22, 35
Anne of Green Gables Foundation, 22
Anne of Green Gables Licensing Authority Inc., 9
Anne of Green Gables, 1, 2, 9, 10, 18, 22, 35
anti-money laundering (AML) enforcement, 144
Asher, David, 160
Aspin, Jason, 138, 139, 200
Atlantic Growth Strategy mission, 40–41, 42
Australia, 20, 56, 74, 106

B
"Backroom Boys", 51
Ball, Dwight, 42
Banks, Tim, 21
Barbados, 202–203
Beaton, Michele, 121
Belt and Road Initiative (BRI), 20, 27, 130, 158
   Trudeau government's strategic vision and, 38–39, 42–44
Bill C-70 (*Countering Foreign Interference Act*), 32, 37
Binns, Pat, 4, 24, 93
"Birthplace of Confederation", 3, 34, 190

Blackbush project, 21
Blair, Bill, 30
Bliss and Wisdom Monastery, building, 157–159
Bliss and Wisdom, 12, 23, 55, 57, 60, 70, 74, 75, 98, 88, 101, 114, 174, 175, 177, 197, 200, 205
   Beijing-aligned perspective, 70
   expansion into PEI as strategic, 164–165
   Facebook page, 175
   followers, role of, 165
   investigation, 13–18
   Jin's arrival at, 102–103
   land holdings of, 11, 12–13
   leadership, 165–169
   origin of, 102–106
   origin of the funds, 149–57
   roots in Taipei, 61
   stories and denunciations, 103–104
   United Front connection denial, 150
   See also GWBI, monastic life; land grabbing; money laundering activities; Tibetan Buddhism
Brison, Scott, 41
Buddhist Association of China (BAC), 66, 80, 81, 101, 102, 106, 150, 174, 175, 189
   leadership, 76–78
Buddhist nuns. *See* GWBI, monastic life

INDEX

C

Campbell, Spencer, 50
Canada Revenue Agency, 60
Canada-China Year of Tourism, 41
Canadian Security Intelligence Service (CSIS), 30, 88, 107, 111, 122, 126, 127–128, 130, 159, 166
Canadian Telecommunications Association, 7
Cardy, Dominic, 54, 56, 57
Caribbean, 24, 25
Carney, Mark, 23, 32
Cartier, Jacques, 2
cash-handling activities, suspicious, 139–140
CBC, 7, 51, 86
centennial goal (2049) (China), 34, 202
Central Tibetan Administration (CTA), 81
Charlottetown Accords, 4
Chiang Tsan-Teng, 104
Chiang, Paul, 32
China Nexus, The (Roger), 79, 199
China's 2049 strategy, 34, 202
China's Criminal Code (Article 300), 99
Chinese Communist Party (CCP)
    American political institutions, infiltration of, 28–29
    Canada, elite capture and economic leverage, 29–33
    dismantled Zhong Gong, 99
    hybrid warfare, 55
    Panchen Lama controversy and Dalai Lama succession, 72–74, 80, 81, 176
    real estate connection, 33
    See also Bliss and Wisdom; "elite capture"; Tibetan Buddhism; United Front Work Department (UFWD)
Chinese People's Political Consultative Conference (CPPCC), 29
Chinese triads, 12
Chrétien, Jean, 9, 37, 93
Chris Hu, 29
Chrustie, Calvin, 160
Claws of the Panda, 9
Cold War, 202
Cole, Michael, 179
Colonial era, 3
Compton, Russell, 194, 139
Confederation Bridge, 2, 4
Confucius Institutes, 24, 27, 33
Connidis, Angela, 49
Cooper, Sam, 30, 89
Cox, Carolyn, 11
CTV, *W5* documentary, 52, 58, 85–86
Cultural Genocide and Asian State Peripheries (Sautman), 71
Cultural Revolution (1966–1976), 101, 102

D

Demick, Barbara, 71
Deng Xiaoping's economic reforms, 27
Department of Justice (DOJ) (US), 29
Dharamshala, 64, 65, 69, 79, 80, 81, 82, 150
Di Nino, Consiglio, 44, 60, 79–80
Dickson, Kathryn, 89
Dorcay Church, 172–175, 185–186, 187
Duheme, Mike, 164

E

Easter, Wayne, 125–128, 196–198, 201
Eat the Buddha (Demick), 71
Eftimiades, Nic, 28
"elite capture", 9, 20–25, 130
    in Canada, 29–33
    in United States, 28–29
English as a Second Language (ESL) training program, 46, 47–48, 86, 193
Epekwitk, 2

INDEX

F
Falun Gong, 98, 99, 101, 198
Fan Yin, Abbott (Zhen Ding), 79, 101, 154, 156, 170, 172, 173, 180–183, 186, 188, 189
Fan Yun, 184–185
Fang Fang, 28
fentanyl trade, 158, 160, 161
Fife, Robert, 31
financial instruments
  intermingling funds, 148
  layering techniques, 147
FINTRAC, 160, 161
Fo Gang Shan, 174
Foreign Agents Registration Act (FARA), 29
Foreign Influence Transparency Registry coalition, 30–33
Foreign Interference Commission, 30
forward operating base (FOB), 25, 202, 204, 205
FPT Settlement Working group, 49
Freedom of Information and Protection of Privacy Act, 89–90
Fu Zhi Buddhist group, 155–156
Fung, Gloria, 30–31, 32

G
Gallagher, Mike, 36
Game-of-Go, 190
Ganzhou School PEI Curriculum Program, 40
German, Peter, 130
Germany, 34
Ghiz family, 4
Ghiz, Atallah Joseph, 4
Ghiz, Joe, 4, 146
Ghiz, Robert, 2, 12, 18, 37, 39, 51, 96, 112, 146
  Bank's relationship with, 21
  lawsuits, 7
  Liberal leadership (2003), 4
  political capture, 23
  relationship with Frank Zhou, 21
  resignation, 2, 7
  See also Provincial Nominee Program (PNP)
Globe and Mail, 30, 31, 119, 164–165, 166
Graham, Shawn, 56
Grant Thorton, 139, 148–149
Great Deportation (1755), 3
Great Enlightenment Buddhist Institute Society (GEBIS), 18, 65, 75, 83, 116, 131, 146, 149, 157, 165, 198
  See also Bliss and Wisdom; land grabbing; money laundering activities
Great Leap Forward (1958–1962), 101
Great Wisdom Buddhist Institute (GWBI), 18, 60–61, 75, 83, 116, 131–132, 146, 157, 165, 198
  See also Bliss and Wisdom; land grabbing; money laundering activities
Guaranteed Investment Certificate (GIC) funds, 131, 139
GWBI, monastic life, 61–68
  Heather, 63
  Jingli, 60, 62, 65, 67, 68
  Joanna, 63–64, 66, 67–68
  nun's vision for the monastery, 67–68
  Sabrina, 62, 64, 67
Gyaltsen, Kelsang, 175–178

H
Haines, Avery, 85, 86
Harper government, 43
Harper, Stephen, 44
Here We Stay project, 8
Hidden Hand, 9, 173
His Holiness, the Dalai Lama, 44, 61, 62, 63, 66, 67, 69, 75, 79–84, 150
  Bliss and Wisdom, conversation about, 79, 81, 82, 83
  CCP control, 80–84

INDEX

Panchen Lama controversy and
    Dalai Lama succession, 72–74,
    80, 81, 176
  picture of, 60
Hogue Commission, 128
Hogue report (2025), 107
Holland College
  Educational Joint Ventures (EJV),
    39–40
  ESL contract, 46, 47–48
  Service Agreement (2018), 40
  Study Abroad Partnership (2018),
    40–41
Holmes, Susan, 5, 52, 86, 192–194
  employment in Yukon, 50, 51
  ESL contract, 47–50
  ESL training program, 46
Honiara province, 19, 25
Hopetown project, 120–121
HSBC Canada, 160
Hsing Yun, Master, 174
Hu Jintao, 43
Huang, Jimmy, 164
Huang, Paul, 156
Huang, Sherry, 9, 21, 23, 29, 37, 39,
  147, 193
  ESL contract, 46, 48
Huawei, 28–29

I
Île Saint-Jean, 3
Immigrant Investor Program, 157
immigration program. *See* Provincial
  Nominee Program (PNP)
International Campaign for Tibet
  (ICT), 75
Island Regulatory and Appeals
  Commission (IRAC), 118, 120, 121

J
Jiang Zemin, 98
Jiangsu Commerce Council of Canada
  (JCCC), 33

Jih-Chang, Master, 70, 102, 103, 104,
  107, 150, 156, 175, 176
Jinling High School Affiliated Program
  (2015), 40
Joske, Alex, 107

K
Kennedy, John F., 162
Kenney, Jason, 43, 44
Ke-Zhou Lu, 165
Khan, Genghis, 202
King government, 108–114
King, Dennis, 12, 23, 24, 121
Klaus L., arrest of, 34
Kolga, Marcus, 30–31, 32
Kuomintang (KMT), 172, 186–187
Kwan, Jenny, 31–32

L
Laliberté, André, 106
"Lamrim Study Group", 104
land grabbing, 3
  alleged crimes, 122–123
  cash, contracts, and corruption,
    118–120
  Hopetown project, 120–121
  investigation, 13–18
  Land Protection Act (LPA),
    115–116
  monastic invasion, 120
  public accountability, avoiding,
    121
  stories and testimonies, 117–118
  touring PEI, 116–117
Land Protection Act (LPA) (1982),
  113, 115–116
Land Use Task Force, 113
landscape (PEI), 1–2, 115
Lee, Christine, 34
Legislative Assembly, 2
Lei's Real Talk, 147
Lennox Island, 2
Li Hongzhi, 98

INDEX

Liberal Party/Liberals, 4, 5, 23, 32–33, 51 28
    financial ties with United Front, 44–45
Linda Sun, 29
Lobsang Sangay, 66
Lobster Shanty (motel), 60, 150
Lucy Maude Montgomery Foundation, 9

M

MacAulay, Lawrence, 41
MacDonald, Edward, 113, 114
MacIntosh, Duncan, 9, 22, 35
MacLauchlan, Wade, 9, 10, 12, 22, 23, 35, 37, 39, 41, 51, 112, 121, 146, 203
MacLean, J. Angus, 115
MacPhee, Alan, 35, 58, 86, 90
Maher, Stephen, 90
Malaita, 19, 20, 24
Mallard, Jane, 47–48, 49
Mao Zedong, 15, 26, 27, 101
Martin, Paul, 44
Matejcek, Jan, 11
May, Elizabeth, 31
McKelvey, Stewart, 50
Meech Lake Accords, 4
Mercer, Greg, 164
Mi'kmaq, 2
Michael Chan affair, 29–30
Ministry of Foreign Affairs (China), 28
Ministry of Foreign Affairs (MOFA) (Taiwan), 178–180
monastic life. *See* GWBI, monastic life
money laundering activities, 33, 44, 122, 129–62
    anti-fraud investigative experience, 129–31
    behaviour of individuals or entities, 149
    complex financial instruments, 147–149
    documentation and recordkeeping, 149
    origin and destination of funds, 145–147
    real estate transactions, 140–145
    suspicious cash-handling activities, 139–140
    suspicious transactions patterns, 131–139
    "Vancouver Model", 33, 89, 142–145, 152, 160
Montgomery, Lucy Maud, 1, 35
Mosaic Effect, The, 9, 11, 12, 15, 36, 46, 53, 55, 173
Mulroney, Brian, 88
Mulroney, David, 43
Murphy, Martie, 50
Myers, Stephen, 10, 12, 23

N

Namgyal Choedup, 79, 82
National Endowment for Democracy, 9
National New Farmer Coalition, 125
New Island Opportunities Inc., 89
Norbu, Gyaincain, 72, 81
NSICOP (National Security and Intelligence Committee of Parliamentarians), 197
Nyima, Gedhun Choekyi, 72, 73, 81

O

Operation Dragon Lord, 44
organized crime, 93, 142

P

Palantir Technologies, 36
Papineau Federal Liberal Association, 44
Parks, Deborah, 147
Pascal, Cleo, 19–20
People's Liberation Army (CCP), 12–13, 203–204
People's Republic of China–Prince Edward Island engagement, 38–45

INDEX

Permanent Residency Card, 96
Plourd, Cora (later Plourd Nicholson), 5, 50, 51–52, 86
Pratt, Michael Van Velt van, 75
protests (1860s), 3
Provincial Nominee Program (PNP), 5–7, 12, 14, 47, 51, 85–91, 146
   applications, handling of, 14–15
   Auditor General's report (2009), 7
   case study, 93–98
   CBC report (2009), 7
   as a "$400 Million Scandal", 5
   Ghiz views on, 23
   Here We Stay project, 8
   immigrants investment, 92–93
   land acquisitions, investigation, 13–18
   launched, 93–94
   premier's office involvement, 15, 17
   reports, 17–18
   retention rate, 8
   shut down, 7, 96
   W5 documentary, 52, 58, 85–86
   See also Zhen-Ru, Master (Mary Jin)
PT109, 19

Q

Qiao Liang, 204
Qigong, 98, 99
QUAD (Quadrilateral Security Dialogue), 20
Quebec Referendum, 4
Quiong Zhonggong group, 101

R

real estate market, 33
Recall Movement, 172, 173, 185, 186, 187, 189
Rizong Rinpoche, 103
Roach, Allen, 138
Rogers, Benedict, 60
Romans, 202

Royal Canadian Mounted Police (RCMP), 7, 44, 108, 111, 120, 122, 129, 147
Ru-Zheng, Abbot, 174

S

Samuel Holland's survey (1764), 3
Sautman, Barry, 71
Serviant, Serge, 51
Seven Years' War, 3
Sherwood Inn and Hotel, 7–4
Sidewinder Report, 12, 44
"sinicization of religion" strategy, 65–66, 75, 100, 174
Solomon Islands, 19, 20, 22, 204
Soviets, 202
St. Dunstan's Cathedral (Charlottetown), 1
St. Patrick's Day, 53, 86
State Administration for Religious Affairs (SARA), 72, 76, 106
Study Abroad Canada, 46, 48
Suidani, Daniel, 19, 20, 24, 25, 60
Sunrise Group, 8, 41
Sunrise Immigration and Investment, 146
Swalwell, Eric, 28

T

Taipei Times, The, 156
Taiwan People's Party (TPP), 186
Taiwan, 12, 13, 60, 61, 74, 163–189
   Bella's testimony, 169–171
   Dorcay Church, 172–175
   Tibetan Buddhism, co-opting, 74–76
Talifu, Celsus, 19, 20, 22, 24, 25, 60
Tay, Joe, 32
TD Bank, 160
Tenetko, Svetlana, 5, 50, 51–52
Tenzin Gyatso, 14th Dalai Lama. *See* His Holiness, the Dalai Lama
Thompson, Bloyce, 121

262

INDEX

Tibet Policy Institute (TPI), 71, 75
Tibetan Buddhism, 18, 56, 61, 70–78
   BAC leadership, 76–78
   CCP control, 80–84
   co-opting (Taiwan experiment), 74–76
   expansion of, 70–71
   Panchen Lama controversy and Dalai Lama succession, 72–74, 80, 81, 176
   urgent fight to protect, 71–72
   weaponization of religion, 71
   See also GWBI, monastic life
TikTok, 28
Toronto temple (Tibetan Community Centre, Etobicoke), 60
Trans Mountain Pipeline project, 43
Trent, Bill, 13
Trudeau government
   business and trade relations, 41–44
   cultural and educational engagements, 39–41
   strategic vision and the Belt and Road Initiative, 38–39, 41–44
   UFWD and the Liberals' financial ties, 44–45
Trudeau, Justin, 184
Truscott, Steven, 13
Tsering, Penpa, 79, 82
Tuan-Liang, Chien, 103–104
Turkel, Nury, 36

U

U.S. Board of Immigration Appeals, 100
U.S. State Department, 24
Under Cover, 11, 12, 53, 130
United Front Work Department (UFWD), 12, 15, 18, 21, 26–37, 56, 69, 74, 106, 107, 150, 161, 165–169, 190
   affiliates, 28
   BAC under, 76, 77, 102
   elite capture and economic leverage (Canada), 29–33
   Frank and Sherry as part of, 47
   historical foundations of, 27
   and the Liberals' financial ties, 44–45
   from Mao to Xi, 26–27
   PEI as softest target, 22, 35–37
   political institutions, infiltration of, 28–29
   responsibility of, 27–28
United Kingdom, CCP's influence, 33–34
United States, 43, 45, 74, 158
   political institutions, CCP's infiltration of, 28–29
Unrestricted Warfare, 204

V

"Vancouver Model", 33, 89, 142–145, 152, 160
Vanyin, Abbot, 103
Ven Xuecheng, 77
Victor Oh, 174
Villemure, René, 31, 32
Voice for the Voiceless, 83
Volkswagen, 34
Vuong, Kevin, 184

W

W5 documentary, 52, 58, 85–86
Wajung Jiang-Li Xiaobai, 145
Wall Street Journal, The, 150
Wang Xiangsui, 204
Wang, Jeff, 166
Weale, David, 53, 54–55, 116
Who Killed Lynn Harper?, 13
Wilful Blindness, 9, 89, 173, 179, 183, 185
World War II, 4

X

Xi Jinping, 15, 26, 28, 33, 41, 43, 100
xie jiao, 99, 100
Xinjiang, 10, 33, 34

INDEX

Y
Yan, Andy, 160
Younker, Colin, 7
Yuen, Peter, 33
Yunlin University of Science and Technology, 104

Z
Zhang Hongbao, 98, 99, 100
Zhang Jiang-hui, 167–169
Zhen-Ru, Master (Mary Jin), 60–61, 64, 65, 68, 77, 79, 101, 150, 156, 158, 165, 189, 199
  appearance, 92, 95
  arrival in PEI, 94–98
  as a claimed spiritual Guru, 83–84
  emerged within Bliss and Wisdom (BW), 102–103
  Gyaltsen on, 176, 177–178
  history, 105–106
  immigration application of, 86, 87–89, 91, 95
  intelligence assessment, 106–107
  "Marco Monks", 97
  See also Bliss and Wisdom
Zhong Gong, 98, 99, 100
Zhou, Frank, 9, 12, 15, 21, 22, 29, 35, 37, 39, 86, 93, 145, 193
  connection with GEBIS and GWBI, 146
  ESL contract, 46, 48
  Myers relationship with, 23
  relationship with Chrétien, 146
Zhu Weiqun, 73
Zuberi, Sameer, 31

www.ingramcontent.com/pod-product-compliance
Lightning Source LLC
Chambersburg PA
CBHW031432160426
43195CB00010BB/705